# VALUE AND EXISTENCE

Studies in

Philosophic Anthropology

# VALUE AND EXISTENCE

## STUDIES IN PHILOSOPHIC ANTHROPOLOGY

by

**FREDERICK PATKA**

---

*PHILOSOPHICAL LIBRARY*
*New York*

Philosophical Library, Inc.

15 East 40th Street, New York 16, N.Y.



Library of Congress Catalog Card Number: 64-13326

Printed in the United States of America

# FOREWORD

Our age has been variously categorized. Among other terms used to describe it one has become almost a cliché; it is an "age of anxiety."

Uneasiness and uncertainty pervade all fields. Barry Ulanov in his *Seeds of Hope in the Modern World* sees them taking the form of an excessive preoccupation with process, which preoccupation, he says vitiates the work of scientist, scholar, and artist alike and contributes to the very loss of the sense of purpose.

Discussing education in his *Man in the Modern Age,* in words written thirty years ago but still retaining their relevancy, Karl Jaspers bemoans "in the absence of any unified ideas on the subject . . . the perpetual amplification of the didactic art," the "breaking up of substantial education into an interminable pedagogic experiment, its decomposition into indifferent possibilities."

It may well be that this fragmentation and unrest are symptomatic of a deeper malady: a disintegration of man as man, of man versus machine in his losing battle of automation, a crisis in human values and, therefore, a crisis in our very civilization.

To quote a pertinent passage from Dr. Frederick Patka's work *Values and Existence*—writing this foreword to which is truly a privilege—

> . . . human values have been devaluated, diluted, transvaluated, depreciated, and transformed in two ways; first, their original, authentic, and intrinsic meaning has been destroyed by pseudo-philosophies such as materialism, positivism, naturalism, and pragmatism; second, the unified system and hierarchy of values has been equally disintegrated by the theories of relativity and subjectivity of values, leading to the attitudes of false individualism. Correspondingly, human existence has lost its mean-

ing, significance, and goal-directed transcendence, decaying into the abyss of materialism, scepticism, and collectivism. Man as an individual human being, as a person, has lost his relative subsistence and absoluteness. *The devaluation of values led to the devaluation of man himself.* For it is the values alone which can give meaning and significance to existence. Accordingly, our question about the integration of personal existence can be answered only through a new revalidation, accreditation, reconstruction or rehabilitation of human values in conformity with their authentic meaning and the ethical obligations derived from their normative must-nature. Therefore, in order to recover a unified idea about the meaning of personal existence and the possible levels of existential integration, there is the imperative of recovering a unified system of human values which support, justify, inform, and direct man's thinking, feeling, and acting.

"As a man advances in life," Johnson the eighteenth-century Lexicographer once remarked to his biographer Boswell, "he gets what is better than admiration — judgment — to estimate things at their true value."

Those exposed to Dr. Patka's philosophical writings and his *Logos* lectures, the basis of this book, need not wait till they "advance in life" to attain this desirable "judgment of estimating things at their true value." In this stimulating work of his with its emphasis of the axiological interpretation of human existence those who are confused with regard to value problems, value outcomes, and even value-goals will find a true orientation.

It is good to know that there are men of his stature who not only see perceptively into the ills of our harassed world but "seeing steadily and seeing whole" can happily communicate to others their sensitive insight and understanding of the need for integration of human values with absolute values for true self-education.

Sister M. Florence, CSFN, Ph.D.
Academic Dean
Holy Family College

# CONTENTS

# VALUE AND EXISTENCE

Studies in

Philosophic Anthropology

# CHAPTER I

## THE CRISIS OF VALUES

### I. Man's value directed condition

By the time the evolving human individual emerged from the state of mere bio-physical consciousness into the condition of a critico-reflective awareness of his own self (self-consciousness), he had already experienced his being as a living reality, an instance of life, imbedded in a world of things, phenomena, and other forms of life which build up his profiles and horizons of existence.

Man finds himself already given to himself in a world-about-himself as the constantly changing frame of reference for all his goings and comings. Man's existential condition is, therefore, always situational, circumstantial, and relational. At any moment of being man is never alone, he is always surrounded by other beings which he finds already there in the field of his experiences or just merging on the horizon of his wandering about. While in a given situation, at a given time and place, and encompassed by other beings, man may recollect having been in other environments and enclosed by other beings; he may also recall having "walked out" of that circumstance (things and people standing around him) and "moved into" the present "set-up" of things; finally, he may project himself into future possibilities and imagine himself already embraced by the new "make-up." All this amounts to the insight of man, who is a part or a member in the never-ending procession of beings. On the other hand, the condition of loneliness comes about as the result of man's having cut himself off from the common ground of co-existing by which he prevented or stopped the process of communication with other beings. This seclusive isolation is usually prompted by a false degree of egocentrism. Thus the lonely existent comes close to the condition of someone stranded on a distant island after having wrecked his own ship on the ocean of universal being.

Since man's existence is relational, it also follows his condition of being dependent upon the things or other existents to which he is related. Every relation presupposes and consists of at least two beings that are mutually related to and therefore dependent upon each other. His being related to others and the others being related to him expresses, from another angle, man's situation of being concerned, tied up with and submerged in the world of his immediate milieu. The condition of dependence, however, takes away, at least in the bio-physical and social dimensions of life, the perfection of absolute freedom and self-sufficiency. Consequently, man must identify himself as a related (relative), dependent (contingent), and limited being (curtailed in his freedom). On the other hand, being necessarily related to others may also be interpreted as evidence that one belongs as a member to the community of beings around him. Thus man appears to be only a link in the uninterrupted chain of beings. The meaning of his existence will reveal itself only if man can succeed in finding, describing, and interpreting his proper locus and condition in the universe of being.

Man experiences himself as a living subject who knows of himself and about the beings belonging to his expanding microcosm. Man as an instance of self-conscious life puts himself apart from, maybe even above the things and objects which do not possess the quality of immanence and spontaneous activity as the essential difference between living and non-living. Non-living things and objects do not possess the power of disclosing their inner reality; they do not communicate with man and man does not know how to communicate himself to the objects. The knowledge man possesses of the physical reality of objects is limited to the quantitative manipulation of material properties. Communication, however, is essentially qualitative. Consequently, there is no communication between the world of objects and that of living subjects. On the other hand, man knows enough about their outer behavior for the manipulation of the physical world. Thus material civilization stands as proof for this pragmatic conquest of matter, time, space and energy.

While things and objects are and remain strange, mute, and closed to man, his being as related to the beings of the bio-sphere (plants and animals) assumes a new character. A common denominator, Life (although differing in its forms of manifestation), brings man closer to the other living organisms. The phenomenon of life and the experience of being alive disclose something about the inner principle of the living (*entelecheia*) which creates an affinity or community among all living beings through the similarity of basic vital processes (nutrition, growth, reproduction of the plants; knowledge, locomotion, and sensitivity of the animals). Accordingly, man's concern with Nature is more than an abstract or pragmatic interest. Nature is present in man's cultural life as the Mother of Life, the Universal Soul, and the source of all creativity in the world of arts, philosophy, and religion. Plants and animals are more than dead things and inert objects; they are regarded by man as instances of Nature's fertility, the same source accounting also for man's life. Poets, artists, philosophers and men of religion of all ages have tried to communicate with Nature and to find themselves as parts of an infinite life process. There has always been in man a longing for Nature. The desire to return to Nature as man's proper locus and habitat finds its expression in the writings of every epoch. Whenever civilization removes man from Nature, man finds himself outside his "natural" milieu. Modern man, for instance, is a "displaced person," "uprooted" in his existence, trying in vain to compensate for the lost "natural" environment by producing the "artificial" organization, a poor imitation of the real thing. This is a vain attempt at compensation, since it is impossible to express nature's symbolic revelation to man in scientific formulae. Scientific positivism is helpless in the presence of the mystery of being and life.

Man's close relationship to Nature brings about an emotional attachment to it, the basis for which can be found in the fact that man knows through experience that his own life depends on Nature's generosity toward his needs and their satisfaction. Man depends directly on nature's resources for the satisfaction of his needs which in turn guarantee his own survival and happiness. Under this perspective man's relation to nature appears to be a vital condition for his being and well-being. This "earth-bound" condition throws further light upon man's existential condition as situational, circumstantial, and relational.

Man's relational existence is more than a mere accidental situation of being surrounded by and dependent upon the other beings around him. It is rather a necessary and essential constituent of man's struggle for survival. Instead of man being completely established in the domain of being and existence, he is called upon to face the continuous task of providing the means by which he may keep himself alive. Accordingly, self-sufficiency may be man's ideal without ever being or becoming man's achieved goal. And at the end of the fight man is always the loser: he loses the life he wanted so much to keep. It is, therefore, more accurate to describe man as a being insufficient in and for himself; he is a needy existent faced with the never-ending task of supplying the necessary fuel to keep himself going for another period of time. Thus one may conclude that man's relational existence signifies his permanent state of necessary dependence on Nature as the store-house of the means needed for his survival.

The imperfect condition of man's existence will appear in a more impressive perspective if a brief analysis of the basic dimensions of his vital concerns is undertaken. Life has been identified as a spontaneous and immanent activity (*motus ab intrinseco*), directed by an inner life principle (*entelecheia*), and aimed at the satisfaction of basic needs which maintain and develop it to the maximum of its potential. The early philosophers of human nature believed in the presence of many powers and instinctual dispositions as the instrumentality needed for the attainment of the chief purpose of living organisms, that is, survival. The number of powers, faculties, and instincts was determined by the number of vital activities displayed by the living. They originated the concept of a tripartite division of life into the vegetative, sensitive, and rational spheres. Modern psychology, having divorced itself from its philosophical heritage, discarded the doctrine on the powers of the soul (life principle) and tried to construct the science of psychology without a soul after the model of the positive sciences (physics, chemistry, and biology). But, in truth, the information thrown out through the front door has been smuggled in through the back door after carefully changing the old labels for new ones. Accordingly, instead of powers and faculties of the soul, modern psychologists speak of a host of "drives, urges, strivings" which populate the living organism, all of them belonging to the complexity of "motivated behavior." While speaking of "motives, needs, wants, desires, goals, ideals, and values" as the discoveries of experimental results, modern empiricists do not realize that "motive" is merely a derivative expression of the old "motivus." (They should not be blamed for this shortsightedness for they have never been "exposed" to Latin as the subject of the authoritarian school system!) Similarly, the traditional wording of the instinct for survival has been substituted by doctrines on "life adjustment", a revival of the Darwinian doctrine of "adaptation" of the organism to its environment.

Having established the principle of motivation, modern psychologists proceed to present the map or classification of motives underlying the overt and visible forms of animal and human behavior. Once again the criteria used for a hieratic classification reminds us of the above mentioned division of vital activities into vegetative, sensitive and rational. The wording, however, is different and less precise. Organic needs include the "motives" or the needs of vegetative and sensitive life processes; the latter are subsumed under the vague term, "psychic needs," and subdivided into personal and social motives; the social needs include of course, the cultural, moral, and religious motives of human animals. If considerable confusion and overlapping results from this random classification of needs and their outlets, the blame should go (so one is told) to the complexity of the subject matter and not to the confused state of the mind who attempts a classification without possessing clear cut criteria needed for the establishment of definite lines of demarcation between the different forms of life. Nonetheless, the impression on the reader of modern psychology texts is basically the same as that which had been had on the student of traditional philosophical psychology, namely, that man appears to be a dependent, imperfect, and insufficient being whose vital activities are constantly directed at the basic drive to maintain and improve the conditions of his existence. One may conclude, therefore, that life as spontaneous activity consists in a sustained process of need satisfaction aimed at the organism's being and well-being. Since concern here is limited to the meaning of human life as an activity from within, it will be restricted to a consideration of the basic human needs whose satisfaction effects the hieratic structure of human values.

Man as a microcosm represents the vital synthesis of the elements and perfections of inorganic, vegetative, sensitive, and rational forms of being. Each element reflects a specific dimension of human existence as manifested by a set of activities aimed at the satisfaction of specific needs for the perfections to be appropriated thereby. Considering man's existence from this aspect of dynamic vitality, success in interpreting its immediate meaning will be better achieved by viewing man as an agent engaged in vital action.

Action implies the duality of the agent (the subject and its term the object). The relation established between subject and object can be best described by analyzing first the dispositions and the attitudes of the agent toward the object of his actions. Man's attitude toward the world of objects is selective. The direction and the contents of his conations are determined from within by the set of specific needs related to the order of particular goods or perfections to be incorporated and assimilated by the subject who is in a constant want of them. Each vital activity, therefore, is necessarily goal directed, finalistically aimed at the possession of a particular good which specifies one or more innate tendencies or dispositions of the subject. The acts of vegetative life (nutrition, growth, and reproduction) guarantee the subsistence of the individual existent and the survival of the species as well. Their proper functioning brings about the state of a temporary balance (*homeostasis*), an equilibrium attained by the assimilation of nutritional values needed for the chemical integration of the organism. This highly complex process of selective activity implies choice, acceptance or rejection, preference manifested in approval (assimilation) or disapproval (elimination of the unwanted or waste products of the body).

On the level of sensitive life the chemical integration is improved by a higher system of complex vital activities (sense knowledge, affective dispositions, desires, likings and dislikings, and motor reactions) made possible by the sense organs and neural integration of the organs' varied reactions to the world of stimuli. Though still on the level of sensory experiences, there is no doubt of the highly selective character of related activities which suggest the presence of a rudimentary form of consciousness, the power of estimation, or a primitive form of value judgment such as the working of an elementary intelligence. All these activities (sense knowledge, affection, and locomotion) are goal directed attitudes of the organism aimed at the maintenance of bodily equilibrium and its further development. The field of perceptions, the objects perceived, the interpretation of the stimuli, the affective reactions of desire, tension, fear, and passion, followed by corresponding motor reactions, all demonstrate the tele-directed activity of the living organism determined from within by the coordinating and integrating efforts of the immanent life principle.

Man's selective attitude toward the world of goods and perfections appears in its full capacity on the level of rational conation directed by an intelligence which is conscious of itself and of its existential condition in the world of reality. The degree of self-consciousness represents, therefore, the highest synthesis of the vegetative, sensitive, and rational acts of man which takes him beyond the limitations of mere bio-physical needs and their appropriation. There appears at this point the expansion of man's motives into the region of the psychic, immaterial, cultural, and spiritual. Consequently, the range of human needs and wants is transferred from the level of animal integration to the perfection of the personal self-identity of an intelligent being who is conscious to a higher degree of the source, development, and functioning of all his desires and motives.

Knowledge moves from the region of perceptions and imagery to the realm of abstract concepts and reasoning; conation and the related affective states are no longer the blind demand of bodily necessities for they are illuminated by intuitive insights into a superior meaning of life made possible by the appropriation of the goods of a higher order. At this point man is called to the crucial task of allocating the proper value to all his activities by constructing a hierarchy of goods or perfections which takes into account the quantitative criteria along with the qualitative differences among values. Thus man's judgments of value take up the whole field of human existence with all the dimensions of his vital concerns. Life becomes more than a biological process; over and above the goal of chemical, neural, and motor integration of life activities, man is face to face with the problem of determining the boundaries of his personal life. Man experiences the need for personal integration on the level of intellectual and reflective insights. At this point, man should work out a hierarchy of values, an order of goods and perfections, which can be used as a personal guiding system in the search for an ultimate meaning of his self-conscious existence.

The significance of the hierarchy of values to be constructed and appropriated by man can be adequately weighed only if one becomes aware of the difficulties intrinsic to this problem. The idea of a hierarchy suggests, first of all, the coexistence of many elements to be brought into relative harmony and unity without the loss of any of the primary or secondary elements which should be included in the structural synthesis of values.

The plurality of divergent and often conflicting elements is the result of the complexity of human nature itself. Most obvious is the coexistence of two different principles, body and mind, each of which presents a full range of demanding needs and wants. Besides the conflicts between material and immaterial concerns, there are other dimensions of life suggesting further possibilities for conflicts. For instance individual goals are often opposed by collective tendencies. The individual has to find the right proportion between his personal and social values. There is always the danger of overemphasizing any one element of the pair of opposites and thus bringing about the symptoms of imbalance, disequilibrium, and tension. Whenever these symptoms appear in the life of individuals or communities, one may ascribe them to the deficiencies in the value system as a unilateral construction.

The history of philosophical systems offers the best illustration for the impressing variety of value structures arranged according to the basic assumptions of the philosophers regarding man's nature and his place in the world. From an axiological point of view it seems legitimate to consider the different schools and systems as so many variations on the same basic theme of values. Each system is, therefore, an attempt to construct a hieratic synthesis of values as the expression of man's thinking and valuing concerning himself, nature, and God. Materialism, idealism, realism, spiritualism, personalism, pantheism, and their divisions and subdivisions, represent the most important forms of philosophical value systems dictated by the different cognitive, affective, and volitional attitudes of certain thinkers at a given time and place.

The theoretical solutions are followed by a host of practical conclusions and consequences regarding man's individual, social, national, biological, economic, cultural, moral and religious concerns. Whenever one of these aspects gains a dominant position in respect to the rest of the collection, it is promoted to and sanctioned as a new philosophy, a new doctrine, a new system presenting a new attempt at the structural synthesis of human values. Individualism, collectivism, socialism, communism, capitalism, nationalism, pragmatism, positivism, scientism, moral and religious dogmatism stand as so many proposed solutions for the basic problem of the final and ideal hierarchy of values considered as the supreme norm and revelation as to man's existential condition. The disillusioned minds, while losing their faith in the possibility of any ideal synthesis of values, propose their own "isms," such as skepticism, subjectivism, agnosticism, and relativism. The only inconsistency in their attitude lies in their presentation of just another "ism" to prove the impossibility of any legitimate "ism" as such.

Cultural and philosophic anthropology, also called by the Germans the science of the Spirit (*Geisteswissenschaften*), approach the problem of human values and their hieratic arrangement from a historical, national, bio-social, and psychological point of view. The interpretation and phenomenological analysis of human civilization and culture, including their historical, spatio-temporal, and ethnico-geographical differences consists in trying to identify that particular set of ideal values which stands as the underlying organizing norm or principle (the normative spirit), which produces a given structural disposition of objectised values (the objective spirit) as they can be seen in the contents of a given civilization and culture. *Wilhelm Dilthey* is the philosopher of culture and history who is credited with the first attempt at this new method of disclosing the meaning of human existence in the light of man's cultural achievements.

The axiological (*value directed*) interpretation of human existence initiated by *W. Dilthey,* induced his followers to apply the same method to the critical evaluation of human values. This reflective analysis undertakes the difficult task of answering *the crucial question about the value of human values.* This question actually formulates the fundamental problem of value philosophy as the problem of what is "better or worse" among human values as we find them objectised in various philosophical systems, in science, morality, religion, arts, society, politics and economic life. Since the criteria used for the evaluation of values vary from one philosopher to the next, there had to appear a wide range of proposed diagnoses, some of them quite optimistic and others radically pessimistic, predicting the necessary decline of western civilization within one or two generations. Their disagreements indirectly demonstrate the lack of and the urgent need for an ideal hierarchy of values to be used as the right measure for something "better or worse."

## II. Value Antinomies

Man has always been with the world of objects as the potential locus of values apprehended as the order of goods or perfections man needs for the achievement of his well being. In this sense it is correct to say that the value problem is as old as humanity itself. On the other hand it is also true that the problem of values as a philosophic concern was explicitly formulated and discussed in its own right only by the modern and contemporary philosophers. The explicit concern with the critical question about *the value of our value judgments* has been conditioned by the historical development of human ideas.

The advent of modern philosophy, following the decline of medieval scholasticism, meant more than a change in the method of philosophizing. The *Cartesian "cogito"* is already the symptomatic expression of a radical reform, rather revolutionary in the world of values insofar as it adopted the anthropocentric view, radically opposed to the previous theocentric concern of medieval philosophers. This new mental attitude proves the presence of another revolutionary change in the form and contents of human values. Modern rationalism, illuminism, and idealism on the one hand, and pragmatic empiricism and positivism on the other, should be regarded as the necessary results of the *"Copernican revolution"* enthusiastically sanctioned by *Kant.*

Every revolution is both against the traditional order and for the establishment of a new one. It is its purpose to overthrow the existing order and to make room for the enthronement of the new one. The shortest way toward the attainment of this double purpose is to discredit or destroy the foundations upon which the old system of values rested and to find an immediate successor for the vacant throne, that is, to bring to power and authority a new hierarchy of values introduced as better than the old one. In this case the anthropocentric value system replaces the theocentric world view.

In the world of progressive ideologies the dynamic process of change occurs dialectically. The new is such only insofar as it opposes or revives some previous position. Being opposition, the new necessarily presupposes the position which now appears to be the condition of its possible emergence. The position, therefore, while asserting its own being, calls forth a denial. For "only with the fall of twilight does Minerva's owl take wing."

The emergence of the opposition occurs easier and sooner whenever the normative character of preceding values is violated by their original subscribers and their heirs. From a psychological point of view this process of crisis, leading to a decisive turning point, is prompted by man's failure to live up to the original commitment assumed on the occasion of putting together an ideal hierarchy of values as the expression of his faith in the meaning of life and existence. This is the tragical moment when Moses is ready to break the table of commandments, for a new idol is being worshipped. The normative character of values holds true and valid only as long as the persons who are committed to them live up to them by their faith and actions. In this regard the crisis of human values is preceded by a crisis in human faith.

Lacking an exhaustive insight into the absolute validity of a given value system, man may also be tempted by the conflicts of his very condition to question its absolute must-character and reliability. Man's limited knowledge always opens the door to the spirit of contradiction by which the authority of previous positions is put on trial. Doubt is the prosecutor of the case. The verdict is bound to be "guilty" if the jury of human actions supersedes the weight of ideal norms.

Adequate analysis requires, furthermore, an answer to man's actual failure to stay faithful to an established way of life, organized after the directives immanent to the leading hierarchy of values. To point merely to the gap between ideal norms and the actual mode of living appears to be only a statement of fact which says nothing or very little about the causes which have led to that specific situation of conflict.

While looking for a solution to this problem one must come across the qualitative differences existing among the value categories themselves. By qualitative differences is meant certain degrees of incompatibility among values when related to one another or forced to coexist in a given civilization and culture. If preference is given in a value category and thereby prominent position is reserved for one value, the other values must necessarily be relegated to the second, third or even the last place in that hierarchy. This juxtaposition implies the very serious conclusion that there is no final balance no matter what combination of values one may attempt. Every value system is an explosive structure because man's nature and existential condition are paradoxical.

By way of illustration it suffices to call attention to the polarities existing, between religious, philosophic, scientific, and aesthetic values on one hand, and the social, political and economic on the other. The first group is rated higher on the ground that it represents "values in themselves" and the foundation of cultured life; the second group is labelled as "means or contributory values" only, belonging to the realm of material civilization. These value antinomies come to expression even in traditional common sense, sanctioned by public opinion, in the form of well-known classical dichotomies such as: material and immaterial; natural and supernatural; temporal and eternal; relative and absolute; good and evil; virtue and sin; finite and unlimited; body and soul or spirit; nature and God; man and God; mystical and rational; reason and faith; etc.

In the process of the dialectical unfolding of human ideas and values, objectised in the history of civilization and culture, several attempts have been made by philosophers, theologians, scientists and political leaders to reconcile the above opposites by assigning to each element of the conflicting pairs its proper *"locus axiologicus,"* thus working toward an *"ideal hierarchy of values"* as the absolute measure of being. The countless number of systems which have been constructed by the thinkers of each generation throughout the centuries should provide sufficient evidence for man's repeated failure in attempting, again and again, the final reconciliation of the conflicts. A few historical examples could well illustrate the correctness of this rather pessimistic conclusion.

Without going into a detailed survey of philosophical systems and schools, it is to the point to recall the opposition between materialism and idealism of monistic, dualistic, and pluralistic versions. Idealism in all forms gives absolute priority to the spiritual, thus necessarily subordinating to it whatever falls into the category of material values. Materialism of all kinds claims an exclusive validity by denying its spiritual opponent. It is an obvious fact that each position has had its followers and reactionaries.

The situation is not altogether different in this generation. The conflict between world-immanence and world-transcendence is the inherited lot of modern man of today. It seems, however, that one now lives under the materialistic regime, the successor of its idealistic predecessor. This is the justification for writing on crisis, a critical turning point in human history. This crisis, however, can be identified more precisely as the crisis of values.

## III. Transvaluation or devaluation?

Christian religion is the undisputable foundation and expression of world-transcendence in the history of western civilization and culture. From its very beginning Christianity taught, and still teaches its fundamental thesis; that the human situation demands redemption through God's direct action. Man and the universe must and can be redeemed by God only, for man cannot transcend himself by himself in his condition of forlornness in the universe. To this day Christianity establishes a theocentric conception of life as the measure of all human and divine values. It is the transcendent, metaphysical, and mystical interpretation of human existence and the answer given to the problem of sin, evil, salvation, and eternal happiness. The Absolute, God, becomes man's highest value and the foundation for all other value categories.

Christian philosophy emerges as the synthesis of this supernatural knowledge, interpreted in the light of rational insights and inherited from the tradition of Greek thought. However, long before reaching maturity in the wisdom of Thomas Aquinas, Christian theology and philosophy had already developed a form of life saturated with its own hierarchy of values. The ideal norms expressed in theology, ethics and philosophy shaped and developed the organization of medieval culture and civilization. As a synthesis it reconciled the material and finite creature with his heavenly Father and Creator. Only from this aspect of other-worldliness was the condition of man acceptable.

Undoubtedly Christianity represented an ideal reconciliation of the natural and supernatural in the light of faith and reason. The absolute priority of the spiritual was the organizing force of an ideal value system in which each area of human endeavor was measured by the criterion of its transcendence. Theology and philosophy stood as the coordinating and integrating values of unity, truth, and goodness, presiding over the values of the beautiful, the just, and the useful. Faith, reason and action — artistic, social, political, and economic — were the hieratic disposition of man's powers which achieved the outstanding works in theology, philosophy, science, arts, education, and the socio-economic organization of medieval way of life.

The objective spirit of medieval culture, molded in the ideal frame of a metaphysical spirit of normative value-judgments, could last only on the assumption that each subsequent generation was successful in appropriating it by philosophic insight and religious faith. Unfortunately, there is no guarantee to insure that the heirs will possess the same nobility of spirit and ability of mind to live up to the challenge of greatness achieved by their fathers and forefathers. History exemplifies quite to the contrary via the dissipation of inherited values by incompetent epigones.

*W. Occam's* nominalism already contained the germs which disintegrated the system of critical realism of high scholastic philosophy. Mediocre persons appreciated only the values of mediocrity, located below the position occupied by the supreme values of a theocentric vision of the universe. This shift in the structural arrangement promoted the subordinate values to a place of eminence which they were not qualified to hold. In order to give at least a relative stability and justification to the new order of mediocrity it was necessary to let the previous norms fall into a gradual oblivion.

Renaissance and classical humanism were the responsible agents which revived part of the Greco-Roman cultural tradition in order to find in anthropocentrism, naturalism, and individualism a substitute for the ideals of medieval world-transcendence. The horizon of human existence became narrowed from the supernatural to the natural profile of human existence.

The disintegration of the original unity and harmony established by the theocentric scale of values was brought to daylight by *M. Luther's* rejection of reason illuminated by faith. The classical formulae: *"intelligo ut credam"* and *"credo ut intelligam"* lost their meaning in the Lutheran interpretation of faith deprived of a critico-reflective foundation. The separation of reason and faith leads to the separation of the natural from the supernatural order. The latter was justified now by mere blind faith which necessarily invited reason to challenge its legitimacy. Furthermore, the individualistic and subjective tendencies, inaugurated by an inadequate interpretation of personal freedom confronted with authority, paved the road to either rationalistic or pietistic interpretations of religious doctrine, leading to the fragmentation of religious communities so well illustrated by the increasing number of new church organizations.

Once the ultimate foundation of a value system is questioned, its progressive dissolution occurs by necessity. The split of theology was followed by a rupture of philosophic systems. This was the accomplished work of *Descartes. His "cogito ergo sum"* classically exemplifies the divorce between thought and reality. There is no bridge to close the gap between *"res cogitans"* (man) and the *"res extensa"* (matter); the ontological order remains unknown, for, according to Descartes, the *"terminus ad quem"* of knowledge is the mind's innate ideas only. Similarly, the integral unit of human nature, as explained by *Aristotle's* hylemorphistic doctrine, is destroyed by the opposition created between matter and form. *Descartes'* attempt to break through the circle of subjective immanence by an appeal to God's veracity ended in failure, due to the inconclusive character of his ontological argument on God's existence.

Cartesian dualism of the ontological and intentional orders set the pattern for the bifurcation of modern philosophic and scientific inquiry. The priority of the *"cogito"* started the idealistic mode of philosophising. There had been several attempts at regaining the lost order of unity between the transcendent and the immanent on the one hand, and the material and psychic on the other. *Malebranche* put forward his ontologism and occasionalism in order to establish some communication between God and his creatures; *Spinoza's* pantheism and psycho-physical parallelism was just another trial and error on the same problems; *Leibniz* optimistically professed a pre-established harmony.

On the other hand English sensism, laboring under the weight of the *"res extensa,"* created the systems of subjective relativism and materialism as they can be seen in *Hobbes, Locke, Berkeley,* and *Hume.* Moreover, the emergence and the discoveries of incipient modern science (*Copernicus, Galileo, Kepler, Newton*) seem to offer further justification for the use of empirico-mathematical methods of inquiry demanded in the works of *F. Bacon.* Consequently, there came into being the divorce between the speculative order (philosophy) and empirical order (science). The empirion gains the upper hand in being used for even the discussion and apparent solution of man's truly spiritual values.

The influence of this new naturalistic and rationalistic frame of mind on the development of modern civilization and culture can be seen in the development of *English deism* (*H. of Cherbury, Toland, A. Collins, Tindal, Blount, Woolston and Blongbroke,* the British Voltaire), *French rationalism* (*Voltaire, D'-Alembert, D'Holbach, Diderot, Helvetius* and *De La Mettrie*), and *German illuminism* (*Aufklärung*) represented by *Reimarus, Wolf, Lessing, C. F. Eichhorn, H. G. Paulus,* and others. Free thinking imported from England into the Continent set off the period of radical anthropocentrism and atheism, a form of romantic worship of human reason emancipated from "medieval obscurantism."

*Emmanuel Kant,* the philosopher of Königsberg, is the outstanding architect of modern rationalism who undertook the gigantic work of critically establishing the boundaries of human reason confronted with the regions of reality. What was meant to be the reconstruction of science, philosophy, and religion actually resulted in widening the gap between mind and being (*Ding an sich*), a position taken to its ultimate consequences of pantheistic idealism (through *Fichte and Schelling*), in *Hegel's* transcendental logic.

English empiricism of the XVII and XVIII centuries developed further in the systems of modern positivism by *A. Comte* in France and *J. S. Mill* and *H. Spencer* in England. The positivistic mode of thinking is applied also to the field of behavioral sciences, and brings forth modern sociology of *E. Dürkheim,* modern political science and economics of both capitalistic (*A. Smith*) and socialistic structure (*K. Marx*). The advent of technology and progressive industrialization condition the emergence of socio-political unrest as the outcome of the radical shake-up of Western civilization founded on the premises of subjectivism, relativism, agnosticism, rationalism, naturalism, pragmatism, positivism, militant atheism, capitalism, and communism. All of them display the symptoms of the same heretic disease of anthropolatry. *Friedrich Nietzsche's* work can be held as the best example of man's divinization through the myth of the coming superman. The reliability of this boundless faith, which man put in the powers of his reason and scientific progress, can be best tested in the light of present day world-wide crisis in an age of anxiety while mankind faces the imminent threat of total self-destruction.

Contemporary existentialists speak for the tragical condition of human existence, torn apart by the disrupting feelings of fear, anguish, dread, self-estrangement, and nausea. Existentialism, however, does not offer any reconstructive solution for man's situation of modern uprootedness. It merely draws, with impressive colors and vivid vocabulary, the depressing profile of a modern man as a frightened pessimist and nihilist, whose practical hedonism is the only compensation left to give him symptomatic relief from his inner conflicts and spiritual frustrations. As *Heidegger* emphatically concludes: the only reason that man is in the world is to wait for the hour of death (*"in der-Welt-zum-Tode-sein"*).

## IV. Symptoms of Crisis

The experiences of loneliness, thrownness, and anxiety are the sure symptoms of modern man's basic maladjustment in the present world of socio-cultural crisis. On the other hand, since culture and civilization represent the objectised synthesis of individual and collective values, one is fully justified to describe this socio-cultural crisis in terms of a crisis in man's value judgments and corresponding value hierarchy. For it is evident that every individual or collective way of life is "a priori" conditioned and shaped from within by the form of value-directed attitude and productivity. This is also the original meaning of the Greek word for "crisis," i.e., an act of decision, resulting from the previous acts of analysis, selective discrimination, choice, which leads either to an active acceptance or a negative rejection of a particular good or perfection. This is what contemporary axiology means by a value-judgment or the act of valuing. The common sense interpretation of crisis dates back to the Romans, precisely, to the medical jargon of the Aesculapians by which term they meant the decisive phase of the turning point in the process of a disease. Since the change was very frequently for the worse, crisis became associated with something with a negative outcome.

Man's value-judgments may also reach a critical turning point insofar as he has to "decide" what values, in what order of importance and structural disposition, should be taken into the world of human civilization and culture. Using again the biological term of metabolism and homeostasis as one term of the analogy, one may speak of cultural metabolism and cultural homeostasis too. The balance of a cultural organism depends on the presence of all necessary values in a hieratic disposition, according to their qualitative differences and normativity. If some important value category is omitted from the unity of the whole system, imbalance, or "crisis" occurs out of necessity. Along with the error of omission, there can also be the error of placing undue emphasis upon some values while disregarding the position of eminence demanded by others. Imbalance results again, this time, however, because of an error in the architectural design of the value structure. Cultural equilibrium is brought about by the coexistence of all human values according to their superior or inferior normativity.

Cultural balance or imbalance, however, is conditioned by man's value-judgments. Its adequate or deficient, rather unilateral character, will decide the fate of cultural progress or decline.

In the light of the above analogy it is suggested that present-day socio-cultural crisis is reducible to modern man's inadequate or erratic critical attitudes toward the world of ideal and practical values. His value judgments are unilateral, and deficient; undue emphasis has been put on the values of material civilization while the ideal values of a cultured life have been either totally neglected or moved to the lower end of the hierarchy. In other words, religious, theoretic, and aesthetic value categories — known as "values in themselves" — have been devaluated or rejected, and the categories known as mere "contributory-values" — such as the social, political, and mainly the economic — have been promoted to an undeserved position of excellence.

This diagnosis seems to be sufficiently documented by the brief historical survey of modern philosophy presented above. To provide more evidence and thus create a broader foundation for the problems under discussion in this book, the symptoms of crisis will be presented by analyzing, at this time, the condition and position held by the different value-categories which do or do not belong to modern civilization and culture. As these considerations are meant only as an introduction to the value problem, the discussion will be limited to a critical analysis of six fundamental value categories, i. e., the religious, theoretic, aesthetic, social, political, and economic values without committing the error of omission or of arbitrary allocation of values.

The *theoretic value,* truth, is found in the enunciations of abstract, pragmatic, and normative sciences as the results of experiential, intellectual, and reflective modes of knowing the different regions of objective reality. The superior synthesis of scientific knowledge should come to expression in the philosophy of science as the ultimate foundation and integration of partial insights aimed at the vision of the whole.

Critically reviewing the rise and development of modern science, there is no doubt as to its progressive differentiation into many fields of specialization achieved by disengaged and applied research. In fact, scientific progress revolutionized man's socio-economic organization of life via advanced technology and industrialization. Its visible achievements can be seen in modern civilization as man's partial but still progressing victory over matter, time, energy and space.

On the other hand, one cannot lose sight of the negative aspects equally inherent in the systems of scientific positivism. For ages science has divorced itself from inherited philosophic principles to the extent of claiming exclusive competence for passing the last, exact, and tested judgment on the whole meaning of human existence. While taking a standing against theology and metaphysics as historically conditioned, inferior stages of human civilization, positive science optimistically promised unbounded progress by which all problems would be solved and human happiness achieved. The apostles of unlimited progress did not suspect that atheistic science might be a dangerous weapon to annihilate itself and its responsible agents.

Furthermore, given the limitations of a strictly empirical and quantitative method of scientific analysis, the most modern science can offer to man is better provision and easier satisfaction of his material needs as a bio-physical organism. However, man's higher needs, conditioned by his cultural and spiritual ideals—the aesthetic, social, political, moral, and religious values—cannot and have not been solved by mathematical calculies or biochemical formulae. The failure of scientific positivism in solving the truly human problem of existence and coexistence indirectly testifies to the need for an integration of human knowledge from a metaphysical point of view. The moral implications of this desideratum could offer the only guarantee for man's survival in spite of his monstrous science.

The *economic value* is the useful. It stems from man's organic needs in his spatio-temporal situation which dictate a recurrent sequence of organized activities by which material well-being and security can be achieved and guaranteed. All useful activities are dominated by the economic law of "maximum achievement with a minimum of energy expenditure." It involves the efforts of practical intelligence, the art of know-how, directed toward the progressive control of matter, energy, time, and space, subordinated to man's use. The totality of material wealth and progress produced by means of modern techniques (industrialization, mechanization, and automation of the economic process within the boundaries of its experiential dimension) is made possible by the application of pragmatic scientific discoveries.

It should be emphasized, however, that a civilization subordinated predominantly to the principles of a utilitarian life-order hardly deserves the denotation of true human culture. There is the danger of promoting the economic value to a position of superiority with respect to the other values, thus creating the order of an economic dictatorship (capitalism and communism) which takes possession of the whole human community, organized, subject and enslaved by the supraindividual forces of capital, labor, production, and distribution of material goods. The hypertrophy of the economic process does not result in man's emancipation from his material needs; on the contrary, it leads to the complete domination of all cultural endeavors which come to be regarded as mere byproducts or sublimated effects of man's original demand for material well-being. This crisis is bound to occur whenever a means-value, such as the economic principle of utility, becomes the highest norm and ideal of individuals and social groups. In this sense materialism and its progress indirectly bring about the decline of man's cultural values. From a psychological point of view, radical materialism produces an extravert hedonist dominated by the pleasure principle and ignorant of his condition of cultural starvation.

The *social and political values* can be isolated if one considers the reasons why the individual chooses to live in society rather than in the condition of isolation. Starting with the bio-physical foundation of social behavior, it is obvious that the individual belongs to a species through which it came into being and by which it may survive and take its share in the prolongation of its life. In this sense it is true to say that man is a social animal *(zoon politikon)* whose very existence and survival depend on the existence of an organized form of life within the natural group of which he is a member.

The bio-physical aspect of social life is not sufficient in itself to exhaust the whole meaning of human togetherness. Man's innate social drive or instinct accounts only for the need to protect, develop and guarantee the continuity of physical existence. It is not sufficient, however, to explain the meaning of those forms of human social behavior whose motivation, content, and scope transcend the limited sphere of bare life and its preservation. Human culture as the product of collective efforts and achievement go beyond the restricted area of mere survival and material well-being. The values objectised in culture disclose man's psychic, immaterial, and spiritual needs whose meaningful interpretation must reach for clues beyond the area of bio-physical necessities of organic life. The very existence of civilization and culture identifies man as essentially different from other social animals which do not possess anything in this progress from the biological to the noological horizon of existence. This fact taken in itself is sufficient reason to reject all modern, positivistic, i. e., purely materialistic interpretation of social phenomena.

The organized form of human social coexistence must be regarded as answering the individual's need for self-transcendence through the channels of cultural communication.

Individuality implies, on one hand, the perfection of oneness, unity, self-identity, distinction, singularity, originality, and exclusiveness. On the other hand, the condition of being an individual also includes some negative aspects of existence, such as separation, loneliness, limitation, imperfection, and unilaterality. The individual is only one instance of human life which does not and cannot contain all the perfections which belong to human nature in which he participates in a rather limited measure. Consequently, it is this set of positive and negative attributes of the individual form of existence that lays the foundations for and justifies the existence of human comunication flowing through the channels of organized social life and its institutions. The individual member, living in a cultured community, is thus provided with the possibility of transcending himself in the process of communication by which his social needs are satisfied and cultural values are assimilated. The limited profiles of individual existence can be extended toward the unbounded horizons of cultural achievements.

The fundamental value category which stimulates, supports, and justifies the condition of cultured togetherness is *love,* understood as the awareness of one common human nature, individually represented by individual human persons, trying to establish a communion of all in the treasures of supraindividual cultural ideals. This confrontation of individuals through love does not threaten the freedom of each; on the contrary, it is the ideal atmosphere needed by the individual to reach his goal of personal autonomy.

With the advent of modern science, technology, and industrialization there came the need for a more formal, rather rigid organization of social life, due also to the unprecedented increase in population. The ideals of democracy penetrate more and more the body of human society and bring about the emancipation of the masses. By this time the traditional ideal of one Christian family, inspired by the faith in the provident assistance of God as the father of mankind, has been emptied of its original meaning and replaced by naturalistic, positivistic, purely materialistic interpretation of human society, regressing once more to the criteria of sheer instinctual drives which dominate the behavior of other animals. The individual's demand for being respected in his personal freedom was interpreted as the outcome of basic egocentrism which offset the balance of the whole social organism. Consequently, theories are put forward according to which the individual is divested of his free, moral dignity, and is regarded as a statistical unit, a cog in the wheel, a cell in the organism, without any right to claim any value in himself and apart from the whole. Society, organized on the rigid principles of positivistic political science and economics, is presented as the only value to which all other values — including individual freedom — have to be sacrificed. This change represents the radical reversal of Christian social doctrine, according to which society is for man and man is for himself. The individual human person represents a value in itself, while society provides only the ideal environment (means-value) in which the human person can reach his natural goal of self-appropriation. The emergence of socialistic ideal and totalitarian political regimes speaks by itself for the crisis of social values. National and international conflicts prove the primacy of hate and ruthless competition to be lifeless substitutes for the genuine social value of human love among free individuals. As a reaction to the increasing threat of being totally engulfed and enslaved by the imperatives of mass-society and police-states, some individuals may desert the community of human society by professing the beliefs of individualism.

The *aesthetic value,* the beautiful, is rooted in the emotional perception and subsequent objectivation of concrete experiences of the harmonious, proportional, and well-balanced tonality of internal (subjective) and external (objective) forms within the two extreme poles of either pure impressionism or pure expressionism. The visible projection of this creative experience constitutes the varied fields of art. The artist draws the materials for his creative intuition both from the world of physical objects and the world of ideas, using the latter for the transfiguration of matter through an idea. On the other hand, the artist's vision is also conditioned by the peculiar socio-cultural atmosphere of his generation. Greek, Roman, medieval, modern, and contemporary arts translate into symbolic forms that specific hierarchy of values which identifies every historical phase of cultural progress. Accordingly, one may easily reconstruct the ideological atmosphere of an historical epoch by interpreting its artistic symbolism.

Applying this criterion to the reflective evaluation of contemporary modern art, it appears from the very beginning that the crisis of the modern age is pictured in the crisis of modern art. In opposition to the metaphysical and classical inspiration of previous schools, modern art moves within the narrow field of the sensuous, sensational, and enjoyable. The progressive disintegration of natural forms, the search for something new, regardless of its validity or authenticity, plus the rejection of objective normativity as the measure of the beautiful,—at least its extreme tendencies—all this symbolically communicates the inner crisis of modern conscience and consciousness to the extent of reaching the limits of abnormal experiences. The emphases on disharmony, asymetry, disequilibrium, and distortion appear to be the projection of identical experiences in the soul of the artist. The moral, social, and educational responsibility of the artist and his work has been rejected on the ground of a false interpretation of artistic autonomy. The category of the beautiful, being disengaged from its intrinsic affinity to the transcendentals of unity, truth, and goodness, is at the mercy of subjective and individualistic forms of expression which utilize the experiences of moral and social licence as sources and standards of so called artistic inspiration. Modern man's inner anarchy is being sold to the public as the new dimension in artistic experiences. All this amounts to the conclusion drawn by many students of clinical psychology and psychiatry, that the extreme position maintained by a good number of modernists brings them closer to the region of morbid abnormality than to the transcendental value of the beautiful. The schizoid tendencies of a disintegrated person are being projected onto canvas, into the mass of matter or into the torturing disharmonies of musical compositions. Modern art is, therefore, the most evident testimony for the cause of a mentally disturbed patient, the sophisticated type of modern insanity. Its main symptoms can be described in opposition to the classical values which animated the art of previous generations. Thus we have disharmony taking the place of harmony; disproportion destroying the taste for proportion; disequilibrium instead of equilibrium; distortion of natural form sold as a new dimension in aesthetic insight, lifeless abstraction without the objective carriers to which they naturally belong, the exploration of the sub-social types of human society presented as the heroes of moral anarchy; all this is being rationalized by the untenable sophistry professed in the *"L'art pour l'art"* justification of irresponsible license mistaken for the right use of freedom.

The *religious value,* the Absolute, is the ultimate, transcendent, and necessary foundation of all preceding value categories. It is not, however, a mere synthesis or the sum total of human values put into the superlative. Such an interpretation would only be the deification of human perfections. God would then be the Nietzschean super-man. Nor is it the utopian ideal of an indefinite process of evolution or development achieved by human progress, a belief which inspired the positivistic, rationalistic and socialistic religions of heaven on earth. On the contrary, the Absolute is the unrelated, unconditioned, infinite Being, who freely communicated being to his creatures on a limited scale of participation. Consequently, all perfections of the macrocosm (the universe) and of the microcosm (man) become meaningful and teledirected only if viewed with this metaphysical perspective as their source of origin.

Critically reviewing the whole hierarchy of human values — both taken in themselves for what they are, and in their psycho-cultural and historical significance — we must become aware of their insufficiency to redeem man from his existential condition. Every mature thinker will sooner or later experience the Faustian disillusion and frustration when looking deeper into the limitations of human philosophy and science, into the imperfections of man's artistic creativity, or into the conflicts in his socio-political organizations and the enslaving power of economic necessities.

If today is the age of anxiety, it is because man has been deprived of his faith in the Absolute, thereby losing faith in himself, his fellow man, and in his work. The modern transvaluation of values actually means the total devaluation of values thus denying man the ultimate reason and meaning to be.

Retrospectively summarizing the preceding considerations, the fundamental error of the modern age may be identified as the effect of a gradual breaking-up of the unity, truth and goodness of the ontological order into conflicting pairs of opposites. Thus the metaphysical is and remains separated from the physical; the ontological order of things is beyond the reach of the intentional order of the mind; the empirical order of immediate causes is not substantiated by philosophic insights into underlying ultimate reasons; reason is opposed to faith; body is the negation of the soul; freedom is denied by necessity; instinct dominates the will; and finally, society oppresses the individual, reducing him to the condition of an obedient puppet.

The splitting of the original harmony in the hierarchy of values brings about the inner splitting of man, manifested in his schizoid ambivalence and basic disorientation. In the presence of conflicting dichotomies, without a superior synthesis, modern man acts pragmatically by simply denying or ignoring one element of the opposites, thus hoping to create for himself some room and directive for living. Having inherited the tradition of agnostic rationalism, it is the supernatural, spiritual, and philosophic values which are cast out of the collection of his vital concerns. His mounting anxiety is the immediate proof for this unwise choice.

Instead of opposing values in conflicting dichotomies, it would make more sense to understand the opposites not as conflicting but as actually integrating each other. Accordingly, the relative calls for the Absolute; the limited, finite, and imperfect direct the attention toward the unlimited, infinite, and all-perfect; the temporal, contingent, and material modes of being can be accepted in the perspective of an eternal, necessary, and spiritual Being. Within the limited horizon of human existence the opposites can be reconciled if each value element becomes conjugated with its natural component. Thus the instinctual and emotional drives of human nature can be illuminated by intellect and will; human power and freedom should be confronted with moral responsibility and justice. Finally, the short-sighted philosophy of rational positivism or agnostic skepticism should be improved upon by the powers of natural and supernatural Faith as the only remedy for man's learned ignorance.

The devaluation of values imposes the tremendous demand for their rehabilitation through a critico-reflective analysis of original premises. To undertake such a reconstructive work is in itself worthwhile even though one may not finish it altogether. On the other hand, being conscious of this ideological imperative of our day, the author of the present work hopes to contribute at least the foundations upon which a sound philosophy of value can be further elaborated. Such, and no other, is the scope of the following discussions.

## CHAPTER II

## THE DIMENSIONS OF THE VALUE EXPERIENCE

Human knowledge sprouts, first, on the pure experiential level *(empirion)*, as the encounter of the individual subject with the objects given in his life situation. Common sense experience, therefore, is the needed basis for the advent of either a scientific research into underlying causal relationships or of a higher critico-reflective evaluation of the experienced segments of so-called "reality" from a philosophic or theological point of view. For even the transcendental and metaphysical mode of intuiting of the religious man presupposes the common sense data of lived experiences. Thus religious transcendence — the leap into the supernatural — necessarily presupposes something to be left behind, after being used as a springboard for the ascension into the noumenal regions of existence. Consequently, the empirical, scientific, philosophic, and religious modes of knowing constitute the four ascending dimensions of possible attitudes the individual subject may assume in the presence of the given world.

This much being assumed, and perhaps even granted, it follows that the present discussion on the dimensions of the value experience should take as its starting point the first mode of knowing the world from "the natural standpoint." It is obvious, therefore, that the description of the value experience can be done only by a phenomenological method. Only in later discussions may we move the question about the validity and reliability of our spontaneous valuings.

In order to create this necessary background of personal experiences it is to the point to quote the remarkable passage from E. Husserl's work on phenomenology.[1]

1. *E. Husserl*: Ideen zu einer reinen Phänomenologie und phänomenologische Philosophie, 1913; Tr. by W. R. B. Gibson; chapter on: Ideas: General Introduction to Phenomenology.

"Our first outlook upon life is that of natural human beings, imaging, judging, feeling, willing, from the natural standpoint. Let us make clear to ourselves what this means in the form of simple meditations which we can best carry on in the first person.

I am aware of a world, spread out in space endlessly, and in time becoming and become, without end. I am aware of it; that means, first of all, I discover it immediately, intuitively, I experience it. Through sight, touch, hearing, etc., in different ways of sensory perception, corporeal things somehow spatially distributed are *for me simply there,* in verbal or figurative sense "present," whether or not I pay them special attention by busying myself with them, considering, thinking, feeling, willing. Animal beings also, perhaps men, are immediately there for me; I look up, I see them, I hear them coming towards me, I grasp them by the hand; speaking with them, I understand immediately what they are sensing and thinking, the feelings that stir them, what they wish or will. They too are present as realities in my field of intuition, even when I pay them no attention.

In this way, when consciously awake, I find myself at all times, and without my ever being able to change this, set in relation to a world which, through its constant changes, remains one and ever the same. It is continually "present" for me, and I myself am a member of it. Therefore, this world is not there for me as a mere *world of facts and affairs,* but with the same immediacy, as *a world of values, a world of goods, a practical world.* Without further effort on my part I find the things before me furnished not only with the qualities that befit their positive nature, but with value-characters such as beautiful or ugly, agreeable or disagreeable, pleasant or unpleasant, and so forth. Things in their immediacy stand there as objects to be used, the "table" with its "books," the "glass" to drink from, the "vase," the "piano," and so forth. These values and practicalities, they too belong to the *constitution* of the *"actually present" objects as such,* irrespective of my turning or not turning to consider them or indeed any other object. . . .

That which we have submitted towards the characterization of what is given to us from the natural standpoint, and thereby of the natural standpoint itself, was a piece of pure description *prior to all "theory."*

While it is customary to say that "the world" is given to me in my experience as actually present, and that I am "in the world," it should be borne in mind, nevertheless, that "the world" is never experienced in its global totality by any individual. Even the sum total of experiences, a given individual may have had of the world, cannot be taken as equivalent to the world as a whole in its objective and total reality. Therefore, the terms "world," "reality," "nature," and "life" are rather vague notions both in their extension and comprehension. They do not account for the factual size and dimensions of personal experiences. On the contrary, they represent merely the effects of generalizations and mental abstractions by which the mind moves from a few particular experiences to universal conclusions, thus theoretically extending the limitations of first hand contacts with some of the things which fall into the narrow field of perceived phenomena. So it comes that these abstract ideas are of a wide extension and enjoy a very poor comprehension. This situation makes it rather difficult to exactly determine their precise meaning.

Since "reality" is never given in my experience in its wholeness, it appears more correct to describe the psychic process by which each individual construes, builds up his own limited "world." Perhaps it would be altogether much wiser to discard the impressing expressions mentioned above, and refer rather to the profiles and horizons of personal experiences which occur only in quite concrete situations at any given time and place. In other words, the "world" is not given to me, just some fragmentary aspects of it which I may call "facts," "phenomena," "things," "objects" or "events." Similarly, "reality" is not present to me and I am not present in "reality as such." Even the "objects" of my personal experience are not objects in the abstract; quite to the contrary, at any moment of being "face to face" with something which is not I, it appears to me as some-thing individual, particular, unique, exclusive, and original. This unique individuality of the emergent phenomenon in my personal experience is bound to be lost whenever I try to translate it into a conceptual form of communication. Words are labels to identify only the common aspects abstracted from the singularity of the extant phenomenon.

Should there be any need for justifying this insistence on the gap between personal experiences and the clumsiness of its linguistic symbolism, it would be sufficient to point to the same abyss between the individual and concrete character of personal conation which follows the cognitive encounter and its conceptual formulation: whenever I am motivated by some desire, it is not just "some" desire; on the contrary, I know very well what I desire and want. I do not desire "something" but rather "this" or "that" specific or particular content or element present in my experience.

The conclusion one must arrive at at this point can be stated as follows: just inasmuch as "reality" is made up of unique events, to the same extent the experience of "a world of values, a world of goods" can be described only in the concrete, and never in the abstract. This state of affairs imposes upon us, first, the task of describing the experiential process of building up one's individual profile of existence, and, second, the phenomenological account of the emergence of conation which follows the prehension of particular goods. Thus, it is hoped that the dimensions of the value experience can be reconstructed on the pattern of experiential evidence "prior to all theory."

One's awareness of his position in the ever-changing flux of emergent phenomena is not an immediate or direct experience. The mind of the human individual is closed in, enveloped by a physical organism which mediates through its sensibility the indirect contact with the things pertinent to one's situation in the procession of experiences. In other words, it is through the outer and inner senses that we become introduced to and made aware of something out there. Consequently, our awareness of something which is not ourselves is only an indirect and mediated — second-hand — information. The mind knows only through the channels of the organism's sensory equipment.

Pointing to the mediation of knowledge, our purpose is not to engage into the longstanding dispute over the subjective or objective value of our percepts, imagery, and ideational activity. While recognizing the legitimacy of such a critical analysis, here we are committed only to the description of the process of how the "world of reality" is being mediated to the knowing self. The problem of the objective validity of indirect awareness of the world will be taken up later insofar as it has a definite bearing on the objective validity of human values, their normative character, and the realiability of related value judgments.

Before entering the description of the cognitive process from its initial start on the sensory level up to the limits of discoursive reasoning and related insights, a general discussion on the nature of knowledge is needed in order to create a frame of reference for the ulterior conclusions to be drawn from the facts obtained in the course of phenomenological description.

The personal experience of knowing the world rests on the initial duality of two given elements, usually referred to as the subject and the object. The knowing subject is confronted with some object which penetrates into the field of his subjectivity. The subject's encounter with the object of his experience creates the condition of being related or referred to something which is first identified, rather perceived, as something *not* belonging to his inner world, though now present in the sphere of his subjective awareness. The object is, first, experienced as something thrown at the subject from without in its otherness ("object" from the Latin verb *ob-icere)*.

The object's otherness is interpreted as "something other than I"; it lies outside the subject's inner field with which he is more familiar; therefore, it appears to be something new, different, even strange and unlike. Before any attempt is made by the subject to know the object present in his perceptional field, that is, to get acquainted, familiar with it and to interpret the meaning of the extant phenomenon, the subject becomes emotionally stirred up; he responds by the feelings of awe, wonder, maybe even some fear mixed with desire motivated by curiosity.

The object is present to the subject as unknown and mysterious, though inviting him to overcome the distance in the encounter by moving closer to it. The subject's move toward the object is conditioned by his sensitivity being exposed to the object which affects, stimulates one or more of his receptors (sense organs). Being affected by some objects lying outside the subject's inner world presupposes his sensibility or sensitivity. Being sensitive to the world of objects and phenomena suggests, first, a natural coordination and correspondence between the subject and the object of his physical environment. Second, this natural affinity also suggests the idea that the subject responds by his sensitivity to the qualities of the objects because both were made for each other. Though the objects are different in their otherness from the subject, the latter may and does find it natural to be surrounded, imbedded, immersed, and affected by things belonging to his range of sensitivity.

Because of this natural correspondence and conformity the subject may feel to belong to the world inasmuch as the objects belong to his experiences. As it will appear below, the subject's presence in the physical world stands also for his natural habitat, the only environment in and through which he can live and adjust by satisfying the needs his insufficient constitution brings along. As a consequence the process of getting acquainted with the world is experienced in a spontaneous, natural way, as a need brought to light by the subject's curiosity and satisfaction whenever the encounter results in some pleasurable experience. Thus *"being in the world"* becomes less and less strange until it reaches the condition of *"being at home"* with the objects becoming more and more *"familiar"* to the subject.

On the other hand, the well-known feelings of familiarity in the world are bound to be disturbed, first, when the subject has certain experiences of an unpleasurable tonality, and, second, when the maturing subject becomes aware of the limitations of his knowledge. The growing awareness of being set within the limits of a man-sized world is a frustrating, disturbing experience for all those who get beyond the limited horizons of common sense and make an attempt at transcending the natural boundaries of knowledge either by scientific or philosophic reflections into the world hidden behind the appearance of sense experience. At this crucial point of critical analysis reality once more appears as *"mundus absconditus,"* a hidden world.

The natural certainty of the common man is now interpreted as a subjective illusion to the disillusioned condition of the critical analyst. The world recesses again as mysterious, strange, and wrapped in the veil of its otherness. Due to man's inventive insights certain barriers are overcome again by some major scientific and philosophic break-through just to find oneself once more in front of another door kept under the lock of human ignorance. At this point some thinkers still have the courage, faith, patience, and energy left to unlock the door; at least they hope to succeed in it. Some others, however, may reach a negative conclusion in terms of an *"ignoramus et ignorabimus,"* we ignore and shall ignore it.

The experience of human ignorance is a painful event for every sensitive subject. The reaction to pain may be in the direction of resigned agnosticism, or skepticism; others may react by a radical turn about in their attitude: like Plato and his early or modern followers, leap into the invisible by the postulate of either a philosophic or religious faith. Then the ideal or supernatural knowledge is presented as "superior in range, quality, and validity" because of its divine origin. This is the attitude of the *"credo ut intelligam,"* I believe in order to understand. Finally, those of a less precipitated reaction try to bridge the gap between the limitations of the natural knowledge and supernatural revelation by using the more rational formula of *"intelligo ut credam,"* I understand in order to believe.

No matter which side one will take, he still has to recognize that all men live in this world by faith as the extension of limited insights. It is the faith of common sense, the faith of the scientist, the faith of the philosopher, and finally, the faith of the religious man.

Since faith is a universal human attitude, it appears to be necessary to include it in the dimensions of human valuing inasmuch as it is present in all forms and degrees of human knowledge; it is the supporting criterion also for the validity of our value judgments which rest on knowledge supported by faith. Thus one may conclude and say that man lives, that is, knows, feels, evaluates and acts by faith.

The above considerations on the nature and limitations of human knowledge and valuing were presented in order to establish the reasonable boundaries within which the emergence of knowledge, faith, and value appear. Let us subject the process of knowledge to a closer descriptive analysis.

Using the established terminology in philosophic and psychological dialogues, we might well start with the objective components of the relation, called stimuli, acting upon man's sensibility.

Out of the many qualities belonging to the object's make-up the subject can register only those which fall within the limited range of his sensitivity. The subject's sensitivity is limited in two ways. First, man's sensory equipment—both outer and inner senses—receive those qualities to which they are made sensitive and nobody would believe that these receptors or antennae exhaustively register all the qualities or properties of the objects. Thus the object stands for more than man can know of it. Reality and man's power to appropriate it by knowledge are not commensurate. Second, within the limited number of senses there is another restriction imposed by the maximum and minimum threshold of sensitivity of any given sense organ. Therefore, the stimuli (some primary or secondary qualities of the objects) are perceived only if their intensity and range falls within the boundaries of subjective sensitivity. Once more, the objects stand out and spread beyond the narrow channels of sensations. It is true, therefore, that man is not equipped by nature to perceive either the very small or the unusually large. Hence it has always been the scientists' endeavor to improve upon the subjective barriers of knowledge by developing instruments whose sensitivity reaches beyond the crude elements of natural sensitivity and to extend the dimensions of knowledge in its range, depth, and intensity.

Unfortunately, even the most refined instruments appear to be too clumsy when they come to register the extremely small or the extremely distant. Consequently, whenever the reach of scientific observations falls short of its object, the scientist is forced to use theory and hypothesis to supplement the lacunae in his observations. Besides, even the observed facts do not introduce and speak for themselves; they just stand there waiting to be identified and labelled by some theoretical device of interpretation. These facts alone should be sufficient reasons to state the imperfection and fallibility of human knowledge and subsequent valuing. However, there is still another aspect in human knowledge which will lead to the above conclusion from another angle.

The phenomenon or thing which occupies the field of cognitive concern is not perceived at once and in its wholeness. Sense perception proceeds in a fragmentary fashion and moves only on the surface area of reality. The wholeness of the phenomenon is broken down into fragments of informations channeled by man's receptors. Each sense organ contributes only some specific quality which constitutes its formal object of sensitivity. Now it depends on the amount and quality of registered properties and on the process of *rebuilding the object from within* whether we suceed in constructing a mental *simulacrum* (image) which more or less is like the original elements given in the subject's encounter with the materials of his experience.

Considering the above-mentioned limitations of sense perception and adding to them the amount of distortions made by the receptors and the possible mistakes made by the subject while putting sense data together, one cannot escape but must face once more the imperfections of sense knowledge. On the other hand, whatever imperfections belong to sense knowledge, they will necessarily be present and manifest themselves in man's valuing which presupposes the cognitive process.

With a view to the degree of validity of human knowledge and valuing, it seems to be necessary to go further into the amount of subjective distortion and to explore the possibilities to correct them by critico-reflective reconsiderations of the first impressions.

Most philosophers and scientists have been aware of the principle announced by Aquinas that "whatever is received, is received after the condition of the receiver." The receiver's condition is not pure receptivity as expressed in the naive form of stimulus and response formula of the early Behaviorists $(B = S + R)$. Pure receptivity ignores the spontaneous, dynamic, and living character of psychic processes, trying to force them into the narrow vision of a mechanical conception of psychic life. In fact, however, the subject's role in the process of knowledge should be described as *"receptive creativity."* It is receptive because the subject does not create the stimuli coming from an object or phenomenon given in his experience. It is creative because knowledge is possible only on the condition that the physical mode of existence of the object is transformed, and changed. Thus the object, besides being in its own right apart from the subject, gains a new form of existence in the knower and through the knower's creativity. This mode of existing in the knower is not a physical presence in the subject for the object is not consumed by the subject: the knower recreates the object's *"alter-esse"* from the material of sense impressions collected in the state of sensing, apprehending, perceiving, and reconstructing its possible identity and meaning. Consequently, the adequate formula to express the cognitive experience is that of *impression* and *expression* as its two basic moments. This is what the Greeks originally meant by *"aisthesis."*

The impression is caused by the action of stimuli on one or more of the subject's sensitive receptors. It is the *objective element* insofar as the subject does not create his stimuli. (Even hallucinations presuppose some previous exposure to some outside sitmuli.) By impression is meant, therefore, the change, modification or state of being innerved or stirred up by some physical agent working on the senses. The change in the senses brings forth also a change of that which caused the change insofar as physical qualities are transformed into sensations of light, color, taste, temperature, sounds, odors, motions, shape, size, position, volume, weight, pressure, extension, etc. etc. No doubt these sensations represent both the impression of the subject and the new mode of how physical and bio-chemical agents are assimilated by the sensitive organism. Consequently, the expression of received impressions represents more than mere modifications and changes in the subject's dispositions. They also express the presence of the object in the subject; due to this presence of the object, the subject has something to express or answer to by his inner reactions. So there is no reason to follow either pure subjectivism or naive and exaggerated realism. Subject and object are simultaneously present to each other in the act of knowledge; the very idea of a subject presupposes its counterpart, the object, which exists in the subject insofar as it is known by him.

While the impression implies the idea of passive receptivity by a sensitive organism, the expression which now follows, represents the subject's creative activity. The subject's overt reaction to the known object is conditioned by the specific form of how the subject reconstructs and interprets the object on the ground of the initial impressions and their effects upon him.

It would be wrong to try and isolate the purely cognitive aspects of the subject-object relationship because there is nothing we could call "purely cognitive." Such an attitude and method would presuppose the existence of a purely cognitive subject which nowhere exists. Even the abstract logical forms and relations of discoursive reasoning represent something artificially made up by isolating one aspect from the total human experience and thereby mutilating its original dynamic nature.

Since there is no pure cognitive subject in reality, one has to take into account the psycho-somatic (mind-body) unity of the whole subject. Consequently, the affective contents of knowledge play at least the same important role in human experiences as the cognitive ones. To put it more forcibly, the subject does not experience the object solely by his cognitive power but his whole being is involved in it. Besides wanting to identify the object for what is stands for in itself, the subject first wants to learn what the object means for him as a living organism in his condition of dependence on the world of goods needed for his psycho-somatic balance.

Using the terminology of philosophic psychology, we might well say that the subject's concern is not purely theoretical but a highly practical one. Very often the practical concern dictated by man's needy condition in the world of goods gains the upper hand over the pure desire to know for the sake of knowledge only. Even the advanced philosopher as the lover of wisdom professes by his very name something emotional — love of wisdom — which is more than the insight into abstract relationships of purely speculative concern. In one word, man lives as a whole and not in separate compartments and the necessity of being practical may rule out the ideal of being theoretical.

The psycho-somatic nature of integral knowledge, understood as the dynamic experience moving withing the field of impression and expression, must be emphasized if we want to succeed in our attempt to create an experiential foundation for our value experiences taken in their different dimensions. A purely abstract and artificial analysis of the isolated cognitive elements in human experiences certainly does not leave any room for introducing the idea of valuing which by its very nature brings to light the subject's psycho-somatic concern with the world of goods rather than the "purely detached, disengaged, and theoretical" concerns of the philosopher with the object's being in itself. As we pointed out above, the whole object is present to the whole subject and both of them mean much more than either "pure object of knowledge" or "pure knowing subject."

The subject reacts with his whole being; the initial impression represents just the first condition to call into being the reaction of the whole sensitive organism to the materials of his experiences. As a rule, the subject first wants to evaluate what the object means to him in terms of need satisfaction or frustration; only much later, if at all, the subject may assume a more impersonal and objective attitude by trying to identify the object's inner reality regardless of its impact on the subject's sensitivity. Such a degree of impersonal detachment never occurs on the common sense level which is almost exclusively practical, functional, and subjective. It is the business of the scientist and the philosopher to establish rules and methods needed for the ideal of objective research.

Since valuing necessarily brings along an ego-involvement of a highly emotional nature, we must turn now to the analysis of the basic emotional reactions as the result of how the subject interprets the impressions received from impinging stimuli.

In spite of the great variety of man's emotional responses, it is both possible and expedient to begin with the most fundamental reactions which permeate their more differentiated forms. Starting with the most primitive responses, we have to mention the first pair of opposites, desire and fear, conditioned by the preceding experiences of pleasure and pain respectively. It is to the point of our description to remember that both desire and fear or, for that matter, pleasure and pain, are the reactions elicited by the subject on ground of his own constitution and the specific nature—harmful or pleasant—of the stimulation itself. Therefore, one should not consider emotional reactions (feelings and commotions or passions) as merely subjective expressions. On the other hand, it is true that objects taken in and by themselves are neither pleasurable nor harmful. But it is imperative to recall again that no object as such can be "taken" just in and for itself. We conclude, therefore, that man is conditioned by his natural constitution to react by desire or fear to the objects present in his experiential field. It also follows that no sensitive organism (man's included) can be in the state of emotional indifference or complete neutrality. This also means that man either suffers or enjoys being in the world as long as he is there. The stoic ideal of unperturbed peace (*ataraxia*) is rather the projection of wishful thinking than achieved or achievable goal.

Because man either suffers or enjoys his life, he is naturally inclined to assume a highly *selective attitude* toward the stimuli which may affect and change his subjective dispositions for the better or worse. If man wants to survive, it is of utmost necessity for him to adjust to the world around him by adapting his senses to the stimuli carefully selected by the practical concern with maximum pleasure and minimum pain, a concern controlled by the principle of safety.

Since not all human reactions are dominated by the necessity of innate and instinctual reflex reactions, man learns gradually and by experience how to get along with objects or how to get about safely in the world of his limited experiences. The process of learning by pleasant or painful experiences starts by necessity of nature with the attempts at satisfying the needs dictated by man's bio-physical constitution. Therefore, the experiences of pleasure and pain are necessarily of a sensuous nature. The range and variety of man's vegetative and sensitive needs constitute the range and variety of related pleasures and frustrations, depending on their successful satisfaction or painful frustration.

The classification of man's organic needs may be regarded as man's first scale of values derived from their satisfaction and subordinated to the goal of individual and collective life preservation. Physical integrity, health, and the "values" needed for its maintenance (food, shelter, clothing, exercise, rest, means of transportation and organization of collective efforts to secure the continued supply of goods by the acquisition of expedient skills) represent the first and most imperative goods of life.

The selective satisfaction of organic needs is a process that man has in common with other animals. Therefore, one might be tempted to interpret man's "struggle for life" purely in terms of mechanistic or reflex reactions directed, rather determined, by innate dispositions and learned habits from within, in order to meet the demands and the conditions of life adaptation imposed upon the organism from without. While it is true that many of the organic needs are shared by man and animals, there is still a world of difference as to the forms and modes of how they are met by both. For one thing man created a civilization out of the ways of meeting his organic needs, while animals have nothing of that sort of thing; they still follow the same, i.e., unchanged, fixed, stereotyped and uniform cycles of their purely vegetative and sense reactions. Consequently, the knowledge derived from natural sciences — physics, chemistry, and biology, especially physiology — can be sufficient only for the understanding of animal life; but the same cannot be said of human existence. The universal phenomenon of civilization and culture testifies for man's symbolic creativity and progress; the absence of which in the vegetative and sensitive forms of animal life proves its inferior quality.

The animal only vegetates in his physical environment; man actively changes his environment by trying to transform and control its conditions. Crude nature is the animal's natural habitat; nature humanized by man's creative imagination and action is the new habitat known as the civilized world. One would arrive at the same qualitative differences by examining one by one the different modes of how man and animal satisfy the same organic necessities. There is a difference, for instance, between how an animal devours his food contrasted with man's refined table manners in his dining room. This difference cannot be explained by any formula of biochemistry applied to psychophysiology.

If the naive formula of a stimulus-response mechanism falls short of yielding an insight into the specifically human way of civilized life — even on the vegetative and sensitive levels — one should look for some new dispositions or powers in man's nature as a possible key to the desired solution of the question. Since the difference between animal and human behavior appears to be qualitative, no explanation based on differences of degree or quantity can suffice. If the behavior of man and that of the animal are of the same kind and different only in quantity or complexity, how can we account for man's continuous creativity and symbolic interpretation of his life condition? (By adding more of the same stuff one should not expect something new out of the same. Ten pounds of fish is just the same as one pound of fish of the same kind.) On the other hand, one must close his eyes to obvious facts in order to deny the differences between the ways of human and animal lives.

The conclusion one must arrive at in the presence of these obviously qualitative differences is the establishment of an exclusively new human power never matched by any amount of animal adaptation, evolution and learning ability. This new power has been identified as intelligence or the power of self-conscious and creative thinking and action.

There has been a great deal written on "animal intelligence" or the animal's power to "learn by insight and rudimentary forms of reasoning" suggesting again the same old confusion between being conscious on the one hand, and self-conscious on the other. The impressing experimental results achieved with animals by behaviorists and gestaltists seem to demonstrate that the power of "thinking" can be found on an inferior level among the higher anthropoids.

There is no need to go into a detailed discussion of such fantastic and liberal claims. A few critical observations will offset their validity.

First, whatever an animal performs in an artificially created and controlled experiment should be ascribed to the intelligence of the experimenter who got the animal conditioned in the desired form of reaction. (For instance, no animal smokes out of its spontaneous desire.) Second, whatever intelligence can be detected in the animal's adaptive powers should be interpreted as the manifestations of innate tendencies — traditionally called instincts and powers of estimation — of which the animal is not conscious in the form man is aware of himself in all his doing and making. Moreover, there is a confusion between being conscious of one's bodily needs and of the changes in the physical environment on the one hand, and being self-conscious on the other. Finally, starting with the rise of English sensism, science inherited another misconception regarding the true nature of intellectual knowledge as not being basically different from sense knowledge, imagery, and the processes of associations.

No one denies that the animal knows, feels, and reacts to a

great variety of objects and related signs. Man, however, experiences a lot more: while knowing, he knows that he knows; while feeling he is aware of being affected by pleasure or pain; while reacting he also knows of the process of choice and deliberation by which he anticipated and directed his reactions. In one word, man knows more than his bodily functions in response to his inner needs or outer demands; he also knows of himself; he is more than conscious for he is self-conscious. All this is true because his concern is not locked within the limited field of organ sensitivity; the horizon of his concerns includes also a self-concern and the satisfaction of higher needs which in no ways are related to the acts of vegetation and sensing. Strictly speaking, therefore, only this kind of self-awareness can properly be called intelligence, thought, insight, and creative activity.

The preceding discussion was presented in order to provide adequate perspective for the interpretation of "human values" which lie over and above the aforementioned primitive scale of so-called bio-physical values or sensate goods. The terms "value, value judgment, valuation or valuing" should be applied exclusively to humans for the simple reason that the "value experience as such" and its dimensions, presuppose the existence of that higher power — exclusively human — we identified before as self-conscious thought and action. This matter should become even more evident when we come to the presentation of those values (aesthetic, theoretical, and moral-religious) which cannot be derived from or reduced to sublimated forms of bodily satisfaction. Such an attempt would betray the same amount of naive generalization S. Freud was found guilty of in the field of his psychoanalytic obsession with sex.

The intrinsic possibility for the value experience consists in man's rational and volitive self-consciousness as its *a priori conditio sine qua non.* The validity of this categorical statement can be further substantiated by going into the implicit denotations and conotations of the value experience itself.

A bare approach or avoidant reaction and the possible ambivalent states produced by their conflicting polarities may be experienced on the organic level alone without presupposing or leading toward a critico-reflective evaluation or interpretation of their significance on the level of rational self-consciousness. The experiments conducted in classical and instrumental conditioning by Pavlov and his followers offer sufficient evidence for this point. Animal desire or fear conditioned by the experiences of pleasure and pain respectively do not reach beyond the limits of sheer animal reflex reactions. The animal's reactions are determined by its innate and learned responses to the physical or bio-chemical properties of impinging stimuli. They do not stand for more than a necessary reaction dictated by the animal's sensory equipment. The animal is possessed by the stimuli to which it reacts by necessity in the form of approach or avoidance. There is no subjective interpretation because there is no free subject. There is no subjectivity because this presupposes the presence of self-conscious thought and action. The animal lives its experiences without interpreting them. Without interpretation the organism cannot assume a selective attitude toward the objects of its experiences. So called animal choice is actually determined by the uniform modes of sensory reactions. The pleasurable is sought after by necessity; the harmful is avoided again by necessity. This is what one means by referring to mere animal vegetation as being locked within the horizon of physical and biochemical laws. The uniformity of animal behavior suggests to man the idea of a machinelike, mechanized, i. e., thoroughly predetermined pattern of behavior.

Considering man's modes of reacting to the physical world of stimuli we come immediately across a new element; it is the emergence of *interpretation* followed by a *meaning* attached to the interpreted experience. After receiving the sense impressions and reacting to them after the laws of sensory life, man may and does come back to reflect upon the experience even in the absence of the stimuli or objects. Man is not possessed and obsessed by his sensory life. He forms opinions, ideas regarding the meaning of his experiences which are then expressed in various forms of symbolism. To put it briefly and concisely, man not only lives but his life has *meaning* for him.

Our sensations, percepts, and imagery on the sense level, and the process of ideogenesis stand for more than blind responses to aroused bodily needs by neural processes. The "symbolic transformation" of all human experiences through interpretation is present in the universal phenomenon of speech as the expression of human value judgments whose range surpasses the limited field of bodily pleasures or pains. No matter how "primitive" man's life should appear to the civilized or rather mechanized moderns, it includes nevertheless the expressions of goodness, truth, beauty, and the holy.

For man nature is more than a place where to vegetate; it is interpreted as beautiful or dangerous, meaningful or meaningless. The phenomena of nature are given by man a symbolic meaning incorporated within the overall meaning he gives to his own being and life. All this happens simply because man — due to his rational and free self-conscious condition — is in a position to evaluate his existential situation by assuming a *detached attitude* toward himself and his world in the act of critical analysis expressed in his value-judgments. Detachment implies exactly the power of *disengaging oneself* from the onslaught of stimuli by isolating them and weighing their meaning.

Man can look at himself and around himself with a critical eye focused on the meaning of whatever falls within the profiles of his existence. It is correct, therefore, to call him *"homo arbiter"* — man the judge — in order to express his judiciary power and its constant exercise. As Bergson saw in the laughter the manifestation of a detached intellectual verdict pronounced by man regarding all forms of deviations from the logically expected modes of reaction, so can we extend the same idea to all of human attitudes insofar as the element of evaluation or the exercise of his judiciary power is the constant component of his psychic life. It seems, therefore, legitimate to associate the idea of valuing with that of giving a meaning. In this sense the philosophy of value appears to be nothing more and nothing less than a philosophy of life standing for man's constant *quest for meaning.* Value and meaning are synonymous. Consequently, the dimensions of the value experience will disclose the dimensions of the meanings man gives to his life experiences. Civilization and culture emerge as the expressions and objectification in symbolic form of meanings pronounced by the *"homo arbiter"* in the court of his life.

There is no doubt as to the experiential origin of the contests which are meaningfully interpreted by man. Thus, there is no point in postulating innate "value categories" or "inherited archetypes" as modern variations on the same and old Platonic theme of idealistic utopias. Man's concrete existence in a real world of extant phenomena provides the sufficient raw material out of which the refined meanings expressed in civilization and culture can be translated symbolically. Critical realism of the type first presented by Aristotle and his disciples provides ample space for a sound foundation for the experiential and phenomenological description of man's valuing and judging. We shall see in more detail in the subsequent chapter that the real foundation and value of our value judgments lies between the two poles of existence: man and his world. However, this subjective world-immanence will prove being fragmentary thus imposing the necessity for its completion through a quest for a world transcendence.

The foundation for man's "receptive creativity," "from the natural standpoint," is given with man being present and set in relation to "a world of values, a world of goods, a practical world." Man's primary activity in this "practical world" is that of valuing, that is, the selective attitude toward and interpretation of the objects, facts, affairs, phenomena or events which enter his subjective field of experiences. "Being present in the world" expresses man's *factual situation* in space-time. Being engaged in the process of evaluating the significance of this situation identifies man's *existential conditions* as fundamentally axiological, that is, the activity of interpreting the meaning of his existence in the world of goods.

By the act of giving meaning — either positive or negative —

to his situation and condition, man exercises his judicial power, thus expressing and thereby formally creating his world of values. The totality of man's value judgments, brought into a more or less coherent synthesis, stands for man's *Weltanschauung,* man's world-outlook or, if you please, man's judgment over himself and his existential condition. His actual modes of inner and outer behavior or attitudes — individual and collective — follow the line of his axiological creed. On a more systematic and abstract level of reflective meditation man's axiological creed may appear as a "philosophy," that is, a selected set of critically analyzed and synthesized judgments on the global meaning of the world and man's view of it. In this perspective all kinds of philosophies — no matter how abstract and impersonal their principles may sound — appear to be value-philosophies insofar as they all intend to disclose the meaning of all being. This is true especially of present day philosophers whose almost exclusive concern is rather the personal philosophic experience than the academic formulation and enunciation of systematic doctrines. In this way philosophizing is valuing because both are directed by and toward the desire of giving or disclosing the inner meaning of reality (*Sinngebung, Sinndeutung*). If the preceding statements hold true, then we may conclude that the dimensions of the value experience coincide with the dimensions and horizons of interpreted human existence.

The valuing of any subject is confined within the range, depth, level or degree, and adequacy of his experiences. While discussing the nature of knowledge in general and that of sense knowledge in particular, we had an opportunity to exhibit the sensory foundation of all valuing. It was stated, you may recall, that man's selective attitude toward the world of particular goods is aimed at need satisfaction which could be regarded as man's fundamental set of "values" on the organic level of life preservation. The totality of material goods or useful values — both natural or artificially produced by primitive or advanced manual or technical skills — amounted to the world of civilization, testifying for man's ability to master, at least partially, matter, time, space, and energy. Man's civilized world makes him essentially superior to sheer animal life which moves exclusively on the level of crude struggle for survival in an unmodified natural setting. Finally, we also pointed briefly to the existence of genuine cultural values of a higher order with the purpose of giving further evidence and emphasis to man's self-conscious and free creativity.

Everybody knows, however, that the modern world in which man lives today is of a recent date. Man did not always possess the practical know-how by which he could create his modern, highly organized way of life. The picture of "modern living" immediately changes if we go just fifty, then one hundred or two hundred, years back in the history of civilization. And this picture becomes almost unrecognizable if one moves from the Middle Ages back to the ancient times arriving at the dawn of human civilization and culture. If anything "historical" can be said about man's "pre-historic" condition — contrasted with the present state of affairs — we must imply that the dimensions of the human value experiences are conditioned by the historical development of the human race. It is not implied, however, that "history" gradually brings forth new values into existence. What is actually suggested is the assumption that the very meaning of historical development can be derived only by following up the emergence of new values which make history.

Undertaking the meaningful interpretation of the historical process from an axiological point of view, we may as well start with the so called "primitive" way of life. Cultural anthropologists are unanimous in describing the primitive man's attitude toward life as pre-logical, pre-conceptual, rather an emotionally-dictated than rationally-motivated and understood mode of behavior. It is called "primitive" mainly because of the very low level of judicial power in interpreting man's situation and condition in nature, which appears overpowering to the mind of the primitive. The lack of rational insight is compensated for by the predominance of and significance given to emotional experiences. The primitive, like the child, feels much more than he knows or can account for by understanding. His existence is lived through feelings, emotions, and passions which — being somewhat opposed to reason — dictate the reactions which appear silly if we measure them by the amount of intelligence they carry.

Since most of the primitive experiences do not surpass the limits of sense observation, a high degree of sensibility for physical stimuli — the workings of nature — can be expected. The absence of insight by which man could interpret and understand the meaning of his sense experiences, calls for an almost exclusive emotionalizing of the experiential situations. Thus even the elements of sense perception and imagery become distorted and misinterpreted by strong emotional charges which move within the narrow limits of quasi animal appetites: love and hatred, desire and aversion, joy and sorrow, hope and despair, courage and fear, and impotent anger. The imagination of the primitive being charged with emotions derived from his sensory experiences, will naturally engage in the well known anthropomorphistic, that is, highly subjective interpretation of the natural phenomena. In fact, this anthropomorphism is the projection of personal emotions and passions into natural events which thus become invested with identical dispositions. This animistic projection is but one step removed from primitive symbolism objectised in primitive superstitions, taboos, rites, rituals, magic, and myth-making. This occurs because the primitive has not as yet acquired sufficient self-consciousness or self-identity needed for assuming a more detached, rather impersonal and critico-reflective attitude toward himself and his physical environment.

The peculiar psychic make-up and functioning of the primitive acts as the inner formal principle that organizes the primitive scale of values by which he lives and dies. The sensory attachment to and dependence on the physical environment for the sake of mere survival bring forth the emergence of *the useful* and *the practical* as the most imperative concerns of the primitive engaged day by day in the struggle for survival. The material goods upon which his survival depends being the most needed, they are also interpreted as the most important and, therefore, the most valuable assets of his existence. The useful and the practical are the bases of what in modern terminology we call the *economic concern* directed by the law of highest gains by minimum investments. We may suggest, therefore, that the primitive man's highest value appears to be the economic. Actually, it is not altogether difficult to see that even the apparently "useless" or "unpractical," that is, non-functional primitive symbolisms expressed in their superstitions, taboos, magic, myth, and moral-religious practices, are indeed sub-servient rites, rituals, and worship of the principle of usefulness, functionality, and pragmatism, expressing the axiological concern of the primitive although they are not identified as such by him.

Next on the scale of values appears the socio-political organization of life valued for its functionality insofar as organized social and political communities offer more protection to the individuals and also guarantee the more or less continued availability of particular goods channelled through the established goods of order as the results of mutual effort and cooperation. The social and political ties in primitive societies appear unusually strong because of the actual insufficiency of the individual member to survive outside the tribal community. No wonder then if one finds an authoritarian principle running through the whole socio-political organization and control of social behavior. The leader and his close associates (witch doctors, wise old men, and brave warriors) hold undisputed power over the individual's existence and freedom. Because of the condition of ignorance the state of absolute dependence precludes the emergence of the idea of individual emancipation as something unthinkable. Thus, the value of social togetherness appears beyond any doubt as the only legitimate mode of life and the absolute power of leadership goes on unchallenged because of its necessity.

The outcome of these powerful socio-political relationships of total submission and obedience to the personal or impersonal, rather symbolic incarnation of an omnipotent power, can be seen in the very low degree of individual self-consciousness; the member of a primitive society has identified himself completely with the collective spirit or spirits of his community to the extent of being unable to think of himself as an independent, free, individual person. The idea of individuality and personality took many long centuries to appear on the horizon of human values. Consequently we may identify the primitive socio-economic and political organization of life as the incipient form of communism.

The foundation for the preceding descriptive analysis of the primitive value experiences — the economic, social, and political value categories — rests upon the assumption that feelings and emotions are the predominant functions in the primitive man's inner psychic organization. Hence rational insight or understanding account for a secondary impact on the process of his life adjustment. The primitive is exceedingly emotional due to his condition of ignorance; he reacts emotionally for not being able to direct his life-process rationally.

A closer analysis of the range of the primitive's emotional reactions will tell us that most of them are derived from or reducible to his very limited life concern dominated by the cycles of organic need satisfaction, confined to the narrow dimensions of bodily pleasures and pains. This situation could well be identified, in Freudian vocabulary, as a dynamic process moving between the poles of the subjective pleasure principle and the objective reality principle. The driving energy of this sustained activity has been called the instinct of life preservation or, in modern jargon, the *"libido"* or vital energy (*élan vital*). Consequently, the emotional reactions are responses to the objective impressions gathered in the course of the adjustment process.

Emotional responses can be manifested in more than one form. Subjectively, we find mimicry and pantomime, music, gesture, rite, rituals, bodily posture, dance, and oral communication (incipient poetry.) These reactions are called subjective, though externalized, because their very existence directly depends on their author and they last only as long as the actor performs. However, besides these immediate releases of emotional tensions in the form of outer, visible behavior, the primitive may also desire to lend an independent, objectised existence to his most impressive emotional experiences. Should this happen, the projection of subjective feelings will appear in the form of artistic creativity. The works of art, therefore, represent the objectification of inner psychic processes of emotional nature. Art as a new dimension in man's value experiences comes into being by man creating the symbolic forms in order to objectize, translate and communicate the significance of his emotional experiences and the meaningful interpretation given to them. The work of art thus created exists now in itself and in its own right; it may continue existing regardless of its creator. Its symbolic meaning, that is, its artistic significance and connotation may not be easily understood by persons who stand outside the field of those specific experiences which inspired its projection into time and space. This circumstance makes it rather difficult to an "outsider" to interpret correctly the meaning of artistic creations; at the same time, however, they speak by themselves in the form of symbolic forms to the "insiders." This interpretation becomes even more difficult whenever a modern man, as the heir of Western civilization, sets out to unravel the authentic meaning of primitive art symbolism. Most of these attempts at meaningful interpretation should be taken as intelligent guessing mainly if they refer to the works of nonexistent civilizations.

By its very essence art represents the symbolic expression of lived experiences in concrete form. Being symbols created by man's need to objectise his interpretation of the meaning given to his experiences, the artistic or aesthetic value moves a step higher on the scale of human values. Furthermore, artistic creativity springs from man's inner sensibility; hence it does not rely on rational insight or logical understanding. Consequently, here we discover a truly universal human phenomenon which is not higher or lower at any historical epoch; it is not dependent on man's rational, intellectual, or technical progress. Art symbolism is universal and universally valid.

The symbolic expression of significant experiences in concrete, visible forms identifies the essence of artistic creativity and differentiates it as qualitatively distinct from the previous practical, useful, and functional concerns of daily living. For art is neither useful nor practical; it is autonomous in its own sphere of existence; its only purpose is the manifestation of an abstract meaning in a perceptible form. In this sense art could be looked at also as the fortunate conjugation of the abstract and the concrete. The concrete symbol is the carrier of the abstract meaning which becomes translucent in the forms of artistic symbolism. Or else art may also be thought of as the visible incarnation of an invisible meaning or idea which man can communicate only indirectly, that is, symbolically.

Traditional philosophy of art defined art almost exclusively in terms of an ideal beauty considered as the highest norm of artistic creativity and purpose. The beautiful then appears as the ideal manifestation of harmony, perfection, proportion, symmetry, articulate form, order, etc.; all of these meant to express the ideal of art. While this interpretation of the aesthetic value experience accounts for a good many works of art, it falls short, nevertheless, of those truly artistic creations whose object is everything but the beautiful. This is true of primitive and modern art alike. It is, therefore, necessary to broaden the conceptual formulation of art interpretation and recommend the more general frame of reference we identified above as the "symbolic expression of the abstract meaning of experiences in concrete form," regardless of its harmonious (beautiful) or disharmonious (ugly) dressing. Otherwise one should stretch the comprehension of the beautiful too far in order to accommodate under its shelter the dreadful, the tragical, the fatal, and the ugly. On the other hand, no one would deny that these negative experiences may have even a greater significance for some men than the "beautiful" ones. Their significance dictates the need for projecting them into the outer world. Therefore, the Aristotelian idea of "catharsis" — the soul's purification through intense emotional release — conveys more meaning than the narrow restrictions imposed on art by the ideal norms of the beautiful which would create the illusionary world of naive dreamers. Artistic symbolism is not aimed at the playful creation of compensatory illusions. On the contrary, it is a very deep, serious need of man in search of expressive forms for all the dimensions included within the horizons of his existence.

Turning now our attention to the hidden contents of artistic symbolism, we may detect another new quality of the aesthetic value dimension. For the very reason of its not being useful or practical in the economic or pragmatic sense of the terms, art provides man with the first opportunity to disengage himself from the crude physical necessities and concerns of everyday struggle; thus man has the *opening* needed for transcending the limited, physical and organic boundaries of his earthbound condition by undertaking his journey into the vast world of unlimited, *free symbolism.* The element of free artistic symbolism taken by itself and in its genuine significance should suffice to prove man's esssential distinctness from animals which never attempted in any form to break through the necessities of bare vegetation.

Art is redemptory insofar as it creates the first opening for self-transcendence. Here we identify the moral, but not moralistic, and the religious impact of art as a unique, exclusively human, i. e., free activity. This close affinity between the aesthetic and the moral-religious experiences imposes the need to discuss them first and leave the theoretical and the philosophic dimensions of life for the last. We feel justified in doing so, for the progress of human civilization and culture point to the early emergence of the artistic experience while the scientific and philosophic endeavors appear long after the full blossoming of the aesthetic, moral, and religious values.

Art as the symbolic expression and communication of meaningful experiences stands as a unique human activity because its very essence presupposes the exercise of the superior powers of reflective interpretation and projection into concrete forms of significant life situations. The reflective interpretation of lived or imagined experiences may occur only on the condition of rational self-consciousness, manifested in the process of thinking as preliminary to planned activity. Due to this power of subjective awareness of one's being, situation, and condition, man may and actually does subject himself and his experiences to a critical interpretation or analysis which is aimed at the discovery of their intrinsic meaning. The meaning derived through self-conscious reflection is not immediately given in man's sensations, percepts, and imagery. The meaning emerges only as the abstracted element from the immediately given experience.

Abstraction, however, presupposes again the same power of rational awareness, a judicial power, a self-conscious disposition which demands justification through understanding. Thus man takes a detached attitude toward himself and his experiences; by spontaneous introspection and outerdirected observation of given phenomena he is striving to bring into light the significance, denotation, and connotation of whatever belongs to the stream of his consciousness. All these activities, leading to more or less adequate insights, can be had only if man enjoys *the freedom to disengage himself from his empirical involvement* which thus appears to be not only the condition but also the very essence of personal self-consciousness. Whenever man succeeds in isolating for himself the abstracted meaning of his experiences, he is ready to project it, to express it or to objectise it in the concrete forms of symbolism. The expression is meant first for the interpreting subject himself; only after this moment of personal insight man may also desire to communicate the same to others. This comunication imposes the necessity of finding a medium or an instrument suited for this purpose. Oral communication — articulate human speech resting on the symbolic meaning of invested words used as names — may be preceded by other symbols such as those mentioned above: mimicry, pantomime, gestures, bodily postures, dance, rhythmical sounds of instruments, or else the objectised works of artistic activity in the form of design, painting, sculpture, etc.

Man gives a meaning to himself, to his being and to his existential condition in the world through the means of symbolic expression. If the same meaning is shared by many through the channels of communication and agreement — human convention — that meaning acquires a trans-personal, that is, collective significance. It is an incipient philosophy of life whose language is only symbolic at first.

The activity of giving meaning to one's existence necessarily leads to the experience of one's being assigned to himself. Man being given to himself means free human existence. At times this freedom need not be rationally justified; it is sufficient if man lives his freedom and spontaneously uses it whenever engaged in the apparently useless and non-pragmatic art of varied symbolism. But the spontaneous exercise of freedom will eventually lead to its manifestation through the individual *conscience.* Again, man may not have formulated the universal principles which may justify or prove his freedom; nevertheless, he feels, and acts as a free being.

The emergence of the *moral value experience* through conscience should not be dealt with as the result of environmental or collective conditioning by which the individual acquires the set of his inhibitions. This interpretation of the moral experience deals only with the negative aspect of the problem, i. e., the restrictions of freedom through inhibitory stimuli without explaining the emergence of that which is subject to all sorts of prohibitions, taboos, proscriptions, regulations, principles, laws, etc. (Awkwardly enough the psychoanalytic theory of inhibitions was meant to disprove man's freedom; actually, however, it proves — at least indirectly — its very existence for inhibition as such presupposes an uninhibited, that is, free individual.) Consequently, the positive meaning of freedom and its exercise through conscience must be explained in order to exhibit the foundations of the moral value experience.

The experience of freedom reveals to the subject a great many things. First, it imposes the necessity of *self-determination* which is achieved by choice and deliberation. Choice, however, presupposes again the same rational self-consciousness and the power of judgment; the *"homo arbiter"* is called upon the task to evaluate himself in a given situation and determine the course of his actions. Now, the experience of self-determination through choice leads to *the experience of responsibility.* The dimensions of experienced responsibilities embrace all the aspects of human existence. Thus man is by his nature a moral being. On a primitive level, there is an instinctual basis for it, that is, the necessity to provide the means for physical survival in a hostile environment. The significant fact, however, is that man's responsibility is not confined to the limits of the narrow field of physical survival which is only the basis for other responsibilities man experiences after the bodily needs have been brought to a temporary balance. It would be rather naive to consider man's feelings of obligations, duties, and related forms of behavior as mere sublimations or more complex epiphenomena of the same crude necessities of animal struggle for survival. It is naive for no animal lower than man has ever tried to "sublimate" further after his bodily needs had been satisfied. (No lion, for instance, will draw in the sand the image of the prey he may be after, and it will have no comments to communicate after its possessions.)

The feeling of responsibility derived from the spontaneous exercise of personal freedom is extended to all human endeavors. According to the different levels of more or less differentiated structures of human civilization, it is either the individual or the collective aspect of freedom and responsibilities that may be more emphasized. Prior to the rise of individualism, there was the strong social or collective bond of communal engagement in the business of organized group life. In this case the ideas or values of right or wrong, good and evil, virtue and sin, merit and punishment were directly derived from and referred to the collective conscience of the tribal community. The moral value was derived from the social and political frame of life and it developed exclusively *the ethics of collective conformity.* Only with the progress made in the direction of individual freedom and self-conscious emancipation could *the experience of self-imposed morality* emerge. This, however, presupposes a great deal of individual maturity and courage. Even nowadays the majority of the people prefer the protective shield of collective conformity.

The essence of the moral value experience could be isolated from its foundation in the experience of freedom and subsequent responsibility. It should be identified, therefore, as the experience of personal obligation toward the self and the group; on a more advanced level of philosophic reflection it may lead to the discovery of a natural law and its foundation in the eternal law of the Absolute Being, conceived as man's highest good (*summum bonum*) and the fulfillment of his desire for lasting happiness and immortality. At this point, however, the moral value experience naturally runs into the dimensions of the religious experience. Before turning our attention to the analysis of the religious value experience, we feel that it is necessary to point out the normative character of values in general, regardless of their specific contents or origin.

Whenever man gains full insight into the meaning and significance of any value through the process of free, self-conscious exercise of his judicial power, there also emerges the feeling of commitment or responsibility toward that specific value category. The feeling of "must" "ought to" or "should" is not like a blind reflex reaction developed in the process of a conditioning process; it is rather the outcome of a free rational awareness or understanding of the significance of the value taken either in itself or with reference to the meaning of human existence. Man feels that the perfection or goodness intrinsic to the value in his experience represents a necessary asset needed for the full development of his being in view of the ideal of complete personal self-appropriation and self-integration. Man also realizes that he cannot lead the human form of existence unless he assimilates or incorporates within himself the perfections pertinent to his value experiences. In this sense the feeling of responsibility manifested through man's conscience appears to be more than an external conformity to collectively sanctioned and demanded forms of behavior. On the contrary, the individual person looks upon the values as the objects of his personal responsibilities and as an opportunity for self-enrichment and self-realization. Should an individual reach this level of insight, he has already left behind the collective forms of moral conformity because his morality is now self-imposed through axiological insights.

The considerations laid down in the preceding pages gravitated toward the basic principle of man being fundamentally "ideational," which means that man is naturally disposed to evaluate and express the meaning of his existence. Thus civilization and culture represent the objective manifestation of this creative power by which man transcends all other living organisms. In this sense it seems correct to say that the quest for meaning is the meaning of all man's activities above the level of mere vegetation. Whatever man does or makes is determined by some value judgment which expresses the meaning derived from his experiences.

The universal quest for meaning comprehends the individual, personal, the social, and the objective or spatio-temporal dimensions of human existence. Man being assigned to himself, he should become his first and immediate concern for himself. The social concern would then follow the original introversion as other directed or extravert attitude and behavior. Finally, the physical environment — so-called "reality" or the "world" — demands the same evaluation. However, it goes without further saying that the tridimensional design of human concern does not actually imply any real separation or necessary sequence one after the other of a strict chronological order. Viewing the matter from a developmental point of view, it is more correct to say that man's first attitude is almost exclusively extravert or object-directed. Only after the process of adjustment in the physical environment has been learned within the framework of inherited social forms of behavior, some few men may direct their attention to the inner reality of their being. This qualification holds true not only from a psychological point of view but also historically. In fact, the primitive mind, like that of a child, because of its low level of rational insight and judicial power, is possessed by sensations, percepts, imagery, and their combinations. Consequently, the subjective interpretation and evaluation of sense experiences is bound to be predominantly emotional, reflecting only the projection into symbolic forms of the experiences belonging to the very narrow horizon of an existence lived in a mysterious environment. The quality of these projections reflects the two basic forms of emotional experiences, that is, pleasure and pain. The element of feared mystery is directly proportional to the amount of ignorance. Gross anthropomorphism pervades the incipient attempts at interpreting the meaning of life and magical forces are suspected behind the mysterious working of nature. Hence we have to conclude that the moral and religious value experiences of the primitives disclose only the projections of an earthbound, extravert, and sensate form of life, dominated by the constant concern with physical survival and physical well-being. This necessary world-immanence makes it hard to interpret the meaning of primitive life in terms of traditional religious experiences as the quest for self-transcendence and world transcendence. As we saw above, even primitive morality expresses the norms of rigid social control and conformity, dominated by the principle of collective utility. We come to the same conclusion if we subject to our analysis the fundamental elements of religious experiences within the horizon of primitive life.

The basic religious ideas are faith, sin, the need for redemption, the universal desire for happiness and the hope for immortality. Now it is evident that the primitive man's faith is a blind postulate lacking in some acceptable rational foundation; sin is interpreted just moralistically without ever reaching the metaphysical implications of the problem which it imposes; the need for redemption and eternal salvation does not transcend the desire for physical security and safety in a hostile world, extended indefinitely; the same utilitarian pragmatism and hedonism translate the meaning of happiness; finally, the vague idea of immortality is rather collective than individual insofar as it expresses the survival of the group in comparison with which the individual's life appears to be destitute of intrinsic value.

Turning now to the dimensions of the religious value experience of civilized people, religion appears as *the quest for a total and ultimate meaning of existence.*

It was made clear before that it is not within man's power to experience "reality" as a whole and that the ideas of a "world" of the "universe" represent only the results of mental generalizations and abstractions. The fact of the matter is that any human experience — the economic, social, political, aesthetic, and theoretical — contains just fragmentary and disconnected information about some particular and partial segment of so-called "reality." The fragmentary nature of human experience applies also to man's inner world of his psychic experiences. Man's inner experiences contain only the immediate facts of consciousness, that is, the stream of sensations, percepts, imagery, related emotions, desires and outer reactions anticipated by rational foresight.

Man is forced, therefore, to put the pieces together into a meaningful pattern. It is the work of synthesis which follows the analysis of particular instances of experiences. Thus man understands himself and his world only if he reconstructs these dimensions of "reality" from within, that is, from both man's forms of understanding and the apparent regularity, uniformity, and constancy of natural phenomena. Now there appear to be, generally speaking, five different levels of integration or synthesis. Starting from the lowest, first we describe the "primitive" world-outlook; next on the scale comes the proverbial wisdom of uncritical common sense which is still moving on the level of phenomenal experience (appearance and reality still coincide). The scientific or theoretical attitude introduces the more "objective," "impersonal" and "detached" forms of inquiry. The spirit of scientific motivation reveals the desire to reduce the multiplicity and complexity of phenomena to the universality, regularity, and simplicity of related immediate causes and underlying laws or principles. Thus the world constructed by the scientist appears the system of symbols — mostly mathematical — which disclose the working of nature. Scientific truth is, therefore, eminently functional. It does not claim ultimate validity for it consists only in the progressive appropriation of more knowledge. But the systematic account of natural phenomena still retains the element of fragmentarity and unilaterality for scientific research limits itself to the quantitative and measurable aspects of the phenomenal world, thus leaving out of its field the qualitative and purposeful aspects of life. Consequently, the scientist must sooner or later come to realize that his knowledge does not disclose the global and ultimate meaning of the real. The awareness of the necessary limitations of scientific methods and of the results yielded by it make the unbiased scientist turn to philosophy from which the insight into the ultimate causes and principles or reality can be expected.

The history of human thought from its earliest start up to the present moment presents a discomforting plurality of scientific and philosophic systems. It is a discomforting or Faustian experience for man beholds the frustration of his original desire and hope to disclose by natural reason the meaning of his existence in the universe of being. This experience represents a critical turning point in the adventures of the human mind; some disillusioned persons are ready to fall into despair and hopeless resignation to man's condition of ignorance which actually represents the loss of faith in the power of human reason and in the ultimate intelligibility of the cosmos. Then there are the enlightened rationalists who still believe in the dogmatic postulate of unlimited understanding through scientific progress to be had at some later date because it is not available at the present. In other words, they believe in the advent of knowledge which —according to their optimistic creed—must come at the end. Finally, there are quite a few thinkers who assume a middle of the road attitude as the integration between the already achieved scientific and philosophic insights and the rationally founded faith in the intelligibility and ultimate meaning of being and existence.

The conjugation of faith and reason allows of many different forms, depending on the individual's background, frame of mind, and his inner psychic motivation.

We may conclude, therefore, that the answer to the problem

of the ultimate and total meaning of existence is fundamentally religious both in its formulation and in its tentative solutions. It necessarily operates through faith and reason; it exposes the fragmentarity and the limitations of the different types of human knowledge; it may also throw some light on man's impotent condition, so as to allow him to redeem himself through knowledge, thus making him ready to expect salvation from above as the answer to his unrelenting desire for full insight, happiness, and the hope for immortality.

We left for last the consideration of the theoretical (scientific and philosophic) value experience because we were following the ascending line of human cultural progress. In fact, the advent of a true theoretical concern — knowledge for the sake of knowledge only — emerged only after the economic, socio-political, artistic, and moral-religious needs had enjoyed man's almost exclusive concern. This statement should not be taken as an implicit devaluation of man's original desire for knowledge. For man's genius has always been creative and constantly inspired by his natural curiosity. Aristotle says that philosophy — the love of wisdom — started in wonder. On the other hand, however, it is also true that man could turn to the satisfaction of this innate curiosity only after creating for himself the needed economic and socio-political freedom as the condition for the rise of his purely cultural endeavors. This cultural climate was first achieved by the Greeks for the so-called scientific progress made by the Orientals was dictated by purely pragmatic interests. Knowledge pursued by the practical intellect is alien to the spirit of a disengaged, scientific research inspired only by the pure desire to know. Even nowadays one should make an important distinction between applied research — the business of engineers and research workers — on one hand, and the pursuit of knowledge for its sake only, on the other.

There is another reason why we should associate the rise of purely theoretical concern with the Greeks. For they have been the first to create the logic of rational discourse, the polished and refined terms and expressions needed to formulate and to convey the meaning of fundamental ideas and principles — theories without which science would still be impossible to think of. Greek philosophic thought developed the mental habit of science as being different from mere opinion or proverbial wisdom. At this time period we find the fortunate conjugation of philosophic and scientific attitudes of mind. Philosophy itself was thought of as a universal science and the pursuit of knowledge was considered as the love of wisdom or philosophy.

With the decline of medieval philosophy and the rapid progress made by positive sciences began the separation between these two closely related fields and developed into their final divorce still in existence in our day. However, this artificial separation is of no advantage to either science or philosophy. Paraphrasing one of Kant's important statements on the *a priori* forms of sensibility and understanding, we might say that philosophy without science is empty, and science without philosophy is blind, dangerous and destructive. Doubtless, applied scientific research, technology, enjoys an unmatched reputation due to the devout worship of material civilization on the part of modern pragmatists. On the other hand, the minds engaged in the disengaged pursuit of pure science feel its limitations and the need for new concepts or ideas by which they could transpose the barriers of human knowledge. It is, therefore, safe to conclude that the spirit of science and philosophy are intimately interwoven only in the minds of true creative thinkers, whereas the majority of research personnel qualifies only for the lesser title of ingenious engineers.

The value sought after by the philosopher-scientists can be introduced as the quest for more knowledge, dictated by man's insatiable thirst for more insight. The kind of knowledge the scientist and the philosopher are looking for must possess all the qualifications of truth as the fundamental value category of all theoretical concerns. Unlike common sense knowledge, science and philosophy strive for certain, universal, and demonstrated knowledge of the proximate causes and remote principles which direct the course of the phenomenal world. In order to achieve this certified knowledge science and philosophy developed a methodical and systematic approach to the study of reality. The major steps of this critical attitude involve fact-finding by observation, descriptive analysis and classification, controlled experimentation, measurements, the mathematical formulation of obtained data, and, finally, the painful search for a comprehensive hypothesis — theory — which would reduce the multiplicity, complexity, and mobility of changing phenomena to the unity, simplicity, and regularity of related causes and principles. Some of the theories can be experimentally validated; others are only functional hypotheses or assumptions the scientist comes up with as the result of his creative intuition. In this manner scientific explanations satisfy man's desire to understand, to predict, to foresee, to control and to dominate the world of matter, energy, time, and space.

A purely scientific knowledge of the positivistic type necessarily involves certain imperfections which take away some of its beauty and value. The most obvious shortcomings are given in the artificial and fragmentary character of the scientific research. The scientist isolates only one aspect — usually the quantitative one — from the totality of given experiences; by isolating it from the whole, the scientist also idealizes, simplifies, and generalizes the abstracted element, using the law of average occurrences or probable chance variations. The situation may become even more suspect when the scientist takes his abstractions formulated in mathematical symbols as directly expressing the working of nature itself. Should this happen, the theoretical web produced by the scientist's mind may appear something which in no way duplicates the reality from which it had been abstracted. Moreover, it is rather daring to dismiss all the real experiences which cannot be quantified by direct or indirect measurements. Consequently, the universe constructed, let's say, by a Newton reduces the whole of reality to matter, motion, attraction, and repulsion. This oversimplification due to unrefrained generalizations produces a unilateral world view which can no longer satisfy man's quest for the whole truth.

Scientific knowledge appears to be only functional; it merely describes the working or the behavior of some isolated phenomena. Herein also lies its fatal limitation, for it can say almost nothing on the meaning and ultimate value of whatever had been scientifically analyzed. The mathematical calculus which approximately describes the behavior of so-called electrons, protons, neutrons, neutrinos, mesotrons, etc., does not say anything about the nature and the meaning of matter, energy, time, space, motion, change, life, to say nothing about man's world embodied in his individual, social, political, aesthetic, moral, and religious values.

Those positivists who still profess the optimistic faith in a future answer to the questions for which we have no answer as yet, seem not to be aware of the limitations of scientific knowledge implicit in its method and scope. As a consequence, the value of scientific knowledge is not absolute; it does not reach any unconditioned region of reality from which the very meaning of being and existence could be derived. At this crucial point of intellectual crisis some thoughtful scientists turn to the philosophic study of nature; their concern is now enriched by the natural desire to know also the meaning of what they have been experimenting with. Thus science turns out to be a philosophy of science which eventually may lead the scientist to purely speculative reflections of a metaphysical nature. Whenever this occurs, positive knowledge is elevated to the status of wisdom as the expression of the universal meaning of the universe of being. Its new name now is philosophy, i. e., the love of wisdom. It is the experience of the highest dimension in human values, as a peculiar synthesis of positive knowledge and philosophic faith. The natural faith of the scientist and that of the philosopher may eventually change into a silent admiration of a mysterious universe in which or above which the religious faith may suspect the presence of a known and unknown Being.

## CHAPTER III

## THE CRITICAL QUESTION ABOUT VALUE JUDGMENTS MODERN AND NEO-SCHOLASTIC SOLUTIONS

The descriptive analysis of the dimensions of the value experience, such as presented to the reader in the preceding chapter from the "natural standpoint," must have created the impression and forced the conclusion of the all-pervasive presence of values in human existence. Existence is saturated with values — possible or actual — because the dimensions of the value experience coincide with the dimensions and the horizons of human life, no matter how diverse or differentiated its forms may appear to us in the perspective of time and space.

The universal presence of values embraces, first, all the manifestations of the individual existent whose bio-physical and psychic activities are all organized for, or subordinated to, the imperatives of personal subsistence and development. The collective or social organization of human existents brings forth again, but on a longer, supra-individual scale, forms of organized life such as the family, neighborhood, community, school and education, professions, church affiliation, national unity and, finally, international relationship, representing values of human cooperation or collective efforts aimed at the establishment of the common good of society.

From an historical and cultural point of view it is again the hierarchy of created values which appear as the ideal and normative principles leading to the emergence of different types of national and international civilizations. Finally, the ethical and religious life of human persons finds its only justification in the quest for the ultimate value or meaning of existence contemplated as transcending its spacio-temporal limitations and contingency.

Because of man's existential concern with the immediate (practical) or ultimate (metaphysical) value of his being in this world, it is not surprising that all theologians, philosophers, scientists, artists, political leaders and even the practical *"homo faber"* of all ages have tried to solve the question of human values and existence, thereby creating some validity or justification for their being rather than not. Thus the "philosophy of value" is as old as mankind itself even though this term be of recent usage in the vocabulary of modern philosophers (*F. Nietzsche, H. Lotze, F. Brentano, A. Meinong, N. Hartmann, E. Husserl, M. Scheler, J. Hessen, W. Windelband, H. Rickert, W. Dilthey, Ed. Spranger* and others).

The explicit philosophic interest in an analysis of human values in modern and contemporary philosophy came about due to a new attitude toward the perennial problem of values. The ancient and medieval philosophers were content with putting the rather pragmatic question about "what is better or worse" for the human being in his life in order to construct a hierarchy of "goods" (values) from an almost exclusively moral and religious standpoint. Thus "virtues," their classification based on the powers of the human soul and the ideal of a "good, virtuous life," exhausted the scope of their inquiry.

The Greek and Scholastic doctrines on the meaning of good life, conceived from the ethico-metaphysical and religious standpoint, endured almost unchanged until the advent of modern philosophy and the rise of scientific inquiry. With *Descartes,* however, the whole tradition of philosophizing changed radically because of the fundamental reform in its method and the ends to which it led the philosophers making use of it. For one thing, the theocentric, therefore metaphysical, moral, and religious conception of philosophy as *"ancilla theologiae"* is replaced by the anthropocentric, geocentric, rationalist, positivist, and anti-metaphysical modes of thinking. This *"Copernican revolution"* in the method of philosophizing achieved also the slow but efficient devaluation of the ancient and medieval cultures along with the intrinsic value systems underlying them. Nietzsche's philosophy is the most aggresive denunciation of traditional philosophy and religion and it should be regarded as the end result of a grinding process inaugurated and systematically followed up by the apostles of illuminism, rationalism, idealism, sensism, and militant atheism.

Man, however, cannot live without believing in something worthwhile. The school of phenomenology, headed by *E. Husserl,* brings about a reaction against all idealistic or positivistic dogmas of the previous centuries in order to create a new realism — without going back to the Aristotelian or Scholastic tradition — a reality which will provide some legitimate place for human values once more. This need and desire for a new revision or revalidation of philosophic inquiry stands primarily in the name of scrutinizing the "validity of values." Hence almost all basic problems of philosophy and science are formulated anew from the predominant axiological, that is, value-inspired and value-directed concern.

In this perspective we can identify the problem of values as being both new and different from the interest taken by ancient and medieval philosophers in the question of a "good, virtuous life." Instead of concerning themselves with the question of "what are" the values which may lend meaning to human existence, the modern phenomenologists promote the more critical question about "what makes values to be what they are believed to be?" This new formulation of the problem at hand necessarily brings to the fore the classical question regarding "the value of our value-judgments." Before going into the depths and details of this highly critical approach, we have to bring to light, first, all the other related aspects intrinsic to this universal question.

The value problem in general is of such a wide scope that it encompasses within its bounds almost every region of recent philosophic inquiry. In fact, there are many things a philosopher should question when critically analyzing the idea of value as such. From an ontological point of view, the question which immediately demands the philosopher's critical gaze is: "What should the intimate nature or essence of value taken in itself consist of?" Undoubtedly, this is a loaded question, for no answer can be had for it unless the philosopher moves from the above question on the value's quiddity to that of its specific mode of being and subsistence!

Considering the endless variety of the values desired by men, along with their qualitative differences and implicit value antinomies, some philosophers may dismiss altogether the abstract idea of "value as such" and concentrate instead on the specific nature of different value categories (the Holy, truth, goodness, the beautiful, socio-political and economic values). Such a study of "values" in the plural dispenses with any speculative dissertation on the inner substance of "value as value" on one hand; however, it introduces the no less difficult problem of the hierarchic disposition of value structure to be brought into some kind of balance or synthesis. Thus a question arises about the possibility of constructing an ideal hierarchy of values which would assess once and for all the place and dignity each value should occupy in this ideal and compelling order.

Evidently, no realistic thinker can hope for even a partial agreement on this issue; first, because the exhaustive classification of values is still lacking and those forwarded by some axiologists were rejected as either incomplete or invalid by their opponents; second, because no mutual understanding has been reached as yet as to which values should be considered as "values in themselves," relegating the others to the lesser dignity of mere "use values," "contributory values," "means values" or simply "values of a secondary order." The atmosphere becomes even more heated when the question on "negative values" becomes the topic of discussion.

Most students of values know by experience that one's valuing is conditioned by a host of conscious and unconscious psychic motives from within and no less numerous environmental and cultural factors from without. In view of this endless variety of axiological experiences and phenomena, there have always been some philosophers who yielded to the temptation of settling down with a bare relativistic, subjectivistic, and functional interpretation of man's value judgments. This apparently easy way out of the profound problem complex of values only creates the illusion of a working formula while, as a matter of fact, just ignores the obvious and indirectly aggravates the need for once more attacking the whole series of truly philosophic questions posed by the phenomenon of value.

In order to prevent or remedy the confusing situation created by all shortsighted relativists, subjectivists, and pragmatists, any philosopher of some intellectual insight feels it necessary to earnestly face the metaphysical problem imposed by the existence of values. Obviously, nobody can say any really intelligent word on values unless he tries to formulate at least the basic question about the metaphysical foundation of all values, real, ideal, or possible. As there is no philosophy without metaphysics (*philosophia prima*), similarly there cannot be any acceptable axiology without a metaphysics of value.

Although metaphysics is the "first philosophy" in the order of being, its very possibility has always been conditioned, that is, made possible or impossible, by the principles of knowledge as related to or divorced from the first principles of being. It is, therefore, gnoseology, criteriology or applied logic which determines the fate of metaphysics. We shall see in the course of this chapter that most contemporary philosophers of value are weary of any metaphysical foundation for values (ontology of values) because of their inherited preconceptions — mostly neo-Kantian or pragmatist — concerning the nature and limitations of human knowledge. In this manner, one will usually find a gnoseology and psychology of values as prolegomena to their metaphysical attitudes.

The problem of value ontology comes into focus once more when the normative nature of values is subjected to inquiry. Practically all renowned philosophers of the axiological school not only accept but emphatically underline the "ought-to" or "should" character of values belonging to the sphere of ethico-religious needs and related modes of individual and collective behavior. At this point, again, their fatal shortcoming and learned philosophic prejudice fails to lay bare the ontological foundation for the imperatives of behavior dictated by the normative spirit of ethico-religious values in a given culture and civilization. The rather awkward condition arises when men create, want, and respect certain values without being able to justify their behavior if faced with the obligations consequently imposed on them. While recognizing the undisputable ethical impact of values on human existence, their justification is disregarded by certain tautological expressions devoid of any ultimate meaning and significance. For example, should one ask why we want and respect certain values, the usual "answer" points out that we want them because they are values. In other words, values are wanted because they are what they are, though no one can tell what they really are or what makes them to be that which they are supposed to be!

Adding up the foregoing reflections, we tried to present not only the very broad and general problem of values but the implicit questions, too, which cannot be disregarded in a thorough discussion on the ontological, critical, and psychological foundation of values. We may, at this point, anticipate a conclusion which will receive its full justification, we hope, in the following discussion and repeat anew that just as philosophy without metaphysics is up in the air, likewise the philosophy of values without an ontological foundation has no other alternative but to vegetate on the poor diet of relativism, subjectivism, and functional pragmatism inducing the cycles of crisis in human values.

Since the critical question about the validity of values is unavoidably tied up with problems of gnoseology and metaphysics, it seems imperative to present the reader with a brief summation of the doctrines defended by modern philosophers on these issues, thus creating a necessary platform for our criticism of it before we present the neo-scholastic conceptions. Considering the scope of our problem, we must concern ourselves with two main schools of contemporary thought, namely the neo-Kantian and the phenomenological principles of philosophy, applied to the problem of value gnoseology and value ontology.

Considering the emergence of the modern philosophy of value in the light of the organic unity and continuity of thought in its historical development, there are three important thinkers, *Nietzsche, Lotze,* and *Brentano,* whom we shall consider as predecessors, therefore, the philosophers whose ideas created the basic program and subsequent school of philosophic anthropology.

Philosophic anthropology, as a reaction against both transcendental idealism and pragmatic naturalism, stands as the quest for rescuing man from the danger of his total dissolution and absorption in Hegel's monistic panlogism on the one hand, and from his relegation to the level of pure animality in the process of Darwinian evolution on the other. Philosophic anthropology is, therefore, the study of man's historico-cultural existence in its vital unity, totality, and singular condition in the world as the concrete situation in which he freely goes about satisfying his everlasting need to create the values of his civilization and culture. In opposition to the rationalist conception of man as a "soul" (*Seele*), a "spirit" (*Geist*), a "thinking substance" (*res cogitans*), "pure reason" (*reine Vernunft*) or "pure consciousness" (*Bewusstsein überhaupt*), or, finally, a "subject" of knowledge, all cultural anthropologists emphasize man's mind-body unity, his concrete individuality, and his paradoxical condition of being at the same time both in and above nature. Finally, in this philosophy of human nature, it is man's free, creative act of will which receives the greatest emphasis, leading, unfortunately, to the other extreme of absolute voluntarism, becoming, and atheistic anthropolatry.

Nietzsche, strongly influenced by Schopenhauer and Wagner, is the main exponent of this new philosophy of life (*Lebensphilosophie*) with its prophetic and messianic pathos pervading all his writings.

Restricting ourselves to the theory of human values, we can distinguish in Nietzsche a negative and a positive attitude toward them. In the first instance, Nietzsche demands the radical transvaluation of all values (*Umwertung aller Werte*), referring mainly to the scale of values of the traditional Christian religion and philosophy, which he considers as the moral code of weak, servile, depersonalized slaves who comfort themselves with the dreamlike illusion of a perfect happiness hereafter. In order to succeed in devaluating rather than transvaluating all values of Christian culture and civilization and to redeem man from the condition of a shameful existence, Nietzsche puts himself beyond the boundaries of good and evil (*Jenseits von Gut und Böse*), proclaiming God's death in order to make room for man's absolute freedom to be used for the procreation of supermen (*Übermensch*), the men of genius who are the lords of the world (*die Herren der Welt*), bringing forth the values of a true humanism by the heroic effort of their will to power (*der Wille zur Macht*).

Thus Nietzsche's philosophic and psychological anthropology introduces the most extreme form of anthropocentrism and world-immanence in which the highest value is only the man of genius. Consequently, human values, according to him, are founded exclusively in the creative productivity of a cultural aristocracy whose moral code (*Herrenmoral*) should be the ideal norm for the too many (*die Viel-zu-vielen*), belonging to the herd of mass society. One should not look, therefore, in Nietzsche for any ontology of value, for values are subjective and relative to human genius as their sole source of origin and validity. To put it more forcibly, the condition for the very existence and validity of all values is the death of whatever belongs to the supra-human and supernatural. With the death of metaphysics values will arise again (*mors tua, vita mea*).

*H. Lotze* is rightly considered the father of modern value philosophy. In fact, only through the impact of his works did values become the center of philosophic interest. His ideal goal was the establishment of a workable synthesis between the natural sciences and transcendental philosophy of Kantian origin, which found themselves worlds apart in the middle of the nineteenth century. His theistic system describes the material world as the manifestations or appearance (*Erscheinung*) of spiritual monads (*Leibniz*) whose activities are responsible also for man's microcosmos, established by his cultural creativity in the process of history. Lotze's theory of value (*Wertlehere*) is to be found in his psychological and aesthetic works. The essence of his influential doctrine can be best expressed in his famous sentence: *"Werte sind nicht, sondern gelten."* Since there is no adequate expression in the English language for the German verb *"gelten,"* we may render the meaning of the above categorical statement only through an imperfect description. Thus one could say, with Lotze, that *"values are not, being only normative."*

In order to capture the authentic meaning of this fundamental principle, dogmatically maintained by all of Lotze's disciples, we have to take it apart and comment on its implicit connotations as Lotze himself made it clear in his works.

As to the first part of the sentence *"Werte sind nicht"*—"Values are not," Lotze wants to establish a rigid dualism between the order of being (*Sein*) and that of values. This should mean that values ought not to be identified with actually existing things, belonging to the order of tangible reality; it would also be erroneous — as it actually happened in the traditional Greek and scholastic thought — to identify the order of values with the order of *"goods"* (*bonum, bonitas,* etc.). Should someone assign the proper *"locus ontologicus"* of values to the order of sensible and ethical reality, that would necessarily bring about the tragical relativization of all values. For, according to Lotze, being of the natural order is conceived only in terms of the reality of experiential phenomena, brought to unity and intelligibility by the laws of positive science. It is obvious, however, that scientific laws are relative to the minds of the scientists. Therefore, reality such as known by natural laws and principles is outside of the region of values, that is, it is free of human values (*wertfrei*) which should not be understood as valueless, but rather as not being the *"habitat"* for values.

To the question on the whereabouts of values, Lotze and his followers want them to be completely separated in an "ultimate independence" or autonomy from the world of material reality; values belong to an ideal order of absolute validity, normativity, legality, very much like the Platonic order of subsisting ideas, transcending the imperfections of the illusionary, relative, and changing reality, transmitted by the senses and tabulated by science. This element of absolute validity expresses the meaning of the second clause of the above sentence: *"gelten,"* that is, "to be valid." Let us, therefore, conclude this paragraph on Lotze with the rather paradoxical dictum: Values are not (like things are); however, they impose themselves by their absolute normative character. Perhaps we do not go wrong if we identify the special mode of being proper to values as that of ideal norms or measures of what ought to be, though it may not be of necessity.

*F. Brentano,* logician, psychologist, and a critical realist of the Aristotelian-Leibnizian type within the framework of his theistic system, is the forerunner of the modern value realism insofar as he rejects the idealistic premises along with the intolerable duality of being and value completely separated from each other. For Brentano every judgment of value, like anything else in the speculative order, is directly grounded upon something real, that is, empirical and existential. It remains, therefore, to be established later on, the exact relationship between being and value (*Sein und Wert*) with a view on the possibility of presenting a critical ontology of value.

Besides Brentano's value-realism, we should mention also *A. Meinong's* "theory of objects" (*Gegenstandstheorie*) insofar as it represents another contemporary philosopher who resolutely frees himself from the idealistic (Platonic and neo-Kantian) assumptions regarding human knowledge and reality. Like Brentano, Meinong also worked toward the goal of establishing an ontology which allows the philosopher to contemplate reality in itself as something originally given to the mind without being radically distorted, transformed, or adapted through the channels of man's cognitive powers. Meinong's direct contribution to axiological realism has a definite ethical and psychological character, besides the already mentioned ontological foundation and analysis.

The return to the objective order of reality can best be seen in the efforts of *E. Husserl,* the father of modern phenomenology, whose method of philosophizing had a definite bearing on the exponents of the phenomenological treatment of values, both idealistic and realistic.

In a very broad sense, phenomenology, not to be identified with Hegel's Phenomenology of the Spirit, can be described as the science of phenomena or appearances (*Erscheinung*) given in man's lived experiences and manifested in the state of watchful awareness or consciousness. Consequently, the material object of phenomenological analysis consists of the original contents — both psychic and intentionally objective — immediately present in the philosopher's experiences (*Erlebnisse*) prior to all theory making, that is, from "the natural standpoint." The formal object is constituted by this pre-logical, pre-scientific, pre-systematic, non-causal and atheoretical attitude, better known as the phenomenological method. The ultimate goal to be reached by this introspective and still extraspective analysis is seen in the establishment of a legitimate and indisputable foundation for all sciences which presuppose such an unbiased, purely empirico-intuitive description of the immediate and original reality as the source and material of all of man's experiences.

It is the task of the philosopher to present the full topological and structural map of the states of consciousness by laying out its two different, though inseparable, aspects, that is, the subjective proper (the personal acts of prehension) and its objective counterpart (the objects or phenomena in the acts of subjective experience). This descriptive analysis gets underway by the method of a double reduction (*Einklämmerung*) of the psycho-objective regions of reality. First, the *eidetic reduction* contemplates exclusively the essence (*Eidos*) of the self, his acts of prehension as well as their respective objects in their singular concreteness without any attempt at a theoretical or causal explanation or interpretation to follow. Second, the *phenomenological reduction* contemplates the objects as fundamentally correlated to and tied up to the states of consciousness. Strictly speaking, there is no consciousness as such (*Bewusstein überhaupt*); being conscious necessarily implies its object insofar as man can be conscious only *of* something given in the acts of prehension and analysis. Thus there is no way of speaking of a "subject" abstracted from its necessary confrontation with an object; similarly, the "object" has meaning only insofar as it is the object *for* a subject.

By positing the inseparable subject-object relationship, Husserl wanted to eliminate the Kantian and the post-Kantian — rather neo-Kantian — conception of pure consciousness or pure reason on one hand and its objects to be manipulated through the acts of the *a priori* categories of sensibility and understanding on the other. In Husserl's terminology one should rather speak of a state of consciousness (*Noesis, Bewussthaben*) essentially coordinated to its contents (*Noemata, das Bewusste*) which are intuitively grasped in their essential structural make-up through the act of ideation (*Wesensschau*). Philosophy is, therefore, to be defined as a pure descriptive study of essences known in and through the immanent configurations of consciousness. Since all empirical objects are regulated by their intrinsic essences and as such are related to the acts of experiential prehension, there is an *eidetic science* corresponding to each empirical science, that is, a *regional ontology.* All regions of reality, however, are rooted in pure consciousness which is the first, self-evident reality. Philosophy, therefore, studies this original region of intentional awareness.

No matter how energetically Husserl tried to free philosophy from the dangers of empiricism and psychologism, he still retains the basic doctrine of Kantian subjectivism. In fact, his phenomenology had to develop into a transcendental doctrine which, in last analysis, makes all given contents of consciousness depend, in their very being and nature, on the acts of the subject's becoming aware of them. Therefore, he failed just as all neo-Kantian philosophers did, to give an acceptable account of the basic problem of first philosophy seen in the light of the still unresolved opposites between the order of essence and existence, as well as in the order of being and values.

While Husserl's main concern was directed toward the gnoseological problem of truth and evidence, *M. Scheler* dedicated himself exclusively to the problem of value from the standpoint of the phenomenological method. Following Lotze's groundbreaking efforts in the field of axiology, Scheler goes even beyond Lotze's dualism between the order of being and the order of values. He feels that one should make a clear distinction and separation between three orders of reality: (1) the order of things (*Ding, Sache*) which taken by themselves are indifferent toward and outside the (2) order of values which represent some ideal and objective order of qualities, and may, in their turn, accidentally inhabit certain things as their carriers and thus constitute (3) the order of goods saturated with values.

Quite similar is *J. Hessen's* position with regard to the specific mode of being proper to values. "Values," says Hessen, "do not belong to the order of sensible objects. Their 'modus vivendi' is that of an ideal existence and validity" (in *Wertphilosophie,* p. 23). As far as the concept of value is concerned, Hessen declines any attempt at its definition, for values belong to those supreme concepts like being, existence, etc. which do not allow of any real definition. Any attempt would thus necessarily end in a circular definition.

The ideal being of values is compared by Hessen with the mode of being characteristic of mathematical objects. Consequently, they can be brought into existence only by the subject's creative activity. This circumstance makes all values necessarily subordinated and related to the subject who constitutes value by marrying, in his intuitive contemplation, the object (thing) with some ideal quality. Finally, values are not beings subsisting in and by themselves, for it is of their essence to belong or to inhere in some subject or thing as their carrier (*Wertträger*). It appears, therefore, that, according to Hessen, values have only an accidental being and relation to the order of reality from which they may be divorced without any further consequences.

Closely related to the position of M. Scheler and J. Hessen is the doctrine professed by *H. Rickert* and *W. Windelband* of the neo-Kantian group of Baden. Both start out with the distinction to be made between *nature,* which can be explained by strict causality in positive sciences, and *cultural history,* which can be interpreted and understood only by the criteria of normative value tendencies. The order of values with their unconditional validity represents the normative spirit (*der normative Geist*), which may, rather should, direct man's cultural activities and establish the meeting point between the two separate worlds of physical reality and values through man's acts of valuing (*Weltknoten*).

The historico-cultural aspect of the neo-Kantian value theory finds its full expression in the monumental works of *W. Dilthey, A. Meinong,* and *Ed. Spranger,* as the main representatives of cultural anthropology (*Geistes-Wissenschaften,* literally the science of the spirit). Both Dilthey and more so his disciple Ed. Spranger revive the Hegelian doctrine on the meaning and understanding of the historico-cultural process as the manifestation of the normative spirit (*der normative Geist*) of ideal value-categories, which inspires and directs man's subjective spirit (*der subjektive Geist*) in his value judgments and value creation, rendered visible and projected into the world as the values belonging to the objective spirit (*der objektive Geist*) of culture and civilization.

For the rest, Dilthey and Spranger have the well-known dualism between the order of being and the order of validity in common with Lotze, Rickert, Windelband, Scheler, Hessen, and N. Hartmann. Spranger further postulates the existence of a set of six innate "value categories *a priori* of the spirit" in man — the theoretical, the economic, the social, the political, the aesthetic and religious value tendencies — called the basic configuration or structure of man's inner psychic life (*das Grundgerüst des Geistes im individuellen Seelenleben*). These immanent, ideal dispositions account not only for man's general valuing activity, but also for the individual types of a person's way of life (*Lebensformen*) as well as for the different types of collective cultural patterns and related philosophies of life (*Typen der Weltanschauung,* described by Dilthey).

A reaction against all value-relativism and subjectivism comes from *N. Hartmann* of the phenomenological school of value philosophy. He strongly defends "the ontological character" of values against their fundamental dependence on and subordination to the human person required by Scheler and Hessen. Besides being experienced by subjects, values do have their own subsisting mode of existence apart and independently from any valuing subject. Their precise mode of subsistence is described by Hartmann as "an ideal being in itself" (*ein ideales Ansichsein*), very similar to the mode of subsistence of all theoretical, logico-mathematical entities. With regard to the order of objective reality, values represent only the set of ideal possibilities insofar as they may not become actual through man's creative efforts. Contemplated, however, in themselves, values represent an ideal hierarchy or a strictly determined system of ideal entities, enjoying a more subtle, almost immaterial mode of existence but still lacking in the full weight of real existence. It is rather easy to recognize here once again the Platonic metaphysics revived by N. Hartmann as an attempt at the foundation of a value ontology, designed to safeguard values from the dangers of subjectivism and relativism. However, his value ontology, just as Plato's heaven of ideas, does not stand the weight of a serious philosophic criticism. It still remains, however, the favorite dream of would-be metaphysicians.

Nevertheless, almost all value phenomenologists have something to say on the ultimate, metaphysical foundation of values. N. Hartmann is the only exception, since he denies the transcendental relation of values, considering them as absolute in themselves, that is, subsisting in their unconditional validity. M. Scheler, on the contrary, refers all values to a supreme, infinite, spiritual, and personal Being and Value. However, it is not within man's rational power to prove such a supreme existent, for no one can break through the subjective barrier of subjective consciousness. Therefore, the only opening to transcendence can be found through the experience of a philosophic faith (*gläubiges Denken*) as the modern version of the traditional attitude of *"credo ut intelligam."* J. Hessen, in his turn, proposes several other reasons why values should be grounded in the absolute Being. First, all values are essentially related to the order of reality, possessing a definite tendency of becoming real; therefore, they "must be" emanating from some ultimate reality. The path to be followed by values should be from this original reality to the region of real existents. Second, since values are essentially related to the subject of valuing, one "must think" of them as the ideas of an absolute, transcendental, spiritual reality.

Should one move the question on the form or mode of a human being's reaching this metaphysical region of reality, he should be told that the phenomenologists insist on a new form of knowledge through which the inner nature of values can be known and disclosed. This power, however, is not and cannot be of intellectual or rational nature because the object of human reason is "being" which is separated from "value." Consequently, all phenomenologists and cultural anthropologists postulate the existence of an intuitive, direct, emotional sensing of values (in German, *Wertfühlen, Wertschau, intentionales Fühlen der Werte)* with the exclusion of all intellectual or purely theoretical elements. Already Brentano speaks of a "correctly or rightly characterized love" *(richtig charakterisierte Liebe)* starting the well-known trend of value irrationalism. Also Meinong prefers an "emotional prehension" *(emotionale Präsentation)* and M. Scheler insists on the same anti-intellectual character of grasping values. In such wise, we may interpret this rather peculiar view by declaring that "values are felt, not known," an expression which fits perfectly within Lotze's sentence quoted above: "Values are not, but are still valid." This is what had to happen once the phenomenologists separated the order of reality from the order of ideal validity and normativity.

What are the reasons leading to this unfortunate dualism in the order of universal reality?

Scheler, Hartmann, and Hessen point to the different structural constitution of being and value. In this sense, values are ideal qualities, and as such they may be thought of as eternal, enjoying an absolute validity; at the same time they are totally indifferent toward real existence or its absence. Due to this indifference or neutrality, values still subsist even though their carrier, the real being, may have ceased to be. Thus the value of justice does not lose its absolute meaning and validity when just men and women die. This may happen because the real existents do not possess this absolute autonomy, independence, subsistence, and validity — attributes which can be predicated exclusively of values. Experience tells us that real beings or existents are totally contingent, changing, particular, individual, and limited in time and space. Furthermore, there are certain objective values which may never become real without thereby losing their ideal validity. On the other hand, there are things which do not carry any value at all. From still another point of view, values belong to a definite, organic system or hierarchy in which the qualitative differences among values are structurally organized according to their higher or lower degree of ideal validity, meaning, and dignity, from the highest value to the lowest, leading to the polarity between value versus non-value or even negative value. Since being is opposed by nothingness (non-being) only, there is no way of speaking in the ontological order of a hierarchic disposition of beings. Being either is or it is not and there is no going beyond this. Finally, real being is thought of as something factual, static, disclosing nothing more than the very datum of existence. Values, on the contrary, possess by virtue of their very nature, a dynamic element as the responsible power behind every progression and evolution. All these reasons confirm the maintenance of the dualism between being and value.

The European philosophy of value has had its direct impact on the mind of American thinkers whose doctrines on value reflect a bewildering variety of positions within the extreme poles of subjectivism and utilitarian collectivism.* It is beyond the limitations of the present chapter to provide the reader with an exhaustive discussion of all these conflicting views. Still we may

* *G. Santayana,* for instance, identifies value with the subject's acts of desire, pursuit, and interest, dictated by some irrational tendencies.

construct a representative sample in order to illustrate the truly hopeless confusion which dominates the whole field of contemporary thought.

Let us start first with the subjectivistic, relativistic, and irrational approaches to human values, leaving the pragmatic and social interpretation for the next. The quotations to follow speak for themselves, relieving us from the burden of commenting on their supposed meaning.*

> Our consciousness of an object's value, while it declares the blind disposition to pursue that object, constitutes its whole worth.
>
> The *esse* of value is not its *percipi,* though this is said too; but the *esse* of value is *desiderari.*
>
> If a man does not value fame, what value has it?
>
> All valuation rests on an irrational bias.
>
> No doubt any desire, however capricious, represents some momentary partial interest, which lends to its objects a certain real and inalienable value.

The same line of opinion is professed by H. M. Kallen:

> Value is, in origin and character, completely irrational. . . . In sum, fundamental values are relations, responses, attitudes, immediate, simple, subjectively obvious and irrational.

The special mode of existence and the emergence of values can be seen in the following remarks:

> Do values exist? The feeling of value exists . . . but value as such, is simply valid. That is its objectivity. (W. M. Urban)
>
> Value is the satisfaction of the valuer. (S. Alexander)
>
> Value is created by valuing. (D. W. Prall)
>
> Values are primarily felt. (J. S. Mackenzie)
>
> Value might be defined as the relation of any object to a valuing subject (since) values are held to be functions of certain acts of living minds to which we have given the name

* The reader is advised to relate the quotations to follow to the works of the respective authors given in the bibliography.

of interest. That which is an object of interest is *eo ipso* invested with value. Any object, whatever it be, acquires a value when any interest, whatever it be, is taken in it. . . . To like or dislike an object is to create that object's value. (R. B. Perry) *

Value is the word I use for the intrinsic reality of an event. Value is an element which pervades through and through the poetic view of nature. We have only to transfer to the very texture of realization in itself that value which we recognize so readily in terms of human life. . . . Realization, therefore, is itself the attainment of value. But there is no such thing as mere value. Value is the outcome of limitation. (A. N. Whitehead)

Values simply are. (J. F. Dashiell)

The problem of value is 'why values are valued.' And the really simple solution is, we value values 'for values.' (A. Weinberg)

Coming to the social and pragmatic interpretation of values the following samples will translate the basic ideas of their exponents:

Value is nothing but the efficiency of a conscious agent to promote the efficiency of society, to maintain the equilibrium of forces which society represents. (S. Alexander)

The basic principle is that values are objective because imperative and imperative because collective. It is society that creates values. They express social aspirations or ideals. (R. W. Sellars)

The central values or "these experiences of apprehending truth or error, goodness or evil, beauty or ugliness, are the culmination and the most potent variety of the experiences of cooperation and helpfulness, of conflict and dissidence." The values "involve a relation to the collective mind, and what is true, good or beautiful is not true or good or beautiful except as so combined with the collective mind." (S. Alexander)

* "I do not find worth in others or in myself, I attribute it to them and to myself." (Felix Adler)

Reflecting upon the suggested meanings of the above statements, one could cry out with W. James: "How fantastic a philosophy! As if the 'world of values' were independent of existence. It is only as being, that one thing is better than another."

* * * * *

Before coming to the exposition of the Aristotelian and scholastic principles applied to the ontological foundation of values, it is in order to call the attention of the reader to the precise meaning of the problem at hand. The exact delineation of this question is needed because of the many and varied opinions of the moderns whose views on values very frequently emphasize only the secondary aspects of the problem while ignoring the real issue to be discussed and answered in the first place.

Throughout the presentation of the modern European and mainly the American analysis of values, most authors considered so far, have a great deal to say on the subjective, irrational, and relative nature of values, going even to the extreme position of identifying value with the acts of valuing (value judgments) and the person's psychic, emotional motives (desires, interests, etc.) which direct man's selective attitude in the world of goods and values. It is not our intention here to deny that these elements of the value experience have no bearing whatsoever on the problem of value. Our only point is that they do not belong to the really essential question a philosopher should ask before going into the description of the phenomenal and accidental aspects of the value experience. We think, therefore, that the problem should be presented anew in the following order of questions:

1. What are the constant elements in value, valuing, and the ensuing value relation?

This question, however, must be broken down to more specific ones:

1. What is value in itself?
2. What is its specific mode of existing?

3. What is the immediate (phenomenal and subjective) and the ultimate (objective, ontological) foundation of value?
4. What is valuing, or the acts of value-judgment?
5. What is the value relation?
6. What do we have to say on the form of knowing values?
7. What specific problems arise from the question about value hierarchy and value antinomies?, and, finally,
8. Is there any real gap to be bridged between the order of reality and the order of values?

Only by answering these questions can anyone hope to have approached the proper field of the philosophy of values in its fundamental principles which are, according to the order of importance, metaphysical, gnoseological, psychological, and socio-cultural. Our present concern, however, will be restricted to the metaphysical and gnoseological aspects only, leaving the remaining questions to the third and fourth chapters respectively.

The problem of values in the Aristotelian and Thomistic philosophies can be introduced as being both old and new at the same time, but from different points of view. The ontological principles, such as the nature and attributes of being used for the foundation of value, are as old as the system itself. However, these principles may clarify only the general problem about the *"locus ontologicus"* of value in general, and say very little or nothing about the specific nature of values in particular. Because of this openness and limitation of the Aristotelian and Thomistic tradition, we may consider the value problem as a new one, mainly if one views their theories in the perspective of modern history and the contemporary way of life.

Since the specific problem on the nature of values has not received a thorough analysis in scholastic philosophy as yet, one can expect to find a uniform position, doctrine, and agreement among the modern exponents of neo-scholastic philosophy. In fact, there is no univocal definition of value universally accepted today. It is true that all of them agree as to the ontology of value; coming, however, to the problems of the value relation, value relativism, and subjectivism, the agreement is nowhere to be found.

The metaphysical principle to be used for the solution of the ontological problem is given in St. Thomas' doctrine on the convertibility (interchangeability) of being and the good *(ens et bonum convertuntur)*. This principle is part of the general thesis on the problem of the transcendental attributes of being.

Anyone who is familiar with scholastic ontology will recall the meaning attached to the transcendentals; they represent those modes or modifications of being *(modi essendi)* which are implicitly given with the phenomenon of being as such, though not explicitly expressed or stated. Thus being implies five transcendental attributes: thing (*res*), something (*aliquid*), unity or oneness (*unum*), truth (*verum*), and goodness (*bonum*). Accordingly, any *thing* which *is* some-thing, has a unity and identity, is intelligible to the mind and desirable for the will. Furthermore, it should also be recalled that the concept of being, as interpreted by Aquinas, is both transcendent and analogous: the formal element of being as such is to be found — in various forms and degrees — in the hierarchy of all kinds of beings as well as in the specific differences through which they are set apart from one another. Consequently, the quality of being is attributed, formally and essentially, to the whole range of beings and their differences, according to the proper proportion — in the degree, quality, and intensity of participation in the full dimension of being as such.

From the five transcendental attributes of being we shall concern ourselves only with the quality of goodness (*bonum*) insofar as it implies the basic value relationship between the subject of desire (man) and the desirability of being apprehended by intellect and will.

The good or goodness of being (*bonum*) is identified by Aquinas as that which is desired by everyone, for whatever is the object of desire necessarily possesses the element of quality or goodness. Thus goodness formally accounts for the subject's desire; in other words, being is desired, or, at least, desirable, because it is good in itself and for others. Further inquiry into the reason for being's desirability and goodness leads us to the concepts of perfection and end (*perfectio et finis*). The transition from the idea of goodness to that of perfection is made clear by the formal element which identifies goodness as such.

Proper to the nature of goodness is to perfect something or someone in the form of becoming the very object of desire for those who know of its intrinsic perfection. In more simple terms, being is the end-object of desire because of the attribute of goodness rooted in its perfection which is manifested through its essence or nature. Transposing this doctrine into the terminology of the value-philosophy, we could express the same ideas by establishing the sequence of relationships between the ontological qualities of being insofar as it implies goodness, desirability, and perfection all belonging to the comprehension of being as such.

It remains to be shown now the common root which accounts for the interchangeable character of goodness and perfection. A deeper analysis of the contents of being tells us that the actual exercise of being in the order of existence represents in itself and by itself a fundamental perfection. In this sense being is not a mere *datum* or *factum,* as the moderns would like to have it; on the contrary, to belong to the order of actual existence is not only good but it is better than not to be. In fact, being in any of its forms and degrees manifests, through its essence or substance, a specific mode of an ultimate perfection of the unlimited Being (*ipsum esse, actus ultimus, perfectissimus omnium actuum, actualitas omnium actualitatum et perfectio omnium perfectionum*). It is wrong, therefore, to restrict being to the mere factual datum of existence. There is nothing which only is; on the contrary, whatever is, is because it is something, and we can notice it only insofar as it discloses some specific nature through which it participates in the perfection of being unlimited. In other words, "*esse*" does not mean the bare fact of existing or being outside its causes; it means much more, namely, a fundamental perfection possessed by every being (*ens*) according to the measure and degree of participating in the source of all being, who is all perfection on an infinite scale. Consequently, whatever is, is some specific being possessing and disclosing some degree of perfection, goodness, and desirability insofar as any being is the manifestation, on a limited scale, of the ultimate perfection (*ipsum esse subsistens, actus purus*) in which it participates and through which it endures in existence. Therefore, the ultimate, metaphysical foundation of all values can be discovered only in God as infinite perfection, infinite goodness, and the ultimate end of all conation and desire. The immediate foundation of all values is to be seen in the specific perfection belonging to the nature of all limited beings.

Since being discloses the qualities of goodness and perfection, there is no need to look for another foundation for values outside the universal region of being. Whenever being and value are separated, the latter is up in the air. In fact, what *are* values if they are not even *beings?* Outside being one finds nothingness, that is, non-being. "An ideal realm," says J. Dewey, "which has no roots in existence has no efficiency or relevancy." And Dean Inge insists that "a value judgment which is not also a judgment of existence is in the air. Existence itself is a value, and an ingredient in every valuation; that which has no existence has no value."

The logical conclusion we are forced to reach in the light of the metaphysical principles applied to the phenomenon of values, points to a value ontology conceived after the premises of a critical realism in which the order of reality and that of values necessarily overlap (*ordo ontologicus et ordo axiologicus convertuntur*). Thus we may describe value as the transcendental attribute of being insofar as it contains the qualities of goodness, desirability, perfection, and finality. Consequently, if there is a reason for making a distinction between the order of being and the order of value, it is only a formal and logico-subjective one to the extent that the above elements, belonging to the structural make-up and nature of being and value, are not explicitly signified, though implied by the universal and abstract idea of being. This distinction also indicates why the concepts of value and being should not be taken univocally. However, one should keep in mind that such a distinction is only a logical one with some imperfect foundation in the ontological order (*distinctio rationis cum fundamento imperfecto in re*).

Since being and value are interchangeable from a material, that is, ontological point of view, we may say that whatever belongs to the comprehension of being should be attributed to the inner nature of value as well. In the first place, the analogy and the transcendental attributes of being ought to be applied to value thus making value and being coextensive. Moreover, the ten transcendental predicaments or categories of being could be used as an indication for the different "value categories," in addition to the already-mentioned five transcendental attributes of being. These ontological modalities of being should be regarded as the criteria for constructing the hierarchic structure of all ideal, real, and possible values. To be sure, no one will succeed in constructing an "ideal scale of values" unless he will consider the real relationships existing among beings as the foundation for any "order of reality" in which every value is assessed according to its eminence, nobility, quality, and perfection rooted in being itself.

In order to prevent or to clear up the almost universal confusion and uncertainty about the validity of values, brought about by all kinds of subjectivistic, relativistic, and pragmatic ideologies, philosophers should accept the fact that the only valid criterion to be used in weighing the higher or lower significance and importance of any value should be the degree in the perfection of its being, manifested through its essence as the measure for the mode of participating in *"esse."* If someone does not recognize the fact that there are different, that is, higher and lower, levels of perfection and existence, there remains only one conclusion leading to universal relativism and irrationalism.

We maintain, on the contrary, that in the order of existents there is an evident qualitative difference in the degree and intensity of beings, due to more or less perfection actually possessed or at least latent in their specific natures. If it were true that one being is just the same as any other being, there would arise an anarchic, egalitarian, and equalizing, rather flattening, process which would do away with any "order" based on specific and individual differences. Communism as a so-called philosophy, for instance, should be regarded as "organized anarchy" dictated by the confusion or ignorance about the qualitative differences in beings and values.

Since *"esse"* is the root of all perfections, there can be no doubt as to the place the *"ipsum esse subsistens"* should occupy in the order of being, perfection, and value. The absolute being, God, is, therefore, the first both in the ontological and axiological orders. All other beings and values must be related to Him according to the order of propinquity or distance they assert by the amount of participated perfection.

Using this ontological measure as the criterion for establishing an ideal hierarchy of values, we propose the following scale or systematic arrangement to be used later in the evaluation of the psychological, moral, historico-cultural, and socio-political impact of values on human existence.

In order to avoid misunderstanding, we should make it clear that the value hierarchy to be presented operates with the distinctions to be made between "values in themselves" and "instrumental or contributory values," a distinction based upon the same criterion of ontological perfection immanent to them. Thus we maintain that all values belonging to the realm of the physical, material, organic order of beings represent only the facilities, commodities, and techniques invented by man for the conquest of his physical environment (matter, energy, time, and space) and the establishment of a material civilization (industry and technology). Consequently, the values belonging to the order of material well-being cannot be regarded as "ends in themselves"; their essential utilitarian character identifies them as values of a secondary order needed for man's liberation from his original dependence and subordination to the forces of nature.

"Values in themselves," on the contrary, belong to man's personal, psycho-spiritual and cultural life, which do not possess the element of practicality, functionality, instrumentality, and pragmatic utility. Here belong the values of religion, morality, philosophy, science and aesthetics. The socio-political values (harmony, friendship, love, and the will to power) cannot be regarded as values in themselves because of their explicitly instrumental character; the social and political organization of human life represents only the needed framework for the development and education of the individual human person whose continued efforts are subordinated to the final goal of personal autonomy and perfection. Should one promote the socio-political values to the eminence of values in themselves, one would justify all totalitarian organizations of political life demanding the enslavement of the free person.

In spite of the fact that the "negative values" do not belong to the hierarchy of values proper, some mention should be made of their existence. Actually, every "positive" value has its negative counterpart, such as indicated by the following pairs of opposites: truth and falsity, the useful and the useless (even harmful or dangerous), the beautiful and the ugly, harmony and conflict, the religious and the profane, virtue and sin, and so forth. The reason for bringing them up in this context is given by the problem of value antinomies, value conflicts, or value polarities which should be looked upon as the results of imperfections in the mode of being characteristic of every finite existent, including the complete absence of a due perfection, usually known as evil or the spirit of contradiction.

The ideal hierarchy of values we propose, therefore, consists of six fundamental value categories to be found both in the human person's psychic dispositions as latent value-tendencies and in the objective, trans-subjective, impersonal, or supra-individual achievements of human culture and history. Thus we have:

I. THE RELIGIOUS VALUE — God as the Absolute Being, Perfection, the ultimate foundation of all being and value as well as the eternal law governing the natural, moral, and religious orders.

II. THE COGNITIVE VALUE — Truth, insight, knowledge, understanding, and wisdom, being proper to the spirit of perennial philosophy and of disengaged scientific inquiry.

III. THE AESTHETIC VALUE — The beautiful and its manifestations in the endless forms of the creative intuition of the artist.

IV. THE SOCIAL VALUE — Human solidarity, cohesion, friendship, love, inspiring the spirit of integral humanism.

V. THE POLITICAL VALUE — The will to power, authority, government, and administration of the body politic in the spirit of justice and democracy.

VI. THE ECONOMIC VALUE — The countless variety of all things useful, representing man's progressive command over his natural habitat.

Having thus presented the general outline of the scholastic value ontology, we have to turn our attention to the objections of the moderns against the fundamental correlation between being and value. Their position, already presented above, boils down to the belief in the basic and irreducible structural diversity of these two orders; values, as ideal entities, are necessary, universal, and valid, subsisting independently and apart from a contingent, mutable, limited, and diversified reality. Let us consider now, one by one, whether these objections will stand or fall under the attack of a serious criticism.

The contingency of the limited being is not absolute — no one wants to deny its indifference toward being or not being for it does not exist out of necessity. On the other hand, however, the contingent still possesses some degree of necessity from the point of view of its nature or essence which is said to be

> "unchangeable, necessary and eternal. By the unchangeableness of essence is meant that the essence of a thing is not sometimes one thing and sometimes another, but always the same. It may be the essence of a changeable thing and the thing itself may change and become something else, but the requirements of the essence are unalterable. The essence of man is to be rational and animal. No matter how much the concrete individual being may change, the requirements of the essence of man cannot change. Either a being is a rational

animal or it is not a man. The necessity of essences follows from their unchangeableness. If they cannot change, they must be what they are, and a thing must have the essence that belongs to it in order to be the thing it is. By saying that essences are eternal we mean that what is essential to a thing now, always was and always will be essential. The constitution of essence is altogether independent of the element of time." (J. F. McCormick, S. J., in *Scholastic Metaphysics*, p. 38).

To disregard this mode of necessity and identity would imply the denial of the self-evident principles of identity and non-contradiction.

As a counterpart to "the ideal being in itself" (*das ideale Ansichsein*), peculiar to values as an indication of their "absolute subsistence, autonomy, validity, and independence" from the reality of things, we may show forth our own doctrine on the universals which happen to possess all the qualifications required by the moderns for the intrinsic nature of values. As a matter of fact, our universal concepts, obtained through the process of abstraction and ideation, possess all the ideal qualities of the "value categories"; they are universal, abstract, ideal, eternal (at least negatively), immutable, and necessary, subsisting in these qualities in the mind of the knowing subject, regardless of the condition of the concrete, individual, particular, singular, and contingent objects or things from which they were derived in the process of ideogenesis. The only important difference between the ideality of values of the moderns and our doctrine on universal ideas is the fact that the universals exist potentially in the order of reality, formally in the intellect, and eminently in God's essence, while the ideal beings of the moderns, called values, hang in the air. Thus they have to choose between the positions available to them: exaggerated realism (Plato), idealistic conceptualism or even the treacherous road of pure nominalism. It is really deplorable that the nature of intellectual knowledge and its results (ideas) are so poorly known or misinterpreted by many modern value philosophers!

We turn, now, to the so-called "ideal and objective values" which never become real, without losing, though, their ideal validity. We should remind the moderns of the doctrine on the possible which, contrary to their position, do not float aimlessly in some unknown region of Platonic entities, but are ultimately founded in the divine intellect and essence as perfections which can be made real through the act of communicating existence to them on a limited scale. It is our impression that the "ideal entities" of the moderns, with all their fancy trappings, do not stand for more than extrapolated, hypostatised human concepts, ideas, ideals, and remote possibilities.

Turning our attention to the alleged "static, factual" character of beings, as opposed to the dynamic and inspiring power of values, perhaps it will suffice to point briefly to the really dynamic and progressive conception of all limited beings in the scholastic metaphysics. The ontological principles of act and potency which constitute the composite, finite being, leave sufficient room for an intrinsic teleology or goal-directed process of development and enrichment. The transition from the state of potency to actuality represents a real change by which the limited being may activate all the latent tendencies and dispositions in view of a higher form of being and existence. On the other hand, one does not see how the moderns can combine the immutable, absolute validity and autonomy of their eternal value categories with the ideas of change, progress, and the dynamic, energetic, teledirected tendencies equally demanded from them.

The next bone of contention concerns the "normative character" of values by which they impose themselves as ideal directives with which human beings "should" or "ought to" comply in their lives and activities. Besides Rickert and Spranger, it is mainly M. Scheler who elaborated a new system of morality, exclusively based on the obliging character of values, opposed to both traditional ontology and Kantian formalism in the field of ethics (*materiale Wertethik*). While going along with the "normative character" of ethical values, we do not regard them with Scheler as "ideal essences a priori" imposing themselves on man's actions, but rather as the sum total of perfections (values), rooted in being, to be appropriated by the acts of free will and intelligent choice with a view on the ultimate perfection and destiny to be attained by every human person. The foundation of morality, just as that of values, rests on the perfections of being needed by the finite creature for the fulfillment of his existential commitment. Nevertheless, we might stretch the notion of values somewhat and call them "ideal norms of human actions aimed at the goal of final perfection." (The ethical impact of values on human existence will receive a more detailed treatment in another chapter of this study.)

We have purposely delayed consideration of the critical analysis of the gnoseological aspect of the modern value philosophy, because it necessarily entails certain psychological questions given with the "value relation," that is, the subject's confrontation with the world of values and goods.

Throughout the different versions of the modern philosophy of value there runs the conviction — either explicitly stated or tacitly assumed — that values can be known only through a new act of intentional and intuitive comprehension or sensing because of their different mode of being and nature, which sets them apart from the realm of ordinary beings and the ordinary channels of knowledge as well. We have already had several earlier opportunities to mention the value-irrationalism of some European and American thinkers. One of the first such instances which developed into a radical anti-intellectual attitude, brought to its last consequences in Bergson and the existentialists, is found in W. Windelband's famous distinction between judgment of mere fact (*Urteilung*) and judgment of value (*Beurteilung, Werturteil*). The same position identifies also E. Durkheim's mode of thinking as it appears, for instance, in the following passage:

> All theories equally suppose that value is in the things and it expresses their nature. Well, this postulate is contrary to facts. There is a number of cases where the relationship between the object's properties and the value that is attributed to it does not exist. An idol is a very sacred thing and sanc-

tity is the highest value that men have ever recognized. Well, an idol is frequently nothing more than a mass of stones or a piece of wood which, by itself, is devoid of any kind of value . . . the same thing can or cannot lose the value that it has or acquire a different one without changing its nature; it is sufficient that the ideal change. (Jugement de Valeur et Jugement de Realité, in Revue de Metaphysique et Moral, V. 19, 1911.)

This distinction, rather lack of correspondence between fact and judgment, makes all moderns feel justified in maintaining the mere subjective nature of value, valuing, and things held valuable. Let us now analyze the difference between the two different types of judgment.

The judgments of mere fact, or the categorical type, imply either an affirmation or a negation by which the identity or the non-identity of the two terms (subject and predicate) is expressed (S is P, or S is not P), as, for instance, in the statement: "It is raining" or "It is not raining." The predominant element is the reference to something objectively given in or absent from the field of the subject's perception. Most judgments of all positive sciences and common sense imply this kind of statement which moves within the two contradictory poles of being and not-being. Because of this strictly factual objectivity, judgments of fact demand a universal agreement unless somebody "wants to quarrel with established facts."

Value judgments, on the contrary, imply certain new elements which express, rather, the subject's emotional reaction to a given experience instead of the exclusive concern with the object's pure intelligibility. The first new element in the value judgment — for example, in "It is good that it is raining" or "It is bad, too bad that it is raining" — expresses the subject's "irrational" attitude toward a phenomenon, which follows his acts of liking, disliking, acceptance or rejection, preference, selection, choice, approval or disapproval, in a word, the new complex process or act of "valuing" or "judging."

The second new element in all value judgments is the apparent absence of all factual, objective, that is, demonstrable, experimental, quantitative or measurable criteria, one could use to determine the "truth" or the "validity" of man's emotive evaluations. For almost every judgment of value one can oppose another as the direct denial of the validity claimed by the first. The disagreement runs through all dimensions of personal, social, and cultural regions of human civilization and history. Thus truth is opposed by falsity; what is considered useful today is thrown out as useless tomorrow; certain works of art are evaluated as "beautiful" by some and as "ugly" by others; harmony is destroyed by conflict, and finally, God is opposed by the forces of the underworld, while the principles of justice and virtue are fought against by violence and depravity.

Because of this obvious antagonism between "positive values" and "negative" ones, there are many who are convinced that there are and can be no criteria to determine what is true, holy, beautiful, moral, just, useful, necessary or superfluous. As a consequence, the majority of people "conform" to the collective or social standards of valuing, dictated by public opinion and prejudice. However, the "conformists" are not the only type created by the situation of value irrationalism, for we have the skeptic, the agnostic, the hedonist, the opportunist, the reformer, the rebel, and the angry young men and women as the newest type of the modern subterranean cave generation.

In spite of this uncertainty about the validity of our value judgments, people continue to value out of necessity; they still desire, choose, select, distinguish, approve or condemn, and even try to teach others how they "should" or "ought to" judge, criticize, see and value life and all that it has to offer. There have always been certain "authorities" in the fields of arts, of sciences, in politics, education, morality, and religion, whose value judgments were considered, at least for a while, as the "ultimate pronouncements" on almost anything worthwhile. The only exception to the collection of different types would be the person who stays "indifferent," "neutral," "independent," or "non-partisan," if such an attitude of extreme callousness is psychologically possible at all.

If there are a few specimens, they do not stay around too long, for usually they belong to the self-exterminating species.

The absence of "factual proof or quantitative demonstration" creates the condition of freedom which, being misused by lack of intelligence, establishes the "order of anarchy" in which nothing is of any real value, that is, any better or worse, since everything else is reduced to the same level of no-value in itself. In view of this depressing situation, no one can hope to establish the reversal of the universal trend toward the total nihilistic or anarchic attitudes. Nevertheless, it could be useful to establish the extent to which the emotional, subjective, and irrational elements can be tolerated in our value judgments and where the point at which the prevalent objective element does lie. In order to accomplish this much, a closer view at the "value relation" is in order.

There are three constant elements in the value relation, that is, the subject, the object wanted or rejected, and the very act of choice or preference we could call "the valuing" as such. In order to avoid the pitfalls of an exaggerated value-relativism, these constant elements of the value relation should not be confused, as happens with most moderns, but rather delineated though not kept apart. In other words, we should agree that value, valuing, and valuable are not the same realities, just as the subject and his actions are not to be identified with the qualities of the objects desired or rejected. Finally, the relation between the subject and the object should be considered in its own right as a really existing situation created by the subject's confrontation with the object of his conation and action.

Speaking first of the subject, we refer back to the ideas already presented in the previous chapter on his situation in the world through which he becomes a true *"arbiter"* of his existential condition, a function manifested through his acts of knowledge, conation, action, appropriation, and self-realization. At this point, therefore, we want to call attention only to the fact that man's cognitive, appetitive, and volitive acts are not devoid of ontological necessities. First, there is a universal human nature and essence, individually shaped in different persons, which predisposes, through the set of his "needs," the direction, the contents, and the goals of all that he knows, desires, and possesses. Second, the act of valuing as such can by no means be described as purely emotional and irrational. It is well-known from psychology, that all of men's desires, appetites, conation, and wanting rest on a definite rational and cognitive basis; it is sense knowledge which precedes the acts of sensitive desire, and it is intellectual knowledge which necessarily precedes man's will insofar as it is man who establishes the contact with outside reality or the objects and the ends of all his activities. In the saying of Aquinas, "there is nothing wanted, unless previously known." Since knowledge necessarily precedes all forms of desire and conation there is a definite cognitive and rational element in the acts of valuing which makes all positions of value-irrationalism contrary to psychology and everyday experience.

It is true, on the other hand, that man's instinctual and emotional dispositions may prevail over the cognitive element, bringing about distortions as to the "truth" of his valuing. This phenomenon, however, should be regarded as the deviation from the general rule which requires that man's valuing be in line with his reason and understanding, oriented toward and measured by the order of reality. Even in the instance of so-called irrational, passionate reactions most people try to justify the meaning of their impulsive behavior in the light of reason. Finally, no man would accept the qualification of an irrational being whose valuing is devoid of the element of understanding, meaning, and purpose.

The "world" man is faced with also possesses a definite character of identity, permanency, constancy, and necessity in spite of the many changes that occur in nature. But even these changes themselves follow a definite pattern or law as described by the positive sciences. Only by discovering the inner causality underlying the phenomena of nature — a highly rational and intellectual activity — can man think of manipulating its forces for the benefit of his life. In other words, man's valuing rests on his cognitive powers whose nature is to unveil the intelligibility and desirability of the objects belonging in the field of his experiences.

We are aware, of course, that on the higher levels of existence, that is, in the fields of religion, morality, art, society, politics, and even science there is more freedom for the exercise of man's creative imagination than on the lower levels of vegetation, sensing, and material need satisfaction. Nonetheless, even the higher acts of intellectual knowledge, the acts of will, and man's symbolic activities are measured by his spiritual nature and by the normativity of the ideals to be created by them. In a word, man's life is not a meaningless, impulsive, and anarchic manifestation of blind urges and desires; man has to live according to the law of his bio-physical and psycho-spiritual nature in a world dominated by the necessity of physical laws. Undoubtedly, he is at all times free to violate the laws of his structural make up and functioning. Whenever or wherever this occurs, we meet the degenerated type of man who misused his freedom by distorting the meaning of his condition in this world.

In the process of describing the ontological foundation of values, we made clear enough that the world of objects, insofar as they participate in being, represent the order of perfection, desirability, goodness, and finality. This perfection is manifested again by their inner essences as the measure of their participation in being. Consequently, objects are not and cannot be made just into anything man would like them to be. On the contrary, they impose themselves on man's senses, sensitivity, intellect, and will according to their own nature and thus condition man's cognitive, appetitive, and volitive acts to conform to their inner, objective reality. Here, again, man may set out to destroy the objects surrounding him, but the verdict is just the same as above.

In this sense the "value relation," consists of the subject's cognitive and volitive acts (valuing), directed toward the world of objects insofar as they are valuable, and of "value" which emerges from this confrontation as the qualitative element of perfection and goodness discovered or created by man. Any of these constants of the value relation possesses a definite ontological identity which lends them a certain amount of objectivity, validity, and normativity.

It is not our intention to institute a universal value dogmatism. The preceding critical restrictions do not remove altogether the element of freedom, subjectivity, and relativity from human values. In fact, we are well aware of the fact that man's valuing depends on the range, depth, and quality of his thought as well as on the use he makes of his freedom in the exercise of giving a symbolic meaning and significance to his existence. Our objection goes exclusively against all types of a *radical* subjectivism and relativism, leading to the contradictory situation of an anarchy in which everything is valid, for nothing stands for anything permanent and identical. In order to express, therefore, our position of a critical value realism, we want to conclude this chapter by identifying value with "being as the possible object of man's rational desire and the result of his creative activity." Thus we may also answer our initial question about the *"locus ontologicus"* and the *"modus essendi"* of values: values exist potentially in being, formally in man, if and when its perfection is appropriated by him through his acts of understanding, conation, and free creativity. Therefore, being is the measure of man's valuing.

## CHAPTER IV

## THE PSYCHOLOGICAL MOMENTUM VALUES AND LEVELS OF PERSONAL INTEGRATION

In the course of our discussion on the problems peculiar to the philosophy of value we have touched so far only on two of its aspects, namely, the descriptive presentation of the value dimensions in human experience, and the critical analysis of the validity and foundation of value as such. It has been our purpose to create the phenomenological and ontological frame of reference needed for the presentation of the psychological, ethical, and, finally, transcendental dimensions of the value phenomenon. In conformity with the canons of methodology, it is the psychological impact of values on human existence which demands our attention and without which the ethical momentum cannot be accounted for.

Since the term "psychology" covers an enormous field within which there is ample room for an almost endless variety of methods, conceptions, attitudes, and goals, it seems to be imperative that we identify the meaning we want to attach to it. Negatively, we do not entertain the ideas and principles so dear to the "science" of psychology conceived on the premises of naturalism and sensism. We feel that bio-chemistry, human physiology or the causal, deterministic, and, therefore, mechanical theories of behaviorism, quantitative experimentalism, and the implicit atomization of man's unity into "psychic quanta or elements" cannot disclose the *meaning* values have for human beings. The same restriction should also be applied to the "motivational approach" to the extent that here one must still operate with the strict and rigid principles of empirical causality, thus precluding the possibility of conceiving man's free and creative acts of value symbolism.

Moreover, all "adjustment" psychologies must receive the same treatment for laboring under the influence of a positivistic and materialistic idea of man.

Positively, we refer to the type of psychology created by Lotze, Brentano, Nietzsche, Klages, Spranger, Stern, Jung, and others, conceived after the methodological assumptions of philosophic anthropology and phenomenology (*verstehende und geisteswissenschaftliche Psychologie*). Since these new terms may sound rather confusing, we may convey their meaning by referring to the traditional idea of a "philosophy of man" or "philosophy of human nature" insofar as it reaches back to the Socratic conception of philosophy in which man occupies the whole field of philosophic concern. Although we have already made some brief reference to the idea of philosophic anthropology, some further elaboration on its meaning is necessary from the point of view of its origin, purpose, and relation to the phenomena of value and human existence.

Philosophic anthropology — a term borrowed from biology — came into being as a reaction against the pseudo-metaphysical speculations of German idealism on the one hand, and Franco-English empiricism on the other. Both idealism and empiricism endangered the dignity, value, and autonomy of the concrete human existent as an individual person either by dissolving its unique subsistent reality in the panlogistic process of historical and transcendental dialectics (*Hegel*), or by debasing man's existence to the level of gross sensism and materialism.

In order to succeed in discrediting and surpassing these systems of anthropophagism, both the material and the formal objects of philosophy had to be changed along with the method of philosophizing. First, the new anti-intellectual and anti-metaphysical attitude suppresses the transcendental region of reality to be replaced by the world of human existence in its spacio-temporal historicity, created and lived by concrete persons (*Schelling, Kierkegaard, Nietzsche, Husserl, Hartmann,* and *Dilthey*). Second, man's selective attitude, while defining the regions of reality, is focused on the cultural, therefore, axiological, value-directed aspects of free human creativity, thus eliminating the mere bio-physical and causal interpretation of human life (*Scheler, Hessen, Spranger, Klages, Stern, Cassirer,* etc.). Finally, the method of philosophic anthropology, as distinct from that of idealistic and transcendental criticism, limits itself to the descriptive presentation of man's immediate life experiences, better known as the phenomenological reduction of reality given within the horizons and regions of personal existence (*hermeneutics*). The exponents of existentialism—both literary and philosophic—carried their anti-intellectual and anti-systematic description of the human situation and condition to its utmost limits and consequences (*Dostoyevski, Kaffka, Heidegger, Jaspers, Sartre, Camus, Marcel, Buber,* etc.).

It is, therefore proper to identify philosophic anthropology as cultural anthropocentrism insofar as the scope and problems of philosophy are restricted exclusively to the phenomenon of man and his activities. Herein lies also the limitation of the phenomenological school insofar as it implies the danger of a geocentric anthropologism or world immanence without providing an opening for the metaphysical and theocentric conception and foundation of the human situation viewed in the context of universal being. On the other hand, philosophic anthropology and phenomenology are the best contemporary modes of philosophizing with regard to the need for a new rehabilitation for man's historico-cultural and psycho-social condition. It is with this qualification, therefore, that we may utilize the wealth of materials disclosed to man by this method and supply — on our own account — the missing ontological foundation for the axiological, psychological, ethical, and pedagogical principles, taken from the critical value ontology such as presented in the preceding chapter.

In order to substantiate our charge against the inadequacy of all types of scientism as inappropriate for dealing with the human phenomenon, we shall illustrate what happens to man and what becomes of him in the hands of hard-boiled rationalists and naturalists. From the many impressive critical studies dealing with man's condition in the modern world, we shall take and reproduce here only a few brief passages from *P. A. Sorokin's* classical work *"The Crisis of Our Age"* (pp. 121-124 and pp. 313-315, D.E.P. edition):

> Let us consider contemporary science, noting just how it defines man and what it contributes both to his well-being and to his detriment. The current scientific conceptions of man exhibit him as a sort of 'electronic complex'; 'a combination of physico-chemical elements'; 'an animal closely related to the ape or monkey'; 'a reflex mechanism' or 'variety of stimulus-response relationship'; 'a special adjustment mechanism'; a psychoanalytical libido; a predominantly subconscious or unconscious organism controlled mainly by alimentary and economic forces; or just a *homo faber* manufacturing various tools and instruments. No doubt man is all of this. But does this exhaust his essential nature? Does it touch his most fundamental properties, which make him a unique creature? Most of the definitions, masquerading as scientific, rarely, if ever, even raise such questions. Some, indeed, go so far as to deprive man even of mind, or thought, of consciousness, of conscience, and of volition, reducing him to a purely behavioristic mechanism of unconditioned and conditioned reflexes. Such are the current concepts of our leading physicists, biologists and psychologists.

The behavioral and social scientists, of course, did not waste time in bringing their "ideas" in line with the "scientific account of man," whose image has since been introduced even in the domains of fine arts and literature:

> Other conceptions, such as those of contemporary biographers, historians, and social scientists, follow a similar pattern. The biographies of the Stracheys, the Ludwigs, the Maurois, the Hugheses, the Ellises, the Erskines, the Millars, the Henry Adamses (in part), and a legion of contemporary psychoanalytical and "scientific" biographers, debunk and debase every personage — no matter how exalted — of whom they treat. Everybody and everything they touch — God, as well as noble men and achievements — is mockingly inter-

preted as something passive, commonplace, abnormal or pathological, impelled by prosaic, egotistical, and, for the most part, physiological drives. Genius becomes a species of insanity; unselfish sacrifice is explained solely in terms of an inferiority, Oedipus, Narcissus, or other complex; distinguished social endeavor is motivated by the herd instincts. Sexual libido, schizophrenia, paranoia, and the like are the dominant forces. Saintliness is pictured as a kind of idiocy, and the patriotic 'Father of His Country' as an abnormal sexual profligate. Piety is identified with ignorance and superstition; moral integrity, with hypocrisy; signal achievements, with mere luck; and so forth.

The same pseudo-scientific principles, inspired by high-sounding names, direct also the historical account of human past, present, and future:

> Our historians view history mainly *sub specie* of the New Yorker or Esquire, of the Freudian libido, of Marxian economic factors, of Paretian 'residues,' and other biological, economic, and cosmic forces. The entire pageant of human history turns out to be nothing but incessant interplay of cosmic rays, sunspots, climatic and geographic changes, and biological forces (drives, instincts, conditioned, unconditioned and prepotent reflexes; physico-economic complexes and 'residues') — forces in whose hands man is as but clay, and which stage all the historical events and create all the cultural values. Man himself, as an embodiment of superorganic energy, of thought, of consciousness, of conscience, of rational volition, plays a negligible role in the unfolding of this drama. In our 'scientific' histories he is relegated to the back stage as a mere plaything of blind forces — a plaything, moreover, stripped of virtually every element of attractiveness. While he is deluding himself with the belief that he controls his own destiny, he is, in fact, but the puppet of a blind biological evolution that dictates his actions and thus directs the course of his history.

The socio-political and economic aspects of our "scientifically organized" human life breathe the same air saturated with the same elements of "scientific fallout":

> From the same root have grown the other forms of degradation of man, atomization of values, and disintegration of culture surveyed before: in art and philosophy, in law and ethics, and so on. They are largely the consequence of the major premise for the same reasons. The same root is responsible for present-day society as an enormous number of armed camps, that by direct or indirect application of force and fraud try each to defeat the others. Relationships of employers and employees, bankers and labor unions, of social classes to one another, of rich and poor, of educated and noneducated, of privileged and underprivileged, of political parties, occupational groups, and finally, of nations, are at the present time in an incessant war, controlled mainly by the rude force and trickery which a given group has. He who has greater force triumphs, while the weaker party is pitilessly trampled on and crushed. Such is the root of the crisis of our sensate culture.

The real foundation, underlying the whole system of scientifism, is a crude materialism which view the human element as the more developed specimen among other anthropoids:

> Man himself and all his values were declared to be real only in so far as they were sensory; anything that was in man or in his culture which was imperceptible to the senses of the rank and file of human beings was declared a doubtful or fictitious pseudo-value. In this way man was reduced mainly to anatomy and physiology. Even as the possessor of nonmaterial mind and thought, of consciousness, and of conscience, he was often questioned and denied. In this manner the major premise clipped the wings of man with which he could soar to the vision of more sublime values and the less coarse aspects of reality.
>
> Once the culture entered this path, it had to move along it, toward a greater and greater sensorization of the world

of reality and of value. This path led inevitably to the growth of materialism, because nothing can be more sensory than matter; to a more radical mechanisticism, because nothing can be simpler than mechanical motion; to growing hedonism, utilitarianism and sensuality in the world of the values, because only sensory pleasure and pain, sensory utility and disutility are real from this standpoint. Hence there has been a growth of mechanistic materialism, flat empiricism, superficial positivism, and vulgar utilitarianism bound up with the growth of modern culture. Man himself and his evaluation of himself could not escape the same trend.

Being consistent with this theory, the praxis, that is, the "human use of human beings" cannot be any different but strictly dictated and controlled by the brutal forces of matter:

All this facilitates an explosive upsurge of man's elemental forces and leads men to treat their fellows, individually or in groups, as mere material atoms, electron-proton combinations, or biological organisms. If man is only an atom or electron or organism, why stand on ceremony in dealing with him? (We do not hesitate to scotch a snake or crush an atom!) The halo of sanctity having been stripped from man and his values, relationships and socio-cultural life degenerate into a savage struggle (witness the endless succession of contemporary wars and revolutions!) whose issue is decided by sheer physical force. In this struggle many values are destroyed—among them those of sensory science, or materialistic truth itself.

This is exactly the treatment man generally gets now especially in those groups where this equation between man and organism is taken most literally. Man as a man has no value whatsoever for most sensate groups at the present time. They do not recognize any charismatic value of man; therefore they treat him exactly as we treat other organisms. Only in so far as man is a Communist or a Nazi, or 'New Dealer' or 'Old Dealer,' or at least, in so far as he obeys and serves the rules of the dominant faction, can he exist, without being deprived of the elementary conditions of decent living. If his 'color' is different from the faction's 'color,' then cold-bloodedly, with scientific efficiency, he is crushed, liquidated, banished, and becomes a nonentity or a negative value. This equation manifests itself in such contemporary phenomena as war, revolutions, crimes, and other forms of brutality discussed earlier. Such a practice is but a logical consequence of the major premise of contemporary culture. These evils are its poisonous growths quite as much as science and technology are its marvelous fruits. Both spring from the same root of the limitation of true reality and value to the reality of the senses.

At this point one may wonder how man reacts to the treatment he gets from the specialists in scientific control and manipulation of his life? The answer is, of course, in line with the demand in the sense that he "lives up" (rather "down") to the "ideologies" presented to him as his identification tag. In other words, man being conceived and treated as an animal, he lives like one; his unrelented pleasure hunting and fun introduce him as the perfect hedonist who occasionally hides his greed behind an attitude of hypocrisy and rationalization. This is usually justified and made fashionable as "modern living."

At the bottom of this critical situation we may discover the original cause responsible for it as the crisis in human values. As we pointed out in the first chapter, human values have been devaluated, diluted, transvaluated, depreciated, and transformed in two ways; first, their original, authentic, and intrinsic meaning has been destroyed by pseudo-philosophies such as materialism, positivism, naturalism, and pragmatism; second, the unified system and hierarchy of values has been equally disintegrated by the theories of relativity and subjectivity of values, leading to the attitudes of false individualism. Correspondingly, human existence has lost its meaning, significance, and goal-directed transcendence, decaying into the abyss of materialism, scepticism, and collectivism. Man as an individual human being, as a person, has lost his relative subsistence and absoluteness. *The devaluation of values led to the devaluation of man himself.* For it is the values alone which can give meaning and significance to existence. Accordingly, our question about the integration of personal existence can be answered only through a new revalidation, accreditation, reconstruction or rehabilitation of human values in conformity with their authentic meaning and the ethical obligations derived from their normative-must nature. Therefore, in order to recover a unified idea about the meaning of personal existence and the possible levels of existential integration, there is the imperative of recovering a unified system of human values which support, justify, inform, and direct man's thinking, feeling, and acting.

The ideal hierarchy of values should be regarded as the *normative, directive, and regulatory foundation* for the difficult task of reducing the variety, multiplicity, and conflicting complexity of human endeavors to the unity, simplicity, and harmony of human perfection and happiness.

However, the problem of integrating the dimensions of personal existence into a meaningful whole—the fullness of life—moves in three stages. First, integration is essentially bound up with the system of values; second, the system or hierarchy of values must be checked against its psycho-ontological foundation in man's special mode of being and existing; third, man's being and existence is put in the perspective of his condition as a relative existent who is in need of redemption from his human condition. This implies the opening toward the Absolute in the process of self-transcendence. Consequently, the problem of life integration should encompass the following regions of reality: first, the metaphysical or noumenal region of transcendental reality—the Absolute—as the unconditional and unconditioned source and foundation of all being; second, the ontological order of finite beings which belong to man's profiles and horizons of existence; third, the intra-subjective order of man's psychic dispositions, tendencies, acts, and experiences which build up his fundamental structural frame, better known as the basic articulations of man's psychic nature, substance, and essence; fourth, the precipitations or objectised manifestations of man's creative symbolism to be found in the treasures of world civilization and culture; fifth, and last, the normative hierarchy of ideal values as the measure for the validity, authenticity, nobility, and dignity of whatever man does and makes.

Thus the dimensions of personal integration extend to:

Metaphysics or the problem of transcendence,
Ontology, especially the transcendental attributes of being,
Philosophy of value or value ontology,
Philosophic Anthropology and Psychology, and
Cultural Anthropology and Morality.

Our present concern regards the problems of philosophic anthropology and psychology — the philosophy of human nature — with a view toward the problem of existential life integration. The problem of transcendence and that of cultural anthropology and ethics will receive their due analysis in the fourth and fifth chapters, respectively. The questions of ontology and especially those belonging to value ontology were already treated in the previous chapter.

Taking up now the specific problem of integrated existence, it appears that each and every integrational stage or level imposes certain specific questions whose precise formulation and possible solution may do justice to the whole question complex. Keeping in line with the principles of value ontology, it is the ontological question which demands our attention. Since all values are rooted in the transcendentals of being, those belonging to human existence may receive their validation only by showing forth their foundation in man's ontological and psychic substance, nature, and essence. In other words, the question about the philosophy of human nature must be clarified first, unless we want to make ours the "scientific" account of man presented above.

This Socratic demand for "know thyself" can be fulfilled only by formulating the set of questions pertinent to the "self" and by answering them in the light of the knowledge to be derived from exposing man's full structural constitution. Assuming that the question about *"an sit homo"* (whether man is) can be dismissed on grounds of immediate evidence, the real comprehensive question refers to the *"quid sit homo,"* that is, *what* man is.

This question must be made more specific in order to suggest the possibility of finding the clues for a satisfactory answer.

Perhaps it would be much wiser to rephrase the above question on "what man is" by asking instead "who man is," thus emphasizing from the very start, man's personal, conscious, and psychic character. If we fail to do so, and retain the original form of the question about man's "what"-ness, we might as well end up with the answers or definitions we already presented above from the "scientific" point of view. We saw, however, that science reduces man to the level of an "object" — a highly complex biochemical, organic, and physical structure — thereby completely ignoring man as a "subject" and making our question on "the levels of *personal* integration" devoid of all meaning.

Since we believe that no "scientific" treatment of man can answer any question about the meaning of human existence, we feel justified to disregard this information and restrict our concern to man's psychic, self-conscious, and subjective, that is, personal identity. From this point of view, man should be looked upon as a subsistent value, wanted for himself and in his own right, displaying through his creative acts of symbolism the essential properties of self-consciousness, self-identity, interiority or inwardness of his existence, an existence experienced as given to him thus demanding the free acts of choice, decision, and responsibility (*homo arbiter*). Man as an individual person is called upon to face the task of knowing himself and giving a meaning to his life by creating and incorporating within his own being the values (perfections) which are given with the powers of his rational subsistence and autonomy as potentialities or fundamental dispositive tendencies. Herein lies, we believe, the first foundation and justification for the question about the levels of personal integration. To be sure, if there is no integrated view on man's nature — man the integer — there is no meaning to speak of personal integration as a process of becoming.

The devaluation of man and the disintegration of his unique individuality into the host of impersonal "stimuli," "reflex reactions," and "mechanisms of adjustment" is of relatively recent date. For, looking at the problem from an historical point of view, every philosopher of considerable intellectual stature considered man and the mode of his being as the meeting point (microcosmos) of all perfections found in the universe (macrocosmos). It is simply impossible to ignore or belittle the ideals of Greco-Roman humanism brought to its fullness by Christian philosophy and theology. Without falling into the exaggerations of anthropologism and psychologism, philosophic anthropology taken in its ancient, medieval, and modern interpretations, stands as the key for understanding the true meaning of Western civilization and culture. Given the limitations of our study, we must restrict ourselves to a few highlights or seminal ideas which truly represent the spirit of traditional cultural anthropology.

Aquinas, for instance, refers to the person as "the name of dignity . . . that which is most perfect in the whole nature."

Kant's standing on this problem is well known to all students of ethics; it was he who delineated the unconditional, absolute value of the human person by stating: "Man and every rational being exists as an end in itself, not as a mere means for arbitrary use by this or that will, but he must always be regarded as an end in itself (*Zweck an sich selbst*) in all of his acts directed either at himself or at other rational beings." (in Grundlegung der Metaphysik der Sitten, p. 63-64)

Although Hegel is justly charged with having contributed to the devaluation of man as a value in itself, nonetheless he professes a very noble idea when he refers to the person as "that which is founded upon freedom, the first, the deepest, intimate freedom. In the person I am exclusively for my own self; it is the singular instance of freedom in the mode of pure being for oneself." (Werke, vol. II, p. 159)

During the period of enlightenment, rationalism, and romanticism the praise of man reaches an all time high. Goethe, for instance, speaks for the whole movement of classical romanticism when he urges men to become themselves (*"Werde der du bist"*), for being a person represents for him the highest happiness man can long for (*das höchste Glück der Erdenkinder"*).

M. Scheler does not hesitate to identify man as "the value of all values" (*der Wert der Werte*), thus demanding man's rehabilitation from his condition of existential degradation through philosophic anthropology and phenomenology. Finally, present-day existentialism should be interpreted as the desperate attempt of modern thinkers to save man from his condition of forlorness, loneliness, anguish, dread, and anxiety in a world which threatens his own value and subsistence.

If we pause now for a moment and compare these ideas with the scientific jargon of modern psychologists, sociologists, so-called cultural anthropologists or ethnologists, it is easy to see their narrow and deplorable myopia as an indication of an overall intellectual and emotional impoverishment. Confront, for instance, the ideas of humanism with the Pavlovian interpretation of a conditioned, apelike organism and still call it man.

Since there could be some who would dismiss these claims and ideas as romantic exaggerations of an exalted imagination, we must explore briefly, the wealth of being and perfection proper to the personal mode of existing. Therefore, we shall treat man as:

1. An ontological subject
2. A psychological subject
3. A psycho-somatic subject
4. An axiological subject, and, finally, as
5. A subject challenged by the world of objects.

In order to describe the ontological constitution of the human person, we shall use Boethius' famous definition: "The person is an individual substance of rational nature." (*Persona est naturae rationalis individua substantia.*) By substance is meant the being which is in itself, subsisting by itself and in its own right, without demanding another being as the subject of inherence and dependence thereon. The perfection of subsistence, besides expressing the modes of being in itself and by itself, also suggests the idea of being *for* itself, qualities emphasized not only by the scholastics but also by Hegel (*Insichsein, Fürsichsein, Ansichsein*) and copied by certain existentialists such as Sartre (*être en soi, être pour soi*).

Moreover, subsistence also suggests the perfections of relative self-sufficiency, independence, autonomy, integrity, unity, and wholeness. All these ideas are rightfully associated with that of a "subject" interpreted as the Latin *"suppositum"* or the Greek *"hypostasis."* In fact, these terms convey the meaning of being subject to, put under, spread under (*substratum*) or that which stays or lies under. In our case, as applied to the person, subsistence and its various connotations, represent the ontological root or basis for the person's substantiality, manifested through the unity of its specific and individual nature. Since the ideas of substance, subsistence, and nature were deprived of their ontological meaning by the English empiricists and the German idealists, it became necessary to describe man with the various "scientific" theories, most of which fail to account for the unity, autonomy, freedom, and ethical responsibility of the individual person. Consequently, man appears as the complex structure of psycho-somatic (bio-chemical and physical) elements in a constant need of being "adjusted, re-adjusted" like a machine which is always in danger of falling to pieces unless the screws and bolts are periodically checked and tightened (*l'homme machine-man, the machine*).

At this point we may question the *contents* carried and supported by the ontological *substratum* we identified above as the substance or the underlying *suppositum* (*hypostasis*) of man's personal mode of being. Boethius refers in his definition to a "rational nature" proper to the individual substance of man. The problem of individuality — also included in the same definition — will be discussed in the context of "individual types of personal integration," to be presented below; therefore, we focus our analysis on the meaning of "nature" and "rationality" as belonging to the specifically human and personal perfection of being.

The "nature" of a being — man's included — expresses the dynamic character of the substance insofar as it is viewed as the source and cause of all activities and sufferings. According to Aristotle's interpretation, nature is the source of both motion and rest from within, thus revealing the intrinsic cause of the active and passive behavior of the subsisting being, without losing its own center of gravity and equilibrium (*Principium et causa motus et quietis in eo in quo est primo et per se et non secundum accidens.*) (Physics, 11, 1, 192b, 20.) Only by discovering this principle which directs from within the "behavior" of a being, can we sensibly speak of the "constants" of behavior manifested in the regularity, uniformity, and consistency of overt reactions. On the other hand, disregarding such an ontological common source of activity, there remains only the artificial mental construct of an "unconditioned" or "conditioned" reflex mechanism, viewed from a purely empirical and experiential point of view. One may find the best instance of this "denaturalizing" of man in J. Watson's "behavioristic" concept of man, equated with the sum total of his overt reactions. In such a situation any question about meaning becomes meaningless. Then man is faced with the decision as to whether his life is meaningless or Watson's theories are devoid of meaning and foundation.

Man's subsisting nature, however, is identified as "rational," inviting us to describe with more precision and detail the implications of this added qualification. Taken in its original meaning, man's "rational" nature refers to his power of reasoning (*ratio*-reason) through which man transcends the limitations of sense knowledge, which he has in common with other sentient beings. While sense knowledge explores only the material or physical properties of the objects in the process of stimulation, sensation, perception, and imagery, the object of man's reason is unlimited both in its scope — the intelligible aspects of being as such — and its depth, for man's reason is aimed at the intentional appropriation of the hidden essences to be worked out in the process of abstraction and ideogenesis. This power of abstract ideation and discoursive reasoning identifies man as a "rational" being, *homo sapiens,* from a gnoseological point of view.

Besides this conceptual assimilation of the intelligible structure of beings, man also possesses intellect (*nous,* in Greek), which gives him the power of directly apprehending meaningful relationships in the act of critical reflection and meditation (insight) on the conceptual material presented to him by his discoursive and fragmentary reason. This power of insight is also often called "intuition," taking us back to the etymological meaning of the act of intellection, understood as *"intus legere,"* that is, to read directly the elements of truth, unity, goodness, and beauty belonging to the perfections of being in general. Besides H. Bergson, it was the modern philosophers of value and existence who emphasized the importance of this superior power of direct prehension of the qualitative, structural, and axiological aspects of being.

Both reason and intellect are the dispositions which make man not only rational but also *"cogitans,"* that is, a thinking hypostasis, or substance.

Man's thinking may be either other-directed or extroverted — concerned with the intelligibility of the reality outside himself — or inner-directed, that is, concentrated upon his own inner reality, the world of his cognitive, emotive, and volitive concerns. The latter has been called — since W. Wundt — introspection, that is, whenever man takes a look inside, within himself (from the Latin, *intus spicere*). Whether man thinks as an extrovert or introvert, it always implies the experience of being conscious, the third dimension of his intellectual power. Its implicit or explicit object is the "self" or the thinking subject himself. Thus consciousness is concomitant knowledge (*con-scientia*), which accompanies both the introverted and the extroverted directions of thinking. In common sense terms, man is aware of the world in which he lives and also of himself in the same act of understanding through his reason and intellect.

Since our interest is predominantly psycho-ontological rather than purely epistemological, we shall consider the inner-directed or introvert form of personal consciousness. We hope that it will open the door to the most intimate corners of the personal mode of existence.

The "object" of the inner-directed thought is the "self" (*das Ich, das Selbst*), which expresses man's direct, intuitive awareness of his identity as a self-conscious being. To be sure, it would be an error to confuse the "self" with any or all of the powers, acts, and activities which it contains. As a matter of fact the self is the *"inner eye"* and the common source of all experiences, modifications, and changes. Thus the self transcends all its modifications and states while underlying and unifying them. The self discloses only the cognitive, affective, and volitional (axiological) powers of its nature. Any attempt, however, to go beyond this information is cut short by the impenetrability and mysterious identity of the hidden self. The most anyone can say about himself can be stated in the tautology of *"I am myself,"* but no one can unmask the inner essence of this stranger who is always present. In other words, the self is simultaneously known and unknown to himself. It is known as far as its powers and their activities are concerned; it is unknown with regard to its ultimate nature and identity.

Because of this strange condition, the mode of being as a person can be described only in terms of self-consciousness, self-awareness, inwardness or interiority of being, immanence, self-identity, being within oneself or by oneself, intimately aware of one's own presence to oneself, without ever being able to go beyond this concomitant knowledge called the datum of self-consciousness. Modern depth psychology (*Tiefenpsychologie*) of the type created by Freud and his associates goes beyond the level of consciousness into the subconscious and unconscious regions of psychic life. It is well known, however, that the relationships between the levels of consciousness are explained in a deterministic and mechanical manner from which the self (the Ego) emerges as the victim of either animal instincts (the Id) or of the "mechanisms" of repressions and inhibitions, developed by the pressures of the Super-Ego. The Jungian version on the depths of personal and collective unconscious only adds to the confusion with the introduction of certain oriental, mystical elements, whose conceptual identity escapes any attempt at a clear definition. Consequently, the identity of the "self" still is and remains both known and unknown.

From an ontological point of view, the self is identified by Aristotle and his followers as the substantial form or principle of life (*entelecheia*) understood as the fundamental actuality and perfection which constitutes man as a rational being. In scholastic terms, the self is the soul which informs the body and is the inner, essential source and reason for man's specific nature as a "rational hypostasis," a "rational suppositum, substratum or substance." It is also thought of as the life principle which directs from within all the purposeful activities on the vegetative, sensitive, and rational levels. Thanks to this inner centrum of life, man possesses a unity, oneness, identity, constancy or permanency, enduring in its specific nature throughout and in spite of all his varied interests and activities. In a word, it is the "known and unknown" self which makes man basically self-centered, and a coordinated, organized, well-structured, self-conscious being. Everyone feels, of course, that this is a very inadequate description, hence man still continues to be "this unknown" being to himself and more so to others.

There is another important element in the experience of self-awareness which demands our consideration, namely the experience of inner freedom as immediately subsequent upon the experience of being oneself. In fact, there is no way of speaking of the personal mode of existence unless the perfection of freedom is included in the picture as its essential part. Without going into the traditional discussions and distinctions aimed at the demonstration of free will, we feel that the intimate personal experience of freedom will do more than the logical necessity of the arguments "forcing" its acceptance.

Freedom is experienced by the person as self-possession — I belong to myself — as a personal power to determine the direction, contents, meaning, and significance of one's existence. The mature individual experiences himself as given to himself without any definite, pre-established program to be followed up, save the one the self imposes upon itself through the acts of selection, choice, deliberation, and action. It is this character of "undeterminatedness" which is the root of personal autonomy and the foundation of ethics, understood as a self-imposed way of life. Personal freedom can be described, therefore, as self-determination. There can be no sensible discussion on freedom unless one is aware of the conditions which allow of its possibility. These conditions are given with the experience of self-hood, self-consciousness, manifested through the activity of thinking.

Should someone come across similar experiences, he will immediately understand that the mode of personal existence is a challenge, a task or a problem, if you will, for which only the person can give a solution. In more simple terms, man realizes that life, besides being a gift, is essentially a burden insofar as he must decide what to do with himself by his acts of valuing. Man must interpret his being for himself; he also must lend some meaning to his being and existence; finally, he must set out and work at the actualization of this meaning by appropriating the values which he thinks to be both necessary and worthwhile for the fulfillment of his existential commitment. Whenever such decisions are made, man realizes that the meaning of his life is the giving of a meaning to it. Man must constantly work at realizing or actualizing himself and walk on the road of his self-imposed destiny at his own risk.

These are the main reasons why we must call every authentic form of personal life an existential series of acts and decisions; the same reasons also account for the dignity of the free human person as a value in himself and for himself, demanding respect for his personal autonomy and implicit responsibility. On the other hand, the persons who lead the life of sheer conformity and "good adjustment" have not reached as yet any ultimate meaning for their own "being around." One positive contribution of existentialism consists, therefore, in having challenged modern man to identify himself and commit himself in a responsible form, thus overcoming or surpassing "happy vegetation" as a form of life which identifies the mass-minded. Finally, the goal of a meaningful existence can be achieved only through the aesthetic work of integrating the various and often conflicting polarities of existence.

The various perfections of the personal mode of being, such as its subsistence, self-sufficiency, immanence or interiority, and self-consciousness, along with the powers of reasoning, intuition, and self-determination (freedom or autonomy), ought not to be taken in an absolute sense, unless we want to extend the dimensions of personal existence into the infinite and thus commit the Kantian error of anthropolatry. In fact, to consider man as an absolute value and end in itself means to deify him (*eritis sicut Dii*) in a quite unrealistic, idealistic, romantic, and fanatic form. The different forms of exaggerated anthropocentrism, anthropologism, and psychologism are the identification marks of enlightenment (*Aufklärung*) leading to rational positivism, romanticism, and, finally, aesthetic materialism. All these worshippers of man are responsible for the false ideas of an abortive humanism. The crisis of the modern age is due, to a large extent, to this overindulgent inflation of the value attributed to human reason, power, and autonomy. When Nietzsche preaches God's death, he actually acts as man's funeral director.

A realistic view of man will assess him only as a relative, dependent, contingent being, limited in his knowledge, imagination, feeling, and in the reach of his creative power as a free agent. It was again phenomenology and existentialism which once again pulled man down to the earth to which he belongs and on which he depends in various forms and degrees. Man's existential "condition" or "situation" is unthinkable and indescribable without his fundamental dependence on the physical, psycho-social, and historico-cultural environments. Consequently, all the ideal attributes enumerated above as identifying man as a person, should be taken with a cautious reservation and prudent restriction.

As a matter of fact, the self and all its powers would be empty and meaningless ideas if they were considered without referring them to their necessary counterpart, that is, the world of objects, events, and phenomena experienced by man. Thus we are forced to put down rather emphatically that existence is given as the dialectical showdown between its two poles of reference, that is, the inwardness of the self on one hand, and the world out there, on the other. Life itself, conceived as immanent activity, necessarily presupposes the materials upon which it depends as the objects and the goals of the activity itself. These considerations led us in the introduction to view man's existence as essentially relational, situational, or circumstantial. Any attempt at eliminating any of the two basic elements of this necessary subject-object relationship must lead to a dead end. In Jungian terms, we would say that both introversion (pure subjectivity) and extroversion (complete decentralization and depersonalization of the self) are abnormal symptoms of existential crisis, besides or because being ontologically untrue insofar as they falsify the precise dimensions of personal life.

Traditional philosophy of critical realism expressed the same ideas, however in simpler and more adequate terms; it identified man as the finite composite of two co-principles of being, matter and form, that is, potency and act. It is the idea of potentiality which helps us to describe the limitations and the levels of personal life as well as their integration as an uninterrupted dynamic process of becoming, change, development, progress, enrichment, and fulfillment. This basic idea was already introduced in the passage on man's value-directed concern; at this point, therefore, we shall establish only its significance from the standpoint of life integration and its various possibilities. Since our interest throughout this study lies in man's axiological concern, we shall not illustrate the process of need satisfaction and the theories on motivational cycle on the bio-physical level of vital concerns. All adjustment-minded psychologists covered this route of happy adjustment. Consequently, we shall rather concentrate on that which they have neglected, namely, the answer to the meaning of good adjustment as such.

While recognizing the vital importance and value of need satisfaction along with the studies on the learning process, the development of habit reactions or "mechanisms," etc., we still would like to have an answer for the questions about the end-value of the whole process itself. We feel that the most vital question about the validity of modern adjustment theories has never been formulated. While constantly hammering on the need for need satisfaction and adjustment, these theories usually fail to give the direction, the contents, and the final goal, value, and outcome of their insistent demands. Because they do not include any adequate consideration of the human person, his nature, and the fundamental tendencies of his cultural and ethico-religious values, they cannot answer the question on the very meaning and value of adjustment. Furthermore, since there is no unified system of compelling values and ideals, above and beyond the levels of bio-social vegetation, the horizons of personal existence shrink to the satisfaction of the immediate "functional" needs and wants, though the meaning of the function itself is never asked or challenged. No wonder, then, that most schools of adjustment teach the mechanical approach to life as conformity — adjustment to the given patterns followed by the millions — to a pragmatic hedonism, hypocritically disguised as the "full way of life. . . ."

The root of the problem lies, of course, in the universal uncertainty about human values whose qualitative differences and compelling weight have been washed out in the name of universal subjectivism, relativism, and democratic egalitarianism. The only criterion of good adjustment which still survives is that of functional pragmatism, designed for a man conceived in terms of biochemistry and physiology. However, this universal concern with good adjustment is just another symptom of the uneasiness these "mechanics of behavior" feel in the face of the mounting number of malfunctioning human machines. (Perhaps they need a new "scientifically tested" tune-up kit. . . .)

In the remainder of this chapter, therefore, we shall present the axiological frame or structure of the human person after the psychology of Ed. Spranger. We call it "axiological" because we want to expose the fundamental value tendencies of the self along with the acts, attitudes, preferences, and achievements subsequent to them. We feel that the treatment of man's bio-physical, organic "needs, urges, wants, drives, strivings, and instincts" should belong to the field of human physiology and the "science" of human manipulation on the level of a "well-rounded" existence, bouncing itself in a "well-rounded" society down the road to a "well-rounded" nothing.

It has been man's incessant desire to identify himself through self-knowledge. Even before the rise of philosophy as a systematic and methodical inquiry into the mysteries of being, all the mythical, religious, moralistic, and aesthetic works, belonging to these prelogical or pre-rational modes of thinking, contain abundant "wisdom" or "advice" on the meaning of being a man. It appears, therefore, that man has always acted as a psychologist no matter how naive, primitive, or atheoretical his interpretations may appear to us when weighed by the insight we have reached so far. The countless symbolic forms of objectised meanings man attributed to his origin, nature, and destiny can be seen in the values of human culture and civilization.

The common sense wisdom which speaks to us through the values incorporated in cultural achievements offers a few fundamental ideas which could be considered as the first principles of philosophic anthropology and psychology. For example, there has been an almost universal consent as to the reality of the soul, its powers, its metaphysical origin, nature, and destiny. Man considered himself as standing at the crossroads of the material and immaterial worlds, participating in both through his psycho-spiritual and organic nature, respectively. This conception of man as a *"homo sapiens"* used to be his "classical" identification up to the advent of sensism, empiricism, positivism, and materialism which stripped man of his dignity, superiority, and value on grounds of the new "scientific" evidence.

The "science" of psychology, created by a servile imitation of the methods, principles, and shortsighted prejudices of "natural, positive or exact" sciences, refused to accept the traditional view of man as essentially superior to all the other living and non-living beings. The justification for this refusal was given by the impossibility of "showing forth" the existence of the soul by the quantitative methods of direct observation, measurement, and experimental devices. As a consequence, the unity, wholeness, and integrity of human nature were dissolved by the analytic method of separating the "psychic elements" of man's bio-chemical, physiological, and psychic functions. What remained of man was a collection of unrelated functions, brought under the loose architecture of an organism, somewhat more complex and intelligent than that of his next neighbors.

The questions about the meaning, value, and destiny of human existence were "a priori" rejected as devoid of any scientific significance and relegated to religion, philosophy, and the fine arts. In such a manner, science debased man to the animal level of existence thus failing to fulfill its first duty to make him intelligible and meaningful. This materialistic, mechanical, and deterministic "explanation" called for the legitimate reaction coming from the schools of modern philosophy, cultural anthropology, and psychology whose exponents refused to look upon themselves as a mechanical complex of organic functions only. As we pointed out above, they felt the need to reconsider the premises of human psychology in order to create the conditions which make the understanding of human existence, as a meaningful whole, both possible and necessary.

The first condition for the possible intelligibility of all that man is and stands for, is the assumption of the existence in man of a superior life principle — the rational soul — which is responsible for man's inner organization. Ed. Spranger, among others, makes it clear that psychology as a meaningful interpretation of man's nature, unity, and subsistence must start with the fundamental idea of an "organized totality" in which the parts or elementary functions derive their meaning from the global meaning of the whole. The idea of a *"Gestalt"* (structure, constellation, organization, organized complexity, orderly articulation, meaningful disposition of the parts) is the fundamental principle of the psychology created by *Chr. von Ehrenfelds, Köhler, Koffka, Wertheimer* and others. Although the Gestaltists concerned themselves with the structural patterns of stimulation, sensation, perception, attention, imagery, and association on the level of animal and human sense experiences, no one will deny their contribution for rescuing the meaning of psychic life as a totality from its previous "atomization" into psychic elements.

The application of the *"Gestalt"* principles to the phenomena of man's cultural and value-directed activities is the merit of phenomenology and philosophic anthropology. The predominant idea is the wholeness of the human person whose most important activity consists in creating the meaningful world of culture and civilization. Thus psychology becomes again "humanized" insofar as it considers the understanding of man its primary mission (*verstehende Psychologie*). In order to understand man and any of his activities, it is imperative to start with the idea of a psycho-spiritual wholeness, totality, unity, and to analyze its rapport with the parts (elementary functions) which belong to its structural make-up. The whole of psychic life should not be regarded, however, as the sum total of its possible elements. From the formal point of view of understanding and meaning, it is only the whole which possesses these qualifications of intelligibility. Any of the parts, taken apart or in isolation from the structural whole, lose all meaning, which cannot be recaptured even by trying to add up or put the elementary parts together again in order to reconstruct the original, meaningful totality lost in the process of atomizing analysis. In this sense, the whole of psychic life is much more than its parts, taken either separately or in their numerical totality. Moreover, the parts derive their meaning from the whole and not the other way around. It is correct to say, therefore, that the whole is independent of the composing parts, and, in a certain sense, it exists "before" and "above" them. (For example, a melody is more, different, before, and above any of the particular notes belonging to a musical composition.) In one word, the whole is all, the elements have meaning only insofar as they belong to the whole which alone lends them meaning and validity.

It goes without saying that the organized totality should be identified as the soul or the underlying, substantial, and inner principle which organizes, informs, and directs from within all the elementary functions, acts, and experiences according to the overall meaning which identifies its nature and essence. Consequently, the soul is distinct from all of its psychic functions; at the same time, it is "before" and "above" the so-called "parts" which belong to its inner articulation. Finally, any visible projection of psychic activity derives its meaning from the original value and meaning proper to the soul as such. It also follows that "understanding" man will be possible only if one possesses first an adequate knowledge or insight into the specific nature and structure of the soul. Should these fundamental principles be dismissed, a "psychology without a soul" will be the necessary outcome.

We went to some considerable extent above in order to identify the nature of the "self" as a subsistent, rational, and free consciousness, experienced as self-identity and personal autonomy. At this point, therefore, we suggest the equation of the self with the soul, keeping in mind its ontological, psychological, and axiological character. From the point of view of axiology it is evident that our explicit concern is restricted to those specific personal acts which are directed at the values, inspired by man's desire to create the conditions of a cultured life. Besides, each creative act of the person should be regarded as a complex activity, structurally articulated and made up of elementary psychic functions — sensitive, affective, and intellectual — subordinated to the goal of bringing to light a piece of work which carries the trans-subjective values embodied in human civilization and culture.

Ed. Spranger believes that there are six fundamental value tendencies — the religious, theoretical, aesthetic, social, political, and economic — innate in the human person, making up the basic structure or articulation of the self (*der subjektive Geist*). Each value tendency has its corresponding act which brings forth the specific value as a contribution to the whole of culture (*der objektive Geist*). Finally, there is a formal normativity or legality, intrinsic to both the subjective and objective aspects (*der normative Geist*) which directs the acts of value creation in conformity with the ideal values for which man should strive. Cultural anthropology and psychology study this hierarchic structure of man's axiological dispositions in its subjective, objective, and trans-subjective or supra-individual aspects. It is assumed, therefore, that the understanding of man should proceed from studying, first of all, the original meaning and the qualitatively distinct nature of man's axiological concerns in their static as well as their dynamic forms. This may happen by methodically isolating the genuine meaning and significance (importance) of each value disposition taken not only in itself, but also comparatively, that is, with regard to the other dispositions of the collection, thus identifying the qualitative differences in meaning as well as in the degrees of compatibility, affinity, or else polarity and conflicts.

The descriptive presentation of man's axiological *"Gestalt"* is the material and formal object of this new psychology also called *"geisteswissenschaftliche Psychologie und Ethik der Persönlichkeit"* — a psychology and ethics of personality from the point of cultural anthropology — in contradistinction from all sorts of "scientific," that is, bio-chemical, physiological, and causal interpretations of man, who is regarded as an organism only. It should be noted, however, that philosophic and cultural anthropology do not want to question the validity of the scientific approach as such; kept within the limitations of an experimental science, its ideas, principles, methods, and results should be accepted as valuable information on the material basis, conditions, and instrumentalities of psychic life in general. On the other hand, should the "science" of psychology be presented as the only valid and worthwhile body of knowledge concerning the behavior of man, every sensible thinker would protest against such an arrogant claim. We noted above that the "scientific" treatment of man can disclose nothing on the meaning of man's cultural and ethical endeavors. Therefore, it must be emphasized again and again that man can be understood only as the creative subject of values which alone can lend any meaning to his personal mode of existence. In a word, the philosophy of human nature should precede and inform the scientific account of man.

Consequently, instead of moving within the narrow field of "motivational cycles" and their mechanical rounds, aimed at need satisfaction, human existence should be interpreted as the dialectical process between the subject and the challenge of an objective reality, demanding his thought and action. Only this axiological and dialectical view of man provides the necessary foundation for establishing the conditions of personal life integration. Let us now turn our attention to the concept of integration itself, viewed in relation to the axiological structure of the human person.

The idea of integration imposes the task of analyzing a highly complex set of questions, all of them being immediately tied up with the highest problem concerning the ultimate meaning of personal existence. In fact, personal integration can be considered both as a process and an ideal, and it can be described in a satisfactory form only if its most important elements are brought into discussion. Thus one may speak of the aspects, forms, levels, effects, conditions, means, limitations, and unresolved conflicts of integration. In view of this confusing diversity and range of the problem, the best thing we can do is to start with the analysis of the concept of integration itself. By exposing the comprehension and the extension of this term, we hope to gain some guiding posts for the methodical presentation of the material.

Integration is the abstract term coined to signify some kind of an active attitude toward a variety of elements to be brought into some sort of equilibrium, order, unity, and structural arrangement or synthesis, by discovering the criteria or the common denominators needed for this purpose. Since we speak of "personal life integration" it is evident that the materials shall be drawn from the contents (dispositions, powers, functions, and activities) of psychic life. At first glance, however, there appear to be more reasons for conflicts than affinities. There is, for instance, the well-known mind-body duality, each part bringing forth tendencies which are or may be counteracted mutually. The traditional tripartite division of man's forms of life into vegetative, sensitive, and rational offers further instance of more differences than similarities. Furthermore, it is commonly accepted, since *Pascal,* that *"le coeur a ses raisons que la raison ne connaît pass,"* exposing the clash between the rational and the irrational tendencies of the same human being. Besides, for every emotion there is its direct opposite; for every desire and interest there is the possibility of its frustration. Even modern psychology exposes the conflict between conscious and unconscious tendencies (the Id versus the Super-Ego). On the rational level itself, there is no necessary harmony between thought and action, suggesting the possible discrepancy between reason and will. From another angle still, reason and faith have been divorced only too frequently, just as on the collective level of existence individual interests are opposed by social control systems. Finally, there is for every positive value a negative counterpart, and the polarities or antinomies among the positive values themselves are too well known to allow oblivion. This almost pervasive presence of opposites in human existence forced many philosophers, psychologists, and even theologians to introduce man as the carrier of an unbalanced nature held responsible for his schizoid, anguished, and fallen condition.

This notwithstanding, in man there is still the desire for creating order within himself, just as the philosopher and the scientist work at the same goal of reducing complexity to simplicity, multiplicity to unity, variety to uniformity, as the conditions for the possibility of an intelligible interpretation and understanding of the world and its phenomena. Similarly, the psychologist with some philosophic outlook on existence would like to "integrate" the apparent conflicting opposites given in human nature by designing a formula for their possible reconciliation and relative equilibrium. Without such a desideratum there would be no meaning or purpose in trying to make human nature and behavior understandable, predictable, and—to some extent—even controllable. It should be noted, too, that the integration of personal existence will be attempted here only from an axiological point of view, thus leaving all other aspects open for debate and possible solution. Consequently, we should rather speak of integrating man's basic value tendencies into an ideal hierarchic disposition without losing sight of the individually differentiated types of human life.

From the concept of integration we now move to integration conceived as an ideal, a necessity, and a process. Integration is an ideal, for it stands for the perfections of unity, equilibrium, harmony, totality, and order. The necessity of integration appears clearly from the many conflicts which are immanent in man's psychosomatic, axiological, and socio-cultural concerns. As a process, integration means the personal activity and effort aimed at the appropriation of the perfections belonging to the ideals of integral existence. Viewing the problem in this perspective, we must, first, delineate the "ideal type" of integrated personal life in order to create a frame of reference and to provide the criteria needed for the construction and understanding of the differentiated or individually distinct forms of life synthesis.

In the previous chapter we presented an ideal hierarchy of values, based on the criteria of their qualitative differences, relative prominence, and the degree of their validity. We suggest, therefore, to regard that ideal scale of values as the prototype to be put up as the standard for the evaluation of the lesser forms of personal life organization. In addition to the above criteria, used for the creation of the ideal value structure, we should present a few more which must also be included in the adequate evaluation of the height, scope, and validity of the possible forms of personal life. Accordingly, a value rates higher on the scale, if it reveals and contributes more to the specific perfections which belong to the ontological identity and ultimate destiny of the human person. Since man is a rational and free person, it follows that the values which come closer to the ideal perfections of his nature and the meaning he derives from them while incorporating them into himself, must be considered as necessarily higher. Considering, however, the need for a metaphysical, that is, an ultimate foundation for both man's existence and his values, it should also appear that the Absolute, conceived as the source and reason for all real or possible values, founded in the infinite perfection of the only self-subsistent being in the form of an absolute autonomy (*ipsum esse subsistens*), should be placed at the top of the hierarchy. The other values of the scale are arranged then according to their quality, content, significance, and meaning for man. The degree of affinity or conflicting polarity among values themselves also determines the order of their structural dispositions on the scale.

The ideal human type, therefore, would be the person who possesses within himself the following hierarchy of values, integrated according to the criteria suggested above:

*The Absolute* as the value which discloses the ultimate meaning of man's metaphysical, transcendental, supra-natural, and religious aspirations.

*Truth,* understood as wisdom or insight, that is, integrated knowledge (philosophy) going beyond the level of mere information or useful knowledge.

*The Beautiful* as the symbolic manifestation of such qualities as harmony, order, unity, proportion, equilibrium, etc., created and captured by man's intuitive imagination and feelings.

*Love* introduces the real reason and the only justification for man's higher social concerns, beyond the immediate, useful benefits he may derive from the state of organized togetherness.

*Power* is the consequence of the person's free autonomy which can be either other-directed (political concern) or inner-directed for the achievement of personal self-control and self-discipline.

There is no doubt that such an "ideal" human person has never existed and he never will. For, in order to measure up to this ideal, such a person would be a saint, a philosopher, a scientist, an artist, a humanist, a leader, and an efficient economist! Consequently, this ideal integration of personal life should be regarded only as a frame of reference, a guiding system or a standard to be used for the evaluation of the less perfect, and, therefore, more real types of differentiated individuality which imply certain ontological, psychological, and physical limitations. Perhaps the "religious man," according to Ed. Spranger, comes closest to the ideal of integral humanism.

The individual types of differentiated value structures, integrated in the human person are five, that is, the theoretical, aesthetic, social, political, and economic structures. These types emerge whenever one of the basic value tendencies assumes the predominant position and thus directs the hierarchic disposition (integration) of the other values. It should be noted, however, that there are no "pure" types. Therefore, even the schematic outline to be presented next, should be looked at as the possible inner value structure which identifies the form of an individual type or integration without ever succeeding in bringing the value polarities to a final equilibrium and solution. Since the religious type was already presented above, only the remaining five integrations will follow:

| *The theoretic man* | *The aesthetic man* | *The social man* |
|---|---|---|
| Insight-Truth | The Beautiful | Love-Harmony |
| The Absolute | The Absolute | The Absolute |
| The Beautiful | Insight-Truth | Insight-Truth |
| Harmony-Love | Harmony-Love | The Beautiful |
| Will to Power | Will to Power | The Useful |
| The Useful | The Useful | Will to Power |

| *The political man* | *The economic man* |
|---|---|
| Will to Power | The Useful |
| Harmony-Conflict | Will to Power |
| The Useful | Harmony-Conflict |
| The Beautiful | Insight-Truth |
| Insight-Truth | The Beautiful |
| The Absolute | The Absolute |

It is beyond the limitations of our presentation to go into a detailed discussion on each individual type of personal life integration. We are forced, therefore, to limit ourselves to a few closing remarks on the effects and outcomes of life integration as well as the consequences to reckon with if the person fails to reach any acceptable level, form, or degree of personal balance and inner organization of his life.

Since no person can be everything, integration must occur in the form of choice, conditioned by the individual's innate tendencies and the opportunities for learning and development presented to him by his environment. The choice of one type will be regarded then as a personal commitment to one specific form of existence which the individual person may experience as his self-imposed vocation and destiny. This decision occurs during the stages of personal development, education, and self-education. Its specific aspects and implicit problems would take us into the special fields of psychology and pedagogy. The most philosophic anthropology can do in this respect is to offer the ideal norms and principles based on value ontology which must be respected in the process of self-appropriation and self-integration.

The end result of this personal effort is the possession of a definite inner form of life, usually identified as character and personality. Goethe describes it as "an impressed form which lives and develops" (*"geprägte Form, die lebend sich entwickelt"*). In a more realistic sense, only the person who saturated the potentialities of his self with the values belonging to the perfections of human existence in a highly individual form, can be called "personality." This level of integrated existence identifies itself in the perfections of self-knowledge, self-identity, self-possession, self-appropriation, and inner self-direction toward the "known unknown" harbor to be reached with the winds and wings of time. While on the journey, the person should strive for the perfections of individuality, universality, and totality as the highest identification of man the integer.

The failure to do so leads to what K. Jaspers calls "shipwreck." This condition, however, takes us to the fields of existential psychiatry which lies outside the scope of our present concern. In final analysis, however, even the disintegrated human types disclose a meaning (a negative value) insofar as their condition is an indirect plea for the imperative of integrating the finite existent with the One Who can redeem them. This eschatological aspect, however, shall be presented in chapter seven in which the problem of integration will appear again as the conjugation of the limited human person with the infinite perfection of the Supreme Self. In this sense, the ultimate moment of life integration brings up the problem of redemption.

## CHAPTER V

# LOVE AND JUSTICE
# THE SOCIO-POLITICAL VALUES

Ever since Aristotle introduced man as a political animal (*anthropos zoon politikon*), that is, a social or sociable animal (*homo gregarius*) who can survive and prosper only in the "polis," the organized city life, all noteworthy philosophers and more recent "behavioral scientists" have tried to identify the origins, foundations, causes, nature, forms, and purpose of human togetherness. That no agreement has been reached should surprise no one; for whenever some major issue of life is at stake, there will, of necessity, be as many divergent opinions as there are proponents (*quot capita, tot sententiae*). The bone of contention is not the questioning of the universal phenomenon of social life — except, perhaps, for some extreme individualists who have grown forgetful of their own parents; while no one can deny the factual or objective reality of group life, disagreement is bound to appear when man tries to interpret the meaning and the value of established facts.

The specific issues implicit in the broad formulation of the "social problem" are both theoretical (speculative) and practical (pragmatic). From a theoretical point of view the socially motivated philosophers and scientists have tried to find either within man or outside him the reason for his fundamental social dispositions. Those of a naturalistic or positivistic frame of mind (*A. Comte, E. Durkheim*) and their disciples on the Continent and in the New World point only to man's bio-physical condition in nature which — according to them — accounts for the early emergence of human associations, dictated by the crude necessity of survival. Consequently, all progress achieved in the forms of civilization and culture — including its theoretic, moral, and religious aspects — should be regarded as symbolic epiphenomena of the original bio-physical necessities of animal life. The many forms of radical collectivism took this bio-physical determinism to its political extremes and reduced man, the individual, to the condition of a cell in the social organism as his natural *"locus ontologicus et axiologicus."* Thus even the practical aspect of the social problem seemed to have obtained its solution.

Those thinkers who looked rather within man than outside him, developed the psychological interpretation of group life (*G. Tarde, R. Duprat, MacDougall,* and others). We may consider them the forerunners for the modern ramifications of sociology — founded and named by A. Comte — into social psychology, cultural anthropology, ethnology, social ecology, etc. They believed in the existence of several instincts in man — some collections reach even twelve or more instincts — among which "imitation" and "gregariousness" were held up as responsible for man's organized social life. This explanation amounts to a circular reasoning by saying that man is social *because* sociable. The intrinsic nature of the "instinct," however, seemed to recess indefinitely when submitted to a close, critical analysis. Nevertheless, there remains the fact that man still lives in society though he has not yet found the formula for peaceful coexistence. (Perhaps the "instinct of pugnacity" should be held responsible for the long series of armed conflicts?) This absence of peaceful coexistence may be due to the inadequate interpretation of man's social life in the light of both the bio-physical and the psychological determinism. They seem to deal only with man as an individual (part) without going deeper into the meaning of the personal mode of existence in which they might find the philosophic justification for man's collective needs and the forms of his affiliations.

If the bio-physical and mere psycho-instinctual analysis of the social phenomena cannot disclose its adequate meaning, we should approach the problem from a higher standpoint which identifies man as both an individual and a free self-subsisting person. This personalist approach is a must also for the correct interpretation of man's philosophic, scientific, aesthetic, moral, and religious endeavors whose meaning cannot be derived from or reduced to any set of instinctual equipment. No matter how important the "bios" may be, it will never shed any light on the meaning of "logos." While granting that the bio-physical, instinctual, and environmental factors and causes represent an important part in the social picture of man's life, considered as an individual coming from, depending on, and therefore belonging to an animal species, still we must insist that their significance or value is restricted to being only the conditions and instrumentalities (means or contributory values), needed for the manifestation of *human* sociability as basically different because it is superior to animal herd instinct. In this sense even the material aspects of social life will be invested with a symbolic significance. However, all this may happen only if we identify human sociability as *inter-subjectivity* as opposed to mere physical togetherness and collective combat readiness. The unilateral exaggerations of collectivism and individualism are due to a distorted interpretation of man's bio-physical and psycho-spiritual nature. It appears, therefore, that the synthesis of these two antithetical positions can be derived from the position of *personalism* only.

To start with a general statement, we could say that the origin and the reason for man's social or other-directed behavior and interests lie in the simple fact that *man needs his fellow man.* However, we want to make clear from the very outset that one should not restrict man's needs and their satisfactions to the mere bio-physical and spatio-temporal aspects of his animal nature. Should this erroneous interpretation prevail, we would end up again with the mere utilitarian, pragmatic, and materialistic view such as presented by Hobbes, due to the rather narrow conception he had of the human being (*homo homini lupus*—man being man's wolf). It is our conviction that the direct or indirect use or exploitation of the human beings by his fellows cannot suffice as a foundation of social life even if someone postulates the existence of a mutual agreement of non-aggression (social contract), oral or written. On the contrary, the selfish, egocentric greed of the inferior human type is responsible for the socio-economic and political unrest of all times. Mutual exploitation must lead to social chaos, conflict, anarchy, and the rise of the brutal nullification of misused human freedom by all forms of dictatorships. Thus man will necessarily revert to the state of *"bellum omnium contra omnes"*—everybody's war against everybody or the state of total anarchy. From an axiological point of view we would say that the useful or the economic value alone is too weak to cement human coexistence and lend to it stability of form and functioning. The useful being the lowest on the scale of human values, it must receive its assessment from its superiors.

On the other hand, if it is true that man lives in society because he needs his fellow men, we feel justified in rejecting also the extreme forms of individualism, defended by the psychological and romantic interpreters of social phenomena (*G. Tarde, J. J. Rousseau,* and their followers). Were the individual human being self-sufficient—biologically, economically, psychologically, and morally—there would be some justification for the individualist movements of all times. The fact of the matter, however, is that the individual—considered even as a person—is on no account self-sufficient, for he does not represent an absolute form of autonomy but just a relative one. The condition of isolation, separation, segregation, loneliness could be the ideal of an all-perfect Being only. In reality, however, the individualist actually leads a life which contradicts its own norm: while proclaiming his unlimited autonomy and self-sufficiency, he still depends on and uses his fellow beings whom he resents because of his neurotic egocentrism.

From what we have seen thus far it should follow that the reason why man needs his fellows should be found on the higher level of personal existence. It will be recalled that we identified above the psycho-ontological condition of personal existence as the state of an "imperfect perfection" which expresses both its negative (imperfect) and positive (perfect) aspects. The element of imperfection stands here for the need for acceptance; that of perfection expresses the source for giving oneself to another, thus creating the two basic dimensions of human intersubjectivity as the essence of the socio-political values. Let us follow up now the implications of this existential condition from a social point of view.

Whenever intellectually and emotionally mature persons meet, the encounter consists in "getting to know each other." The first thing which is mutually and tacitly acknowledged is the identification of the "other" as "another" human being, that is, another individual instance of personal existence. This recognition leads to the awareness of a natural affinity, similarity, resemblance or likeness, founded on the *community of nature* and manifested in an individualized form or *Gestalt.* To commune in the same nature means to share the same psycho-ontological condition and destiny, which underlies the ideas of human equality, fraternity (brotherhood), and solidarity. There is no need, we hope, to point out that this is a "person to person" rapport, a personal confrontation, thus transcending the limitations of the physical (racial) identity or difference. Man discovers his fellows as "man" not as white, black, or yellow, although the common ethnic background may account for group cohesion and solidarity on the lower levels of primitive social life. On the other hand the ideal of humanism discovers in every person an individualized instance of "humanity." Thus does Schleiermacher report his enthusiasm when discovering that he, as an individual, represents mankind in a special, exclusive, and unique form.

The awareness of natural community generates the experience of mutual understanding as the basis for the incipient stages of possible *communication* and *friendship.* Thus, paraphrasing on the Hobbesian pessimism, we would suggest that the encounter between two human persons rests upon the assumption that *"homo homini est amicus"*—man is man's friend because of his participating in the same nature and sharing the same existential "human condition." The special quality of intersubjectivity can be rendered even more emphatic if we compare, for instance, man's attitude and reaction when face to face with non-human beings, things, objects, plants, animals, etc. All of them are regarded as "not man," that is, not representing the individual incarnation of humanity. Consequently, man does not and will not try to establish a "personal rapport" or confrontation because the other self is not there. Man's relationship to the world of objects is, therefore, impersonal. Even when trying to identify the meaning and the value which the objects of his experience represent for him, man will not question the meaning man represents for the objects. In a word, objects may be invested with meaning by man's rational and bio-physical dispositions without man representing any specific meaning, significance or value for the objects as such. There is no ground or foundation for an intersubjective relationship because there is only one subject and an object or thing which does not possess the ontological perfections of the personal mode of being. Communication presupposes the opening for intentional appropriation through the powers of knowledge leading to insight.

The process of human communication — made possible through the symbolism of human speech — is not and should not be limited to the factual, impersonal or practical remarks on the environmental (geographic, climatic, and economic) aspects of life. On the contrary, the true purpose of human communication is the discovery of the other self which manifests itself through the physical "Gestalt" of the individual. Thus the human body and its external appearance are first interpreted as the indirect revelation of a hidden, invisible form of existence, possessed by the other self in a unique manner. The impression derived from the impact of the physical appearance should be regarded, therefore, as the foundation for human love on the physical level. Before going into the description of this form of love — to be called "eros" in contra-distinction to "caritas" — we want to point to the fact that it is the community of nature and destiny which accounts for human solidarity and association. The many forms of love, therefore, should be regarded as the value underlying the many differentiated forms of social and cultural dynamics. Furthermore, since the concept of love is truly analogous insofar as it can be brought into existence by whatever perfection the forms of being represent for man, it should be made clear too that in the present discussion we restrict the meaning of love only to the phenomena conditioned by intersubjective relationships thus leaving out all the other forms of love relative to physical nature, its regions, their phenomena, and object. On the other hand, it also follows that love as a social value must have at least an indirect reference to the religious and aesthetic values as will become apparent from the following discussion.

All attempts to deal with the phenomenon of love in terms of scientific analysis have failed and will always fall short of its peculiar make-up. This is true because of the disproportion between the rational, abstract, and general language of science on the one hand, and the eminently irrational, emotional, and intuitive language spoken by the lovers on the other. Furthermore, it is peculiar of true love to be "tongue-tied," silent, and devoid of all convincing proofs of logical insights to be used for its justification. Regardless of this, the topic of love has always been chosen as the most preferred subject in conversation, art, literature, and even popular philosophies. The institutions of civilization and culture on the social, moral, religious, historical, and even economic levels are impregnated with it and determined, in their specific articulations, by the universal concern with the experience of love and its varieties.

In spite of the outstanding universality and popularity of love and the unique place given to it by man, the topic does not become exhausted, worn down, and annoyingly trivial. It is still the most talked about and the most dreamed of experience of people belonging to all age groups, of all walks of life, of both sexes, regardless of all cultural differences and barriers throughout human history. Its importance is not derived from its scientific or economic import; it is rather due to the personal involvement and its supposed connection with the dream of all ages, human happiness. Love is considered as everybody's need, everybody's concern, everybody's problem, and everybody wants to have his turn and share of it. There seems always to be an inexhaustible residue, thought of as something impenetrable, mysterious, ecstatic, mystical, and overpowering in the depths of love. Therefore, it always promises something new and rich in every successive moment of experience.

If happiness is the first idea to be associated with love, there is still enough room here for the tragic, comic, ironic, satiric, sarcastic, skeptic, and so forth, down to the borderline of the criminal and sadistic. However, people think of these negative outcomes of love as unnecessary and not powerful enough to endanger its renewed appeal and temptations. No frustration or disillusion is great enough to discredit the sublime, metaphysical, religious, moral, social, psychic, and aesthetic values with which love has been invested since time immemorial. Poets of each generation find the words to justify, over and over again, the amount of suffering and pain connected with love as the possible sacrifice dictated by it and accepted by man. At times even death does not seem too high a price to be paid for love as long as there is hope for its coming and becoming one of man's most longed-for experiences. Thus the erotic and heroic may become synonymous in the life of men.

The most surprising and paradoxical phenomenon, however, is the fact that this continued grand show of life is put on the stage by an actor and a stage manager who think of themselves as rational beings. Psychology, however, teaches that human behavior is motivated rather by the pleasure principle than logical insights; human choices are directed by our likes and dislikes. But since rationality and love are as irreconcilable as faith and scientific demonstrations, herein lies the primary conflict in man's nature. It is this conflict between the rational, as an academic postulate, and the irrationality of love which accounts for the tensions, fears, anxieties, and insecurities experienced by men in love. It is the same conflict which opens the possibilities for the opposities, like happiness versus misery, dignity versus comical roles, tragedy as opposed to happy ends, morality against depravity, faithfulness contrasted with promiscuity, illusions followed by frustration, union that ends in separation, communion destroyed by mutual estrangement, respect taken over by contempt and scorn, the spirit of sacrifice degenerated into mutual exploitation, and confidence conquered by suspicion, jealousy, and mistrust. These antinomies and antagonisms are themselves conditioned as secondary phenomena by the very polarities to be found in the range of basic human needs and emotions. Love is fought against by hatred, desires were threatened by aversions, joys may change over into sorrows, hope is just the opposite of despair, courage is inhibited by fear, and anger stands alone as the final witness of human frustrations with no compensations to follow.

Conflict implies the coexistence of opposites that make final equilibrium and happiness just wishful thinking or the result of optimistic daydreaming. Still, love is here to stay by popular demand. Undoubtedly, this demand is not backed by the wisdom of the philosophers; it is rather the demand of the pre-logical, preconceptual, and anti-intellectual urge of the life principle, rooted in the instinctual drives and the unconditioned, primary dispositions that man is equipped with. And it is thereby forced to follow the plan of self-preservation and the continuation of human life on earth. Thus love appears to be, at least in its primitive form of manifestation, self-love which, in turn, is the condition of the other-directed love. In such manner, one may understand the opposition described above between the rational and the irrational. This explains also why there is not and there cannot be any adequate scientific account of love.

Love cannot be taught regardless of the many publications on this topic which promise to introduce the reader into the secret labyrinths of love. Love can be felt, given, received, or taken; it can be developed or destroyed, but it can never be defined. Any definition falls short of its very nature which we have associated with the instinctual and emotional. Therefore love cannot be deduced from aprioristic principles, or adapted to any universal formula of functionality. Love is an experience and not a theoretical hypothesis to be demonstrated methodically. This statement is in agreement with the common sense belief which looks at love as irrational, blind, and following its own dynamics, many times as a direct denial of all logical categories. It is this foolishness of love which accounts for so many witty, humorous interpretations, jokes, sarcastic remarks, and other kinds of misuses.

Nor is this all. Love not only refuses to be reduced to the form of the encyclopedic existence of a definition, but further, it cannot manifest itself directly. Though it can be felt directly by the persons in love, it cannot be made visible, tangible, and observable immediately. Words and modes of behavior are only symbols, that is, indirect manifestations of the original and hidden reality of love. However, this symbolic language provides also for the possibility of deceit; words and behavioral forms can be simulated, acted out, without standing for a genuine psychic experience. In this case the communication is untrue, false, and deceptive. Deception brought about by symbolic lies is just another aspect of the tragical potential latent in the experience of love. Deception in love implies self-deception too, which affects both parties involved in the duality of the roles needed for the staging of love. Thus one may believe that he is in love and loves, whereas he is not and does not love in reality. The other person may believe that he is loved, whereas in reality he is just being deceived. Most frequently, however, deception occurs in the form of wishful thinking about the values, qualities, perfections, and distinctions of the partner.

Love is necessarily value-directed. Values or goods, commonly called perfections, are the very object of love. On the other hand, imperfections, deficiencies, and depravity cannot arouse love, admiration, dedication, friendship, and the communion of two selves. The most they can achieve is sympathy for and understanding of human imperfections. Love is always thought of as an experience of mutual enrichment, an integration of values on a higher level of existence. Its direction is always upwards, toward the still unexplored heights of more and more perfections to be discovered and taken into possession.

The desire to love and to be loved is the symptom of one's psychic hunger for more perfection in view of an ascending synthesis of personal life. It is the striving for surpassing the painful limitations of isolated individuality. Therefore, if the partner does not represent the desired form or quality of perfection needed for the incubation of love, imagination will take care of the deficit. Imagination will procreate the trimmings and the decorations needed to produce that kind of an apparent reality which is capable of effecting the same emotional involvement that identifies the love brought into existence by true perfections. This creativity of human imagination is called the process of idealization of the real or the magic of imagination.

The reality of man analyzed from a rational point of view, in the light of an impartial, detached, and logical account of what man actually represents in the nakedness of his existential condition, will bring to light an existence made up of opposites that creates the inner tensions and conflicts in the experiences of the individual existent. This kind of reality cannot and will not produce the emotions characteristic of love which can be stirred up only by real or at least assumed, imagined, and believed perfections. For to every human perfection there is an equal or even greater amount of imperfection as its tragical counterpart. Man is the existence of an imperfect perfection. Without being pessimistic, one cannot deny man's imperfections rooted in his limitations, contingency, temporality, and inner subjectivity. Therefore, the imperfect perfection of man has to be idealized in order to fit the conditions of the emotional experience of love. If someone fails to take into account both man's imperfections along with his perfections, he has to end up with a distorted picture of man.

The idealization of the real occurs in the form of generalization, transfer, projection, and totalization. It is done by isolating, and abstracting only the available perfections from the equal or greater amount of imperfections that are also included in the real situation of man. Imagination considers only the perfections, while the imperfections are excluded. The ideal element thus isolated from its original context will be enlarged, made general and total as if it were now standing for the whole of man's reality. As a consequence, man appears now in a new light, the ideal and artificial light, lit by the artistry of imagination while creating the ideal type needed for the conception, development, and manifestation of love.

Man has never been solely satisfied with the real. Reality appears to be too "realistic," surrounded by and immersed in frustrating limitations, deficiencies, dangers and evils of all sorts. Man cannot think of himself as he is because the outcome of this self-knowledge may result in despair and suicide. Man has to think of himself as the king of the created world, a microcosm, the synthesis of all perfections present in the macrocosm. Man has to idealize himself and his environment too in order to be able to accept himself and think of his life as worth living. Man must decorate himself, put on a make-up, a mask, a second form of existence, designed by the inventiveness of his fertile imagination. Man can love himself only if he creates the illusion of perfection by repressing the unpleasant and disturbing aspects of his imperfect being. Similarly, man can love his fellow man only if he applies the same make up, the same illusion, and same process of idealization of the real by the process of projection and transfer. So, perfection is a must; if it is not forthcoming from real savings, then it must be borrowed and applied.

The repression and the masking of the undesirable aspects of reality occurs in obedience to man's need for maintaining a relatively tolerable and at times even enjoyable psychic balance. Since the imperfect is unpleasurable and therefore disturbing, man defends himself against its disrupting effects by making it invisible, hidden, inaccessible, and he covers this by the product of his imagination, inspired by his desire for happiness, pleasure, satisfaction, and love. There is a definite romantic approach to reality in this flight from the real into the imaginary and ideally unreal.

The idealization of the imperfect perfection given in man's experiences may occur both on the conscious and the unconscious levels.

Here we are faced with the idealization of man by his fellow man and by the same process of isolating the imperfect from the perfect, by repressing the unpleasant to the level of unconsciousness, and by identifying the real with its ideal type which has never existed and never will exist. This is the process created by human imagination in view of the need for an ideal subject fit for the experience of love.

Although there is no science of love and nobody has been able to condense its complex nature into a satisfactory definition, one may try a descriptive interpretation of this important human affair without claiming to have exhausted all that has been written, said, or done because of love. In fact, any description will fall short of its goal, for nobody can express in words the individual, unique, and exclusive experience of love. Every person in love is convinced that nobody before or after him could love so intensely and originally as he did. For every individual his personal experience comes first. What others may have experienced, written, or said on this matter seems to be inferior in quality when compared to the pervasive, possessing, overwhelming, even maddening heights and depths of his emotional upheavals, turmoils, and ecstasies.

Because of the highly individual and subjective interpretation of the love experience, one may rightly call it "a many splendored thing"; the "splendor," of course, varies according to the predominant element or factor which accounts for the subjectivistic and mutually exclusive—even cynical and sarcastic—point of view such as can be seen from the following random collection.

For the religious man love is the meaning of life, the symbol of perfect happiness now and hereafter on the supernatural level.

For the moralist love is the first and greatest of the commandments: "the whole law and the prophets."

For the philosopher love is an idea (logos), a theory, a doctrine, a system very useful for abstract and learned lecturing and discussion.

For the psychologist love is just another psychic process, having a start, a development, peak, and decline; it is a motive, a need, a stimulus and response, an experience with its pleasurable or painful potential and its positive or negative consequences, bringing about some change in behavior for better or worse; a complicated maze-running in pairs.

For the artist love is an inspiration for his creative imagination during the periods of his creative intuition.

For the economist love is a consumer's good and the loving partner's possible prospects for profitable business.

For the social engineer love is a social phenomenon or symptom which became static in the institution of marriage, a traditional value, part of our civilization, or a "function to be measured."

For the politician love is a power potential, an eminently feminine emotion to be manipulated skillfully for the sake of espionage and sabotage.

For the linguist love is words, expressions, idioms, slangs, jargon which disregards even the elementary rules of grammar.

For the physician or physiologists, like Kinsey, love is a biological process leading to procreation.

For the lawyer love is a paragraph in the law to be applied in Reno, Nevada.

For the beauticians, dieticians, and the managers of charm and modeling schools love is the art of the fix-it-men while trying to correct that which mother nature left unfinished or badly finished.

For the hedonist: love is a sensuous pleasure worth its price.

For the movie producers love is an attraction to be staged romantically and presented to the millions as a compensation for the frustrated and hungry ones.

For the scientist love is an embarrassment, an embarrassing phenomenon that refuses classification, experimentation, definition, prediction, and control by measurements, numbers, statistical averages; correspondingly love is dimissed as an unscientific matter, good for the poets only.

For the optimist: an illusion to be cherished and taken seriously.

For the pessimist love is a disillusion to be avoided.

For the child: a basic emotional diet for growing up, a

sort of psychic vitamin to be taken once a day before or after the usual spanking periods or in between.

For the teenagers love is a romantic, mysterious attempt with frequent failures that accumulate feelings of insecurity, anxiety, and doubts about their own physical and psychic worth.

For young adolescents: love is an attempt with more success and, therefore, more emerging concern with the possible consequences and responsibilities of being a success.

For married people love and marriage could be interpreted as double expense and split fragments of half-pleasures, scented with the spirit of true sacrifice and virtue.

For separated and divorced people love is a mixed feeling of liberation and guilt which prompts them to attempt a second or a third trial and sure error; thus they live between the last and the next adventure.

For old people love is the happy memory of those good old days that, unfortunately, will never return; on the contrary, they are headed toward the grave that will take care of the old man and his distorted memories.

Love could be described, in more serious terms, as the emotional experience of a psychosomatic relationship of pleasurable quality and limited duration between two persons of opposite sexes at some definite age level. No matter how artificial and abstract this description may sound, it still includes the main structural elements and moments of this dynamic and very intricate process. Because of love's complex nature, we have to first isolate the subjective and objective aspects; then we may point out its origins, foundations, and sources. They actually stand as the premises, conditions, and causes of love.

First of all, love is an experience. Experience suggests the idea of something real, concrete, and personal. It possesses certain unique, exclusive, and incommunicable characteristics, conditioned by the individual, singular, and particular make-up of the personal existent. All these traits, however, gravitate toward the central reality of existence—life.

Experiences are of many kinds and not all of them qualify for being included in the world of love. There are experiences which do not involve the subject, as happens, for instance, in the field of detached philosophical, theoretical, or scientific speculations about universal principles and laws of the many phenomena man is confronted with in his intellectual concern. They are too abstract, impersonal, and universal to have anything in common with the subjective and personal situation of life.

If the theoretical does not fit into the category of love, the same can be said of the economic, political, and, to a lesser degree, the social experiences of man. The economic is dominated by the law of usefulness, practicality, and functionality. These qualities are diametrically opposed to the unpractical and idealistic concentration of love. Love brought many economists to insolvency. Coming to the political and social behavior of man, the same incompatibility can be found. The political obeys the imperative of the will, motivated by the desire for power and as such cannot afford the risks and dangers typical of the unstable emotions. Politicians manipulate people without loving them. Finally, the social on the larger scale of organized human relationships steals the intimacy and privacy needed for the personal experience of love.

Love is an emotional experience. But emotions are not primary and original phenomena either. By their very dynamic and pervasive nature emotions are always goal-directed toward the stimuli which aroused them. In other words, they are not absolute realities in themselves and for themselves, just directed tendencies. Emotions do not stand for themselves but for the elements which called them into existence. They are not the very first motive for what man does or does not do, rather the opposite is true: they appear as effects or consequences of what the person has learned while in contact with the stimuli given in his experience. At least at the very beginning of the whole process of psychic life, the first element is the encounter of man with the many objects of reality. On the other hand, it is true that once emotions have been called into being, they may become self-sufficient, autonomous, and follow their own free course of development even though the original stimulus may not be present any more in its objective reality. If it is true that emotions are secondary and derived phenomena, we shall look for their first premises and conditions.

The dynamics of emotional experience start on the level of human senses exposed to the stimuli while in contact with objective reality, the world of objects and subjects. Man learns to know the physical properties of his immediate environment by means of his sense impressions, sensations, and perceptions that mediate the information needed for his life adjustment. Feelings, emotions, and passions represent the subjective interpretation of and reaction to the pleasurable or painful qualities of the stimuli acting upon man's senses. In this way feelings and emotions are the expressions of value judgments which announce the psychic reaction of the subject to the presence of the object. We are faced with the duality of a subject-object relationship in which each component plays its specific part.

The object is considered the cause responsible for the impression produced in the subject; the subject is at first the passive element insofar as it receives the impression. It becomes active when reacting to the stimuli by way of an emotional expression, followed by a corresponding motor reaction, as the expression of the impression just received. In this process of experience on the sensitive level a situation of interdependence and interaction is established between the two poles of the relation; the subject is affected and made dependent by the impression received; but the object will also be affected by the expression and the reaction of the receiver. The very essence of this passive and active relationship can best be expressed in the brief formulas of impression-expression, action-reaction, and stimulus-response. It follows that we shall find the same structural make-up and relation between the two persons engaged in the experience of love. There is the initial impression followed by the expression of the other. Mutual dependence, interaction and passivity, followed by periods of more intense activity on both parts — all these constitute the live drama of emotional involvement, love.

The object stands for the impression or modification brought about in the subject. Thus, at first the object plays the active role. Its activity and the effects thereof increases in efficiency with the intensity, duration, and frequency of the stimulation. However, this acting upon a subject of experience is not purely objective. Whatever the nature, qualities, and properties of the objective stimuli might be, the subject still reacts to them according to his specific constitution which establishes the frame of his experience, observation, and system of reference. The dictum of philosophers and psychologists, stressing the point of subjective dispositions and conditioning, is well known: "Whatever is received after the manner of the receiver." (Aquinas.) In this sense the original properties of the stimuli producing the impression are transformed and adapted to fit the peculiar make-up, set, and expectancy of the receiving subject.

There is no doubt that the impression is always of something, but that something becomes meaningful only in the process of being modified by the subject of experience. Nobody will ever be able to draw the line of demarcation between the objective and the subjective. And nobody will ever measure satisfactorily the exact amount of distortion caused by adapting stimuli to our specific nature and its basic needs. Therefore, it seems to be proper to speak of the co-penetration and mixing of objective and subjective components instead of defending either pure objectivity or pure subjectivity, both of which represent the unilateral abstraction of the speculative intellect.

Inasmuch as the subject receives the impression, it is passive. But it also becomes active in the process of stimuli-adaptation and even more so in the process of self-expression while interpreting and evaluating the desirable or frustrating properties of the impinging stimuli. For sure, stimuli in and by themselves are neither pleasurable nor painful. These qualities belong to the subject as of psychic life. The condition of the subject becomes at times his modifications, and it is only by a process of transfer or reversal that they will be ascribed to and predicated of the stimuli as such.

The amount of subjectivity may, and as a rule does, increase as soon as contact with the stimulus is interrupted and the object is removed from the field of immediate experience. When the object is absent, the subject becomes free of external control and restrictions. This freedom afforded by the remoteness from matter, offers the opportunity for further modifications and distortions, dictated by the desires, needs, and wants that populate the field even more important than the so-called objectively given in his experience. The subject may project into the object some or all of its dispositions making the object appear similar to what the subject wants it to be, regardless of whether it is factually true or false. Even common sense wisdom expresses the same insight when saying that one sees only what one really wants to see, or that you will get exactly what you are prepared to get, and so forth. Beyond a doubt, it is imagination, the subjective disposition, which plays the active role in the process of creating one's reality, one's profile of experiences, one's horizon of existence, re-investing the objects with such qualities which the imagination attaches to them by way of projecting subjectivity into the world created by it.

The subjectivization of reality is accomplished by human imagination. However, imagination is inspired and constantly nourished in her creative design by the indefinitely rich scale and tonality of human emotions. Emotions, in their turn, are conditioned by man's basic needs on the organic, psychic, and social levels. No matter how many and how varied these needs seem to be, all of them fall into the fundamental category of the instinctual nature of man which is always present in the original striving for pleasures and happiness. By way of simplification, we might reduce the whole picture to the original relationship between the pleasure principle on the subjective level, and the reality principle on the objective one. This structural set-up applies mainly to the case of emotional involvements and attachments experienced by subjects of opposite sexes, engaged in the process of romantic experiences.

The staging and acting out of romantic plays follow the same pattern described above with regard to sense perceptions in general.

If knowledge is limited solely to the level of sense perception, images and their association, colored heavily with emotional charges, imagination may work wonders insofar as it is free from both the object and the other instance of restrictive control, exercised by reason and intellect. Reason produces an insight into both the objectively given and the subjective processes of sense knowledge as well. It has the reflective and critical power to separate the real from the rational and thus curb the dynamic tendency of imagination supported by the emotional inductions coming from a needy subject always hungry for gratification. From this new perspective one may understand better why logic is the enemy of love, chiefly of the romantic type.

From the preceding considerations we might draw the first conclusions about the structural constitution of love. First, we must emphasize its eminently subjective character. Although the process is set off by an objective element, the complexity of stimuli acting upon our senses, the importance and the weight of the objective decreases in the same proportion as the subjective process and its contents increases in significance. This process is the move from the real to the unreal and ideal; from the external to the internal processes of dream-land; from the objective to the subjective; from the merely given to the created; from the limited potentialities of the subject to the unlimited possibilities of the imaginary which may now appear to the subject not less real than the object—or maybe even more so.

However, the move from the real to the unreal is preceded by a change within the structural disposition and functioning of the person's psychic powers. Thus critical analysis is replaced by naive synthesis of the subjective elements produced by phantasy thinking. The irrationality of demanding emotions substitutes for sober rationality. The logical is thrown overboard for the sake of the illogical, rather a-logical, pre-logical, just symbolic and primitive intuitions. Common sense wisdom appears foolish in the "twilight zone" of emerging new experiences. The barriers of a static and rigid organization are disregarded in this state of psychic anarchy, created by the rule of possessing passions. The reality of factual determination is exchanged for the land of freedom. External control and the censure of public opinion, tradition, morality, and religion disappear in order to make room for the absence of all valid principles and rules of expected behavior from a sober conformist.

Psychologically this process falls under the mechanism of escape from reality, or flight from the outside world and of withdrawal into the new world created by imagination, populated exclusively by the pleasurable images dictated by the hope for final conquest of the secret of happiness. This move from the real to the ideal can be seen in the insistence of the persons in love on isolation, and privacy in order to eliminate all possible disturbing circumstances that might remind them of unwanted reality. Thus we may also conclude that love is against the principle of reality presented coldly by the logical necessities of rational thinking and existence. One simply cannot expect the lovers to be reasonable. No one can fall in love as long as he is being reasonable. Rational reality stands in the way of irrational subjectivity and ideality. Therefore, we might conclude further that love is the beautiful, rewarding, and pleasurable sickness of imagination. Only with the removal of objective controls can imagination effect the state of emotional transfiguration of the real.

The lovers' state of mind can be compared also to the process leading to a gradual narrowing of objective awareness of and contacts with reality and the exclusive concentration of the whole field of consciousness on the object of one's love, an object, to be sure, created by imagination, an imaginary object. Because of this narrowing of consciousness along with a unilateral and exclusive emotional concern, we might call the attention to the state of mental fixation and obsession. In fact, many of the reactions of the persons in love manifest the typical symptoms of compulsive reactions dictated by their mental obsessions. The difference is in the fact that the field of consciousness is not dominated by one idea only but by the image of the beloved or adored person, charged with intense emotions and passions. These passions will take possession of the whole person and dictate the kind of behavior needed for their satisfaction. Thus to satisfy the passions may appear to the person dominated by them as the only "reasonable thing" to do. As long as these passions have not received adequate satisfaction and gratification, there is little hope that the person will recover from this beautiful sickness.

Beyond a doubt, no one can understand the power of human passions without reference to the *libido*, the vital energy rooted in our organic, instinctual, and erotic nature. In Freudian terminology, love would be the predominance of the Id over the Super-Ego while the Ego identifies itself with the demands of the Id. In our traditional terminology all this would look much more simple if viewed in the light of the instinct of self-preservation, the pleasure principle on one hand, and that of the preservation of the species on the other. In such manner the instinctual accounts for both self-love and that of the other-directed love, conditioned by the first.

The passionate ecstasy of erotic experience cannot last too long because it would endanger the whole psychic balance of the person. After reaching its maximum of intensity, the tension effected by it has to be reduced in order to reestablish the original equilibrium on the psychic and organic levels which is the normal state of the organism. The reduction of the tension may occur in the process of actual need satisfaction by way of the psycho-somatic union and communion of the lovers. If such a union cannot materialize because of insurmountable difficulties, coming either from the restrictions, prohibitions, and taboos imposed on and enforced by the cultural control apparatus, or from the lack of responsiveness of the partner, tension will increase until it will dictate a course of action that might at least indirectly or by way of compensations provide a substitute satisfaction for the original need. Whatever the outcome, the original ecstasy will terminate because it must. Let us first follow up the outcomes of erotic union.

The union of the loving partners follows the pattern of need satisfaction and tension reduction, a process known in psychology by the name of motivational cycle. It usually starts with a need which can be either an unconditioned, instinctual urge or a conditioned need, that is, induced or created by the stimuli working on one's organism. As we saw above, the stimuli became internalized and thus increased the need for satisfaction, demanded by the desires created by the triple effect and the conjugated effort of stimuli, needs, and desires, reinforced by secondary stimuli, located in the imagination of the subject. Desires are included because they represent the supporting energy that accounts for the continuity and development of the idealizing activity of imagination itself. All this brings forth the experience of psychic and organic tensions which express the state of imbalance or disequilibrium. Since the natural and normal state of the organism is *homeostasis* or balance, tensions will bring about some sort of active reaction on the part of the organism, directed toward the goal of need satisfaction. The cycle of the motivational process is completed if and when subject and object — in our case the two persons in love — meet again, this time, however, in the form of real union and partial gratification. Thus the tension is reduced and the original balance should be reestablished.

This may sound very logical and simple; in reality, however, gratification is not likely to be completely satisfactory. Therefore, tension does not completely leave and give its place to perfect enjoyment and happiness. There is a considerable amount of frustration and disillusionment at the point where subject and object meet again in the form of psycho-somatic union. Where does this element of frustration, this component of disillusionment, this experience of incomplete, imperfect, and therefore tragical — if not downright comical — union and happiness come from? The answer seems to be given by the disproportion between what the subject expected to get on the one side, and the actual and real amount of satisfaction derived from the union on the other.

We should recall at this point all that has been said about the creative activity of the imagination removed from the original stimulus and its control. It was suggested that the imagination, fed by the primary needs and desires of the subject, created an idealized type of a person, man or woman, dressed in all possible perfections — trimmings and decorations — the only things seen and desired by the other person as the object of his love. This also means that the real persons are much less than their idealized types. In other words, the persons in love, prior to the experience of the real union and mutual possession, are set for much more than reality can offer them. They expect to receive the reward of this ideal land, unfortunately, they only get the real. They are in love with the ideal type of a person and not with its realistic condition.

The ideal does not include imperfection, limitations, distortions, and the possibility of frustrations. But the real possesses all these negative values in combination with the positive ones. Furthermore, the ideal has never existed outside the dream-world of imagination while the real one always has. Consequently, the process which follows the previous period of passionate ecstasy moves just in the opposite direction, toward the real. At this point imagination is not much help either, because the experience of union is objectively controlled by the naked presence of the stimuli which now appear under a new, sobering and awakening perspective.

If this reversal of the process does not occur on the very first occasions of mutual communion and possession, it is just a matter of more time, needed for the onset of a more realistic view. All trimmings and decorations, qualities, perfections, values, and virtues will be taken from, or rather off the subject, if the subject does not really possess these alleged personal characteristics. Surely, nobody possesses them to the extent and degree the liberal imagination presents them.

The reversal of the idealizing process has to occur, regardless of how much the loving partners resent the threatening approach of it. No one is able to be an actor throughout the many years following the celebration of the erotic union. The mask cannot be on all the time. The make-up has to be washed off, because real life situations, demands, stresses, problems, and conflicts presented by the reality principle, would make their continued use both comical and unfunctional. The most important cause of bringing the ideal down to the level of the real is the true existential condition of man whom we saw to be the combination of opposites, the coexistence of conflicting values, the presence of the imperfect in the limited amount of human perfections.

At this point someone may raise a protest against equating love with a mere imaginary illusion which necessarily leads to disillusions and the absence of love. To answer this objection we must remember that love is a "many splendored thing" and its imaginary illusion applies only to the rather immature form of love (*"eros," "bios"* or *"amor concupiscentiae"*), restricted to the area of "romantic" experiences. One should not, therefore, try to derive the meaning and value of love from this particular aspect only; on the contrary, we have to move now on the higher forms of love.

The fundamental error, to be held responsible for the necessary failure of the erotic and romantic love, lies in the misinterpretation of man's mode of being. The misinterpretation is due to a unilateral approach to man's total existence which discloses the coexistence and the co-penetration of two — rather opposite and conflicting tendencies — the *psyche* and the *soma.* While the psychic and self-conscious disposition is inner-directed and rooted in the uncommunicable presence of the self to the self, the somatic is naturally other-directed and constantly motivated by the desire and the interest to take, to possess, to enjoy, to dominate, and to enslave. The so-called love, inspired by instinctual, erotic or libidinous desires, brings about the "objectification of subjectivity" in the sense that its immediate and only purpose lies in debasing the partner to a mere object of desire and the source of pleasures to be exploited and enjoyed. Were man only a *"libido,"* dominated thoroughly by the pleasure principle — the Dionysiac attitude — there would follow no conflicts leading to mutual estrangement, incompatibility, and separation. Thus the *"amor concupiscentiae"* is the form of love which befits a purely organic and physical drive of animal nature. For this reason animal "sociability" is limited to the area of short lived instinctual togetherness, needed for the procreation and rearing of the offspring. Thus one may equate sex and libido with animal desire on the bio-physical level exclusively.

However, man's self-conscious, free, and subsistent personality forbids him to decline down to the level of sheer animality. Though it may sound strange, the truth of the matter is that no matter how hard man tries to become an animal, he cannot escape—on a permanent basis—from his own self. The most he can achieve is to bring about the condition of self-estrangement, self-deception, and self-abandonment. In a word, even the professional hedonist is still a human person, a degenerated type, of course; man can never lose completely his own self which is always present to the I in the form of an inner dialogue, whose voice cannot be completely repressed. Therefore, we must conclude that the love which befits man must be in correspondence with his own nature which demands to be discovered and respected. This human love (*amor amicitiae*) was introduced above as "intersubjectivity." Let us now describe in more detail the meaning of subjectivity leading to the experience of intersubjectivity.

First of all, the individual person has to discover himself by analyzing the implications and the consequences of his fundamental self-centeredness (egocentrism), manifested in the all-pervasive experience of *self-love.* Unfortunately, there is too much confusion regarding the meaning of this psychic imperative, called man's natural love for himself as a subject. The most frequent mistake is the identification of self-love with selfishness. Since the latter has a bad moral connotation, there are many who feel uneasy because of their natural self-concern and, therefore, they desperately try—without ever succeeding—to exterminate all vestiges of this "immoral" and "sinful" feeling. As a necessary consequence, unselfishness, altruism, philanthropic or humanitarian ideas and ideals are held up as the counterpart for selfishness. Many moralists insist on the constant need for self-denial, self-mortification, self-punishment in order to curb or discipline this devil hidden in the human person. Thus they hope to reach their maximum of a total unselfish perfection through complete self-sacrifice.

In opposition to all these ideal aspirations we want to put forward a very blunt statement: man has never succeeded in completely eliminating his own self because that is both ontologically and psychologically impossible. To substantiate our position, it may be sufficient to point to the fact that even the most heroic acts of self-denial and self-sacrifice are still performed by the self which was supposed to step out of the picture completely. Man being the kind of existent he is, that is, a self-subsistent, self-conscious, and free subject (a person), he should not try to overcome the natural mode of his being basically self-centered; no matter what he dreams of, he cannot be but himself, that is, a self present to himself in the inwardness or interiority of his self-consciousness. Consequently, it would be altogether different if instead man concentrated all his efforts on discovering the true meaning of subjectivity and corrected his misconceptions about the value of self-love as basically distinct from selfishness.

Selfishness always takes the place of genuine self-love. A person becomes necessarily selfish as long as he has not discovered the perfections proper to his mode of existing as a subject. A child, for instance, is naturally selfish because of a lack of insight into the depths of his own self, to be discovered and developed as a positive value and not a negative disposition to be disposed of. Similarly, all human persons who remained stationary or fixed on the childish, immature and undifferentiated level of consciousness — not having overcome as yet the original narcissistic tendencies — are of necessity selfish or extremely "self-conscious." This self-consciousness, however, is concentrated on the individual's inadequacies, imperfections, real or imagined inferiorities, insecurities, etc., resulting in the typically oversensitive, timid, shy, withdrawn modes of reaction or else in the development of overcompensations in the forms of aggressiveness, personal disregard, airs of importance or superiority, etc. To put it briefly, the immature, underdeveloped person becomes selfish whose immediate symptom is the constant desire to take, to receive or to get, without being able to give, perhaps, because he unconsciously knows that there is not much he can offer anyway. Consequently, there is no openness or opening in the selfish person who is afraid to show himself forth because of the inner poverty of his inner self. At the same time, however, the selfish individual is desperately trying to enrich himself by constantly trying to "take out" whatever he can from others, without realizing that all his trials will necessarily end in error, frustration, isolation or loneliness. His incessant complaints about not being loved and wanted by the other selves actually indicates his own inability to love or to give himself as a free gift to others without the hidden desire to possess, dominate or exploit them. Let us conclude, therefore, that the inferior type of person is selfish because he is psycho-ontologically poor; therefore, he is capable of only one type of so-called love, the love of desire, of interest, of exploitation, of possession, and domination. This love, however, reduces the other self to the state of a "thing," and "object" or a "consumer's good" and a "nice thing to have as a commodity." The failure is a must because of the pseudo-character of the love in question.

Let us turn now to the opposite of the selfish individual whom we would like to introduce as an intellectually developed, mature or adult person. In fact, we should rather call him a personality whom we identified elsewhere as the person saturated with values. This person has achieved — at least partially — the goals of self-appropriation, self-identity, self-possession, inner security, equilibrium, and the ideal of an integrated mode of existence. Because of the inner presence of these values within his own self, he regards himself as a positive value; consequently, he must love himself. Without being conceited, he is aware of the perfections he represents both as a human subject and as an individual instance of humanity as well. If we analyze his being "self-conscious," we shall find that it is concentrated on the positive perfection of the human or personal mode of existence, committed to the appropriation of the ideal hierarchy of values, according to their qualitative prominence and significance. This "self-loving and self-conscious" person is in the state of actuality, having left behind the inferior states of childish immaturity (the states of potentiality). He regards himself as a value for himself and for others as well. Therefore, he has no need to hide his self, to deny himself, to mortify himself, to repress his natural self-interest, self-love, or self-centeredness. In fact, there are within himself certain perfections or actualities which must be shown forth, thus demanding an openness, or readiness for communication. His predominant social motive is not the claim for more securities, dependence, guidance, and protection. On the contrary, he is there to open himself and to give, to share his perfections with other selves who happen to be on the same level of personal maturity and perfection. Not being psychically poor, emotionally and intellectually a pauper, he need not take, exploit, dominate or possess. His person is a gift of self-offering or self-giving.

Moreover, this self-loving person has learned through experience to love himself as a "self," that is, as a free, autonomous subject who must be regarded—under all circumstances—as an end in itself, a subsisting value whose meaning is none other than itself, known as the perfection of personal immanence or interiority. Naturally, such a person must resist any attempt coming from without—mainly from the selfish type described above—to deal with him as an "object of desire," a statistical unit, a mere cell in the social organism or a "means-value" to be subordinated to individual selfishness or collective regimentation. Consequently, this self-subsisting person is also conscious of his individual worth and autonomy, considering his freedom and responsibility as values demanding an absolute respect.

From all this, it should follow again that there is nothing "immoral" or "sinful" in loving oneself according the right measure of one's ontological and psychic perfection. On the contrary, this "self-love" is the only adequate criterion and condition for loving one's neighbor, that is, his fellow human being. In this sense both "self-love" and the love of another self are rooted in the same ontological perfection which belongs to the transcendental attributes of being. We say that "to be" or "to exist" is a perfection in itself because it implicitly connotes the attributes of oneness (*unum*), truth (*verum*), and goodness (*bonum*). These perfections belong to all things (*res*) which stand for some specific nature (some-thing—*aliquid*). It also follows that the perfection of being increases according to the mode and degree or intensity of participating in the *"esse"* of the self-subsisting, absolute Self of God Who is His own Being without any restrictions (*"ipsum esse subsistens"*). Man, therefore, as a human person (*individualis substantia rationalis naturae"*) or a "subject" is far above the lower forms of being (inorganic, organic, living, vegetative, and sentient). He is not "some-thing"; he is "some-one" or "somebody," an individual instance of selfhood who displays through his developed nature the values of personal truth, unity, and goodness. Beyond any doubt, it would be psychologically impossible for man not to love himself after he developed an adequate insight into the perfections of his existence. Having thus described briefly the conditions of human love, rooted in subjectivity, let us now move on to the analysis of "intersubjectivity."

To love and to be loved as a self-loving and self-conscious subsistence is rooted in the desire for communication, leading to *communion.* It is of the nature of any perfection and goodness to manifest itself, to propagate, to become diffused through the act of self-revelation and self-manifestation (*bonum est diffusivum sui*), without losing itself through the act of giving or displaying oneself. We feel that herein we find the ontological basis for all the ideas presented by philosophers as the primary energies or moving powers (*élan vital*), responsible for becoming, change, development and progress. The adequate meaning of evolution from a philosophic point of view is the process of ontological growth, that is, the process of acquiring more being (the quest for more being). The perfection of the being (actuality) reveals itself in the acts of creation as the communication of being and existence. This is also the reason why love has always been invested with the power of building or creating a new world of its own, opposed to the powers of destruction, inspired by the absence of true love (selfishness and hatred).

We have noted above that the condition of communication lies in the community of a mode of existence which implies community in goodness, unity, truth, manifested through the affinity of ideas, principles, values, interests, aims, etc. The community in the mode of existing, however, does not imply sameness or identity, speaking, of course, of the limited mode of being. For there is the fact of individuation, limitation (imperfection rooted in *taleitas*) which is the proper mode of being of the individuals (*indivisum in se et divisum of quolibet alio*). Therefore, individuality should be added as a further motive for the desire of communicating in the community of individualized natures. This desire, again, is not aimed at taking possession of the other self's perfections; it is, rather, the desire to participate, to share, to expose or exhibit one's perfection to another with the assurance that there will be no attempt at "taking away" the perfection belonging to the selves who are mutually present to each other in the acts of subjective reciprocity.

Although the two selves, confronted with each other, represent the same mode of existence, they do it, however, in a unique, original, exclusive, and singular form. While there is identity of natures, there is also the individuality in the mode of participating and representing it. Thus affinity, similarity, and likeness are accompanied by diversity, distinctness, and uniqueness. Furthermore, besides the fact of limitation and uniqueness, individuality also brings with itself the condition of "being divided from anything else" (*divisum a quolibet alio*), a condition of separation, isolation, and loneliness. It appears now that love as communication in the community of individualized natures must lead to communion (union, common union, union in common, communism) in order to overcome the imperfections of loneliness and separation. The quest of communication and communion also suggest the fundamental desire for more being thus revealing the redeeming power of love as a revelation of more being through which the limited self can transcend himself in the other without losing his own identity. The personal confrontation of the two separate selves (I and Thou) develops into the experience of "we" which expresses the state of communion in the perfections of the selves in their reciprocal consciousness while being open, disclosed or "face to face" for one another. We would say, therefore, in ontological jargon, that the isolated and individual *"esse"* of the self is confronted with the *"esse"* of the second self, developing the state or condition of *"co-esse"* and culminating in the state of mutual fusion, co-penetration or union (*"in-esse"*) without claiming the "selfish" possession of each other. Thus the state of being in love still respects the fundamental perfection of personal autonomy or freedom. The opposite is also true, insofar as there can be no love between two selves, unless there is mutual respect for one another's freedom and independence. (No one can love another whom he cannot respect for the mode of being he represents; only the truly mature self is qualified for the experience of true love which sets one free.)

Summarizing the preceding considerations, we would describe love as the *free, self-giving, and self-transcending act of two subsisting selves, united in and perfected or redeemed through their unique otherness.* Every element included in this statement is here with the definite purpose of differentiating love on the personal level from the many abortive attempts (erotic, romantic) at loving on the lower levels of existence. If the meaning and value of social life is rooted in love, it also follows that justice should be understood as the expression (legal or other) of the respect for the freedom, rights, and responsibilities of the human person. No one would call anyone "just" unless he measures up to the psycho-ontological perfections, belonging to the mode of subjective and intersubjective mode of participating in "esse" (*bonus amor et recta voluntas*). Finally, this should now facilitate the relating of the meaning and value of human love and justice to the transcendental form of love and justice, coming from the Absolute Being, known as the Absolute Self in Whom the relative self of man communicates in the spirit of *"caritas"* and *"agape."* Thus love on the natural and supernatural levels appears to be integrated if interpreted with Spinoza as *"amor Dei intellectualis"*—the intellectual love of God as the Absolute Self. For God is love (*Deus est caritas*) and the source of human redemption and happiness.

The lesser problems of more practical nature, such as the meaning of sex, procreation, and marriage, as well as the place of the socio-political values in the whole hierarchy of values should come easier for their correct interpretation and assessment. The limitations of the present study do not permit us their detailed presentation in this context.

## CHAPTER VI

## VALUES, CIVILIZATION AND CULTURE

Human concepts or ideas, despite their abstract and universal character, embrace a large variety of intelligible notes. All conceptual characteristics are commonly designated as the contents or the comprehension of the idea, as expressing the meaning man derives from the objects of his cognitive experiences. Adequate knowledge presupposes a rational and intuitive awareness of this conceptual richness, abstracted from the materials grasped by man's sensory equipment. Because of the well-known discrepancy between intellection (*intus legere*) and the available forms of linguistic expressions, one often experiences the failure in attempting a more or less complete expression of one's ideas (*l' angoisse littéraire.*) Therefore, we understand and know much more than we are able to communicate.

Communication is the relation of intersubjectivity resting on the objective part of human knowledge, that is, on the world of reality, conceived as the totality of changing and emerging phenomena. Each phenomenon, however, represents a unique individuality (*indivisum in se et divisum a quolibet alio* — undivided in itself and divided from anything else). The inexhaustible singularity and uniqueness of the extant phenomenon may justify, therefore, the flight of many thinkers into the realms of rejective subjectivism, relativism, agnosticism, criticism, skepticism, philosophical idealism, or anti-intellectual attitudes. The underlying causes of these and similar states of mind are rooted in the abyss between the overwhelming profusion and complexity of the concrete, singular, and dynamic materials of sense experience on one hand, and the scarcity of our linguistic symbols on the other. By creating new words, expressions, and terms —

thus enriching our terminology and improving the expressive power of our vocabulary—we try to secure for ourselves a more reliable means for the symbolic identification and communication of our immediate experiences, both material and immaterial.

No wonder, then, that we often find ourselves face to face with a great deal of confusion concerning the right use and interpretation of the meaning, immanent in our concepts, as it happens, for example, with the many antagonistic explanations of one of the most complex and synthetic ideas, associated with the general term of *"culture."* Such confusion and subsequent disagreement are due either to unsubstantiated generalizations of particular aspects, taken for the whole and thereafter developed to the farthest extremes, or to specific assumptions, standpoints, and principles *a priori,* underlying the whole discussion and its methodical implications. The extreme forms of conceptual disagreement are much more likely to occur whenever the term stands for a reality which transcends the boundaries of the physical reality and points to man's free, symbolic interpretations given by him to whatever he considers worthwhile. This is the case whenever people are called upon to specify the meaning, significance, and denotations of the unfortunately vague concept of human culture. The first reactions consist, of course, in associating the term culture with something of a superior value. On the other hand, when it comes to identifying the values and their hierarchic disposition in the organic structure of cultured life, all hopes for agreement seem to vanish. It seems that there is only one way to overcome such logical and irrational pitfalls, that is, by presenting a systematic account of all primary and secondary aspects and qualities which are ineradicably tied up with the thorough meaning of the concept of culture under analysis.

Let us first take into consideration the historical and etymological sense of the term culture in order to create a basis for further investigations.

The word "culture"—from the Latin *colere* = to cultivate—

originally denoted the training, formation, and development of the human dispositions and capacities beyond the mere natural condition. Consequently, the natural state of man (*conditio naturalis*) is compared unfavorably with the condition of cultured existence as being inferior and demanding, therefore, the necessary progress and development out of and beyond the primitive level of natural existence. The synonymous expressions used in antiquity and in the middle ages for the conceptual identification of culture were *"humanitas"* or *"civilitas,"* thus emphasizing the emancipated condition of an educated individual or group of individuals. Any person who was not on the level of cultured existence, was rejected as a mere "barbarian." Furthermore, the term culture, followed by some qualification — the culture of the spirit, the culture of the memory, etc. — has been used since the sixteenth century. But the independent use of the noun originates in the eighteenth century, precisely in the interpretation given to it by *de Fortia* in 1797. "The word culture designates, as one can see, is this thought and the following one, the state of a spirit (soul) cultivated through instruction."

The general idea of culture, interpreted in its historical perspective, rests on the basic principle of personal development; the spirit (the soul, the Self, the Ego) achieves the superior state of cultural life through the process of learning, instruction or education. This conception is, therefore, limited to the subjective, individual, personal aspects only; it is the individual human being, his innate dispositions and tendencies which constitute the object — both material and formal — of the whole process of growth and accretion. The instruction is the means or the instrument needed for the actualization of subjective potentialities. The starting point would be the nature of man which undergoes the formative power of training and learning in order to unfold its hidden capabilities.

The final stage of this evolutionary line of action should be the state of the spirit characterized by the actual posession of the qualities, skills, and values which belong to the structural make-up of a mature personality. The opposition between the mere state of a potential nature on the one side, and the ultimate expression of personal maturity on the other, is meant to emphasize the developmental and dynamic condition of human existence as a constantly emerging phenomenon. Obviously, this elucidation is closely allied to an indirect pedagogical standpoint: the problem of culture is intrinsically concerned with the norms of education and self-education. This explanation, however, fails to take into account the very important trans-subjective, that is, the socio-political and economic aspects and implications of culture.

The meaning of culture assumes markedly new aspects in the interpretation given it by the philosophical trends of the seventeenth and eighteenth centuries, historically known as the philosophy of enlightenment (*Aufklärung*). Rejecting the traditional metaphysical framework of the ancient and medieval philosophies, including their moral, spiritual, and religious implications, the natural human reason is accepted as the only legitimate source of any positive or critically valid knowledge. The gradual emancipation of reason passes through a variety of thought patterns, such as the empiricism of *Locke* and *Hume* in England, the rationalism of *Descartes* in France, the extreme criticism and philosophical idealism of *Kant, Fichte, Schelling, Hegel, Leibniz, Wolff, Lessing,* etc. in Germany, the deistic moral philosophy of *Hobbes, Shaftesbury* and *Bentham,* the ethical pantheism of *Spinoza* in Holland, and, finally, the radicalism and materialism of *Voltaire, Holbach,* and others.

The radical change in the interpretation of culture — its conditions, foundations, nature, meaning, and value — can best be seen in the schools of sensism, empiricism, naturalism, and positivism. According to the epistemological principles relative to the nature of human knowledge, the psycho-educational and spiritual factors of culture had to be gradually de-emphasized and finally doomed, in order to establish a new, extroverted, objective, and naturalistic attitude. Due to the progress achieved in the fields of the natural sciences, more and more emphasis was placed on the external, visible, and empirical outcomes of man's physical and cognitive efforts. The audacious, self-reliant, and critical standpoint introduces the ideal of progress so generously accepted and developed thereafter by the new technical results of modern science and technology in the nineteenth and twentieth centuries.

The primary preoccupation becomes the conquest of the material energies of nature, even at the cost of sacrificing man's essential attributes as free, autonomous, and moral subject. Because of the serious moral, social, and religious consequences of the modern interpretation given to the meaning of man's cultural life, it seems to be necessary to undertake the analysis of the objective side of culture and civilization.

The main characteristic of the objective approach to the study of culture is the strict empirical and scientific method directed exclusively toward the outer, external, and trans-subjective results of human activities and achievements. It is man's rational, creative, and progressive nature in general, presented in the light of his historical, socio-economic, and geographical setting, rather than the value of the individual human being, which is presented as the cause, factor, and agent responsible for cultural progress. Also, the specific goal of this supra-individual point of view must coincide with the methods, purposes, and results achieved by the highly estimated, positive, natural and exact sciences. New science must be created, therefore, within the very conservative tradition of the exact sciences whose material and formal objects are found in man's collective and historical achievements in the struggle with the powers of nature. This new science receives the name of *"Kulturwissenschaften,"* that is, the science of culture or cultural anthropology from the positivistic point of view. (As such it should not be identified with "philosophic anthropology").

Owing to the complexity of the vast materials to be analyzed and systematized, the general field of cultural sciences had to be differentiated into many divisions and subdivisions, such as: history of culture and civilization; morphology of culture; physiology of culture, and finally, philosophy of culture kept within the limitations of a rationalistic and positivistic outlook on man's place, role, and activity in nature. It would take us too long and too far as well — necessarily exceeding the limitations of our discussion kept within the scope of basic principles only — if we were to attempt a more or less adequate account of the whole problem complex presented with the particular realms of cultural investigation. However, a synthetic illustration of these problems, viewed from the standpoint of axiology, will not fail our purpose.

The essential questions implied here deal with: culture and nature; culture and environmental (geographical, historical, and bio-social) setting; cultural dynamics, such as development, progress, cultural exchange or contact, saturation, and finally, disintegration of culture (*L. Frobenius, O. Spengler*); mutual interrelations between different cultural standards, conditioned by particular determinants, such as the proper philosophical, moral, and religious conceptions; economic factors underlying the superstructures of cultural life (*Feuerbach, Marx, Engels,* and their Russian interpreters).

Considering the objective manifestations of human culture as recorded in history and transmitted from generation to generation, we shall encounter some basic phenomena that stand for the typical structural articulation of any culture as such. If we start with the material or economic aspects, the totality of practical inventions, discoveries, and values will respond to the needs and motives intrinsic in the bio-physical nature of man. Thus we have material tools, instruments, products, artifices, machines, buildings, means of communication and transportation, etc., all of which secure material subsistence and welfare. The quality and quantity of such material values — the securities of "homo faber" according to H. Bergson — stand in direct proportion to the developmental degree of creative knowledge, crystallized in the clear-cut systems of exact and applied sciences (technology) as part of our civilization.

Closely allied to the economic functions of culture, essentially subordinated to the material needs of sustenance and correlative equipment, are the exclusively human motives, conditioned by man's rational, conscious, and social attributes. Consequently, every cultural organism must possess the functions which are consistent with the immanent tendencies and necessities of man's psycho-social and spiritual needs. Among these functional aspects we include language as a *conditio sine qua non* for the possibility of any social intercourse and communication, and then its objectifications, manifested by the collective institutions, traditions, mores, etc., commonly designated as coordinated social conduct, law, government, state, education, science, arts, morality, and religion.

One must not assume, however, that the entirety of these objectivities and motivating factors might express the ultimate nature of any culture. They function merely as external expressions, outer indications of internal determinants (ideas, images, feelings, beliefs, estimations, norms, and value judgments), which are inextricably tied up with them as *a priori* conditions of their possibilities. Every standpoint which falls short of considering these invisible, subjective and psycho-social qualities of culture must be rejected as arbitrary and inadequate. This is the cardinal reason why there cannot possibly be cultural understanding within the rigid groundwork of positivism or behaviorism. Their methodological postulates preclude the apprehension of the immaterial and spiritual. Positive knowledge in and by itself fails to exhaust the whole content of cultural richness: "Le savoir est la condition nécessaire de la culture, il n'en est pas la condition suffisante. . . . C'est surtout à la qualité de l'esprit que l'on songe quand on prononce le mot culture, à la qualité du jugement et du sentiment." (*D. Ronstan,* La Culture au Cours de la Vie, p. 15).

If the purely pragmatic interpretation of culture must be given up, as we have already insisted, there then arises the responsibility and necessity to present not only a new standpoint, but a better one in the sense of being suited to the demands of a thorough understanding of the many distinct aspects of culture. Such a viewpoint must provide a synthetic view of the whole, without being superficial. It must, therefore, reduce the external facts to the respective causes, thus instituting an inquiry into the essence, intimate nature and substance which support the complexity of cultural phenomena. Moreover, such a methodical ideal shall be taken up also with the conditions, aims, directions, and ultimate norms of the whole cultural process, in order to critically establish its intrinsic moral and metaphysical normativity.

Undoubtedly, it is only the philosophy of culture or philosophic anthropology which can measure up to such universal and profound goals. It seems reasonable to us to call this *"forma mentis"* the axiological interpretation of culture.

The methodical supposition of the axiological attitude consists in the assumption, based on the principle of mutual dependence and causality, that the ego-structure (the subjective make-up of personality) is similar to the objective counterpart of cultural realizations. In other words, there is a structural correspondence between the two basic poles of cultural synthesis: the basic frame-work of the spirit in the individual psychic life — understood as the culture creating subjective spirit — on the one hand, and the basic articulation of different cultural domains (the objective spirit embodied in any culture) on the other. Besides the subjective and the objective spirits, one must also include the principle of normativity, regularity, necessity, and universality (the normative spirit), pervading both the subjective and objective aspects of culture, by which means the possibility of cultural and historical understanding is granted. The specific structure of normativity is given according to the basic scale of values, immanent both in the human personality and culture as well, since the essence of values involves a relation to an "ought to" or "should" as the ideal directives of cultural activities. Placed in such a perspective, the problem of culture and its understanding can be solved, if we take the analysis of the personality structure as our starting point, moving further on to the explanation of the subjective structure of culture, in the light of the norms dictated by the basic categories of values.

As we have pointed out on several occasions in the previous chapters, human nature should be considered as a substantial mind-body unity without stressing this bipartite division too much into the rational and the animal. Furthermore, taking into consideration the dynamics of human nature as manifested by its wide scale of activities, we shall find that they are essentially determined by its peculiar existential condition, that is, the situation of a necessitous, indigent being. In other words, self-sufficiency can be only an ideal, a never-to-be-realized goal of a nature which in and by itself offers nothing more than potentialities waiting for actualization or development. The active extraversion of man has to be regarded, therefore, as his basic and normal attitude toward life. To illustrate this matter it suffices to recall the physical and psychic dispositions, tendencies, and faculties that constitute the articulation of the human organism. Besides the physical and organic needs — whose instinctual orientation toward corresponding objects and goods is more than obvious — even our psychic equipment (the intellect, emotionality, and the will, as well as other secondary functions) must be activated through external stimuli as corresponding objects, qualities, and values.

We can arrive at the same conclusion if we study the peculiar elements or ingredients of any action: on the subjective side we shall find an innate, dynamic tendency (needs, desires, interests or wants, both conscious and unconscious) with a definite direction toward the material object, along with a specific interest in the achievement of the value (the formal object) which is perceived as the motivating factor, represented by the outer object. Stated concisely, this means that the insufficient human nature must constantly be supplied with correlated goods in order to maintain and develop its existence. Any single human attitude is finalistic, related to and determined by some value category. Thus we come across the fundamental relation between the natural human value — proneness on the one hand, and its objective counterpart, that is, culture and civilization on the other. In the terminology of cultural anthropologists, the dimensions of man's value experiences coincide with the dimensions of his horizons and profiles of existence.

It has been our explicit purpose, throughout this chapter, to present the axiological standpoint as the most comprehensive approach to the study of civilization and culture. The predominant theme consists, therefore, in the idea of the organic unity and structure (*Gestalt*) of human culture which we consider the condition for the understanding of the meaning instrinsic to man's cultural endeavors and achievements.

> "Any great culture," says Sorokin, "instead of being a mere dumping place of a multitude of diverse cultural phenomena, existing side by side and unrelated to one another, represents a unity or individuality whose parts are permeated by the same fundamental principle and articulate the same basic value. The dominant part of the fine arts and science of such a unified culture, of its philosophy and religion, of its ethics and law, of its main forms of social, economic, and political organization of most of its mores and manners, of its ways of life and mentality, all articulate, each in its own way, this basic principle and value. This value serves as its major premise and foundation. For this reason the important parts of such an integrated culture are also interdependent causally: if one important part changes, the rest of its important parts are bound to be similarly transformed." (*P. Sorokin,* in "The Crisis of Our Age," p. 17).

Allowing, however, for the skeptical attitude of the professional dissenters who embody the spirit of contradiction, we shall now undertake the outline of a philosophy of culture from the same axiological point of view. It is our hope to expose thereby also the fundamental principles of a possible integration between philosophic anthropology, cultural anthropology, and psychology, brought together on the common meeting-ground of general axiology.

In order to prevent misunderstanding, it is best to identify, first, the meaning of the philosophy of culture. From a negative standpoint, philosophy of culture — as part of general axiology or value ontology — should not be equated with the history of human civilization and culture for the simple reason that the latter is limited, both in its scope and formal method, to the mere descriptive or phenomenological presentation of man's cultural progress within the categories of space and time. On the other hand, it is of the inner nature of any philosophy to move from the phenomenal sphere to the noumenal regions of the invisible causal reality. The move from the factual (*le tout fait*) to the theoretical and abstract expresses the first condition for the possibility of any scientific or philosophic integration and understanding. In other words, it is the priority of the ideal which gives meaning and validity to the factual or phenomenal materials present in our experiences.

It should appear, therefore, that the task of a philosophy of culture consists in: 1. to reduce the variety of cultural phenomena to a few constants with the help of a comparative study in their qualitative differences and similiarities; 2. to go beyond the phenomenal regions of culture and into their inner essence and nature by laying bare the conditions and causes responsible for their manifestations; 3. to provide the criteria for understanding the meaning of all cultural life, insofar as it contemplates its varied forms in the perspective of their general and specific purpose, direction, and structures.

This program, of course, can be actualized only within the ideological, conceptual, and methodical framework of axiology or philosophy of value. We saw, however, that axiology does not and cannot fulfill the demands of such an impressive scope without relying on the other fields of universal philosophy from which it will borrow some of the needed principles, insights, and conclusions. Since culture is eminently and exclusively a human achievement, aimed at the eternal goals of ideal humanism, the philosopher of human culture should start with certain truths concerning the nature of the human person. Consequently, philosophy of culture depends on:

1. Philosophic anthropology or philosophy of human nature which tells us what man is;
2. Ethics or moral philosophy which goes beyond what man

is and points to the ideal form of life for which man ought to strive in order to fulfill his psycho-ontological destiny;

3. Natural theology or theodicy, insofar as it is the part of universal philosophy which provides the answer for man's origin and destiny;
4. Metaphysics, since nothing permanent and binding can be taught in the preceding fields of human knowledge unless they are founded upon and supported by the first principles of reality (being) and knowledge (truth).

All the secondary problems which refer to the conditions, opportunities, and instrumentalities needed for the emergence and development of cultural life, should be treated by the "science of human culture" (*Kulturwissenschaft*) from a descriptive and phenomenological point of view only. The philosophy of culture, however, depends on the history of human civilization for the materials to be critically analyzed and assessed according to their universal meaning and validity. Moreover, it is cultural morphology, anatomy, and physiology which circumscribe the regions and the dimensions of cultural activities. We learn from them, for instance, that the two permanent poles, within which the dynamics of culture develops, progresses, and eventually dies, are man and nature. In other words, culture and civilization can be understood only if viewed as a dialectical process between man and his natural *habitat,* the world. It is true, on the other hand, that it is man's definite desire to go beyond the original, rather primitive condition of natural states. As a matter of fact, all progress in civilization bears witness to man's success in bringing the powers of nature (matter, energy, time, and space) under control, thus providing himself with the securities needed for his survival and well-being.

In this sense it is correct to say that both the origin and the goal of culture lies in nature, meaning, this time, man's nature in the first place and his physical environment (the world) in the second. While it is also true that is is man's desire to "transcend the conditions of an earthbound existence," still he finds the necessary motivation for this move mainly in his latent capacities, desires, and needs belonging to his nature. The same should be said also when we restrict the meaning of culture to the more specific goal of "personal formation" (*Bildung*); in a very strict sense, man develops himself and tries to subjugate the physical environment only insofar as he wants to be a "better" human nature, living in a "better" world. Thus both human and objective natures are not left behind, only improved.

There is a definite danger in emphasizing the progressive aspect of civilization and culture, superseding the "natural" state of existence. For example, whenever the "artificial" replaces the "natural or original" or the "metaphysical" oppresses and kills the "physical," a definite harm is inflicted upon man's essence, understood as a "mind-body unity." History gives us many illustrations as to what may happen to men, should this schizoid separation occur either within man or in the attitude he develops toward the world. For one example, even the Church condemned as heretical all the doctrines which demanded man's complete rejection and mortification of his physical organism, looked at it as necessarily " evil," "sinful," and "devilish."

On the other hand, nowadays we can see in full blossom what had to occur after man had been removed, closed off from the outside nature and shut into the "artificial" world created by modern science and technology. Perhaps this was the reason why a Rousseau protested against the anti-natural condition of civilized society. He could see the condition of existential displacement of persons living in a world God has not created. And there are today many psychologists and psychiatrists who recant the same nostalgic notes for a "lost world" in which man enjoyed better physical and mental health. In our opinion, the true cause lies in the diseased state of modern civilization which does not take into consideration man's need for his natural milieu, no matter how sophisticated or pleasure-packed his life is or otherwise can be. To some lesser extent the "existentialist revolt" and the protest of the "beat generation" are clamoring for the same return to the lap of mother nature; they interpret the scientifically organized and controlled mass way of life as a real threat to the original meaning and value to the original form of existence. Even though one might not subscribe to the whole of their protests, there is still some room left for understanding and sympathy. Finally, from a pedagogical point of view, it was *J. Dewey* who fought for the "humanization" of science in order to create a humanized world for true human beings who know the balance between the physical and moral values in their lives. It seems, therefore, that the solution for these problems may come from the integration of the two natures — the nature of man and of his environment — into a higher harmony of cultured existence or in the fortunate term of *J. Maritain* — of an "integral humanism."

It should now appear sufficiently clear that this desirable state of harmony can be achieved only through the wisdom derived from the meaning of human values, both personal and collective. There can be no integration within the human person or outside of him — in the world — unless the ideal hierarchy of values is used as a criterion while allowing the measure, importance, place or prominence, and the symbolic significance to be assessed for each value category. There should be, therefore, a relation of mutual correspondence between the levels of personal integration — presented in the preceding chapter — and the trends followed by its visible projections into the objective field of culture and civilization. We may go even further and suggest that the value, meaning, and historical impact of a culture depend directly on the success or failure of man in trying to identify, integrate himself, and assess the ultimate meaning of life. Consequently, the problems intrinsic to man's cultural life are essentially philosophic.

Man derives the meaning for his life from the values he believes in, for it is the specific value structure within him which directs the "form of life" he develops. Should he lose his faith in his values, or else, disturb their ideal validity, manifest in the order of their intrinsic qualitative impact, man might as well die, for spiritually or culturally he has been dead for a long while without realizing it.

As an illustration of the inner and outer crises resulting from the "devaluation of human values" we can refer to the present condition of personal, social, national, and international symptoms of conflict, disharmony, and the threat of total destruction of life. Since we dedicated our first chapter to the "crisis of values," we need not enter into repetitious commentaries on what has already been presented. Nonetheless, one more remark should be made: at the root of the present condition of cultural bankruptcy stands the split between the material and the spiritual dimensions of human existence. Just as man can be himself only as an integrated "psycho-somatic" unity, similarly, all the symptoms of crisis must appear also on all cultural levels of life whenever the values belonging to the totality of integrated life are split up. Because of the divorce between the super-natural and the natural orders, between theology and philosophy, between philosophy and science, between science and the moral, political, and social dimensions of life, one may speak today of the almost exclusive predominance of civilization at the expense of true culture.

Since the above terms are frequently taken and used as synonyms, it is advisable to describe them and draw the necessary lines of demarcation between them.

*Civilization* is the totality of those values which stand for man's bio-physical and psychic powers directed at the control of matter, energy, space, and time in order to secure increasing material well-being in the form of scientific and technical progress.

*Culture* is the totality of the religious, moral, theoretical, aesthetic, social, and political values which correspond to the psycho-spiritual needs and aspirations of man's nature, involved in the realization of personal and collective ideals, needed for the fulfillment of his ontological destiny.

The above descriptions do not intend to install any extreme dualism or necessary conflict between civilization and culture. They emphasize exclusively the different subjective and objective structures of both phenomena, suggesting, at the same time, the primacy and superiority of culture over civilization. These distinctions could be used as criteria for an historical and critical diagnosis of cultural syndromes, atrophies, and hypertrophies. The reason for this opposition may be found also in the antagonistic polarities of the different value categories, due to their different meaning and quality.

Undoubtedly, it is not easy to find a lasting harmony between the conflicting value tendencies both within man and in his world. Nevertheless, we insist that civilization and culture do not necessarily go hand in hand, unless they are integrated in a dependable and compelling hierarchy of the values they should represent. If we apply this distinction to both man as an individual and to society, we may also assert that a man may be only civilized without being cultured; vice-versa also, a man may possess a very high degree of personal integration and formation without making use or even being aware of the wonders of modern technology. The person who is only civilized can be regarded as an individual spending his lifetime and his cash to satisfy his lust for pleasure and enjoyment. (In fact he is closer to a mechanized barbarian than to a respectable person!) On the other hand, the person who is more cultured than civilized is much better off in the sense that — though he may be guilty of not having conquered matter, energy, time, and space — still he has a deeper meaning and validity to his existence, derived from the culture of his self, being saturated with the values of religion, morality, philosophy, and art.

As long as the subjectivistic and relativistic interpretations of values are defended for the pragmatic purpose of justifying the killing of culture by man's exclusive extraversion to the sensate pleasures of life, there is no hope — immediate or distant — for a rehabilitation, revalidation or resurrection of true humanity and humanism. As we pointed out above, it is the business of the philosophy of culture — enlightened and guided by universal philosophy — to provide the criteria for the final assessment of human values to be integrated in man's cultural life. This task, however, cannot be accomplished unless the issues under discussion are resolved from an ethical point of view.

Right from the beginning of our study we made formal reference to the ethical character of values to the extent that their intrinsic perfection establishes a relationship of obligation or commitment for man. Since the ethico-religious values will be presented in the chapter on the Absolute, it may suffice right now to point out only the fact that it takes much more than simple interest, desire, motivation, knowledge, etc., to guarantee the actual impact of values on human existence. We mentioned above the element of faith; we might as well add to it the experience of respect, awe, and reverence, required for the understanding and appreciation of the higher values of existence. All egalitarian wholesale dealers in values, however, do not know or, perhaps, even do not want to know anything about something "better = higher" or "worse = lower," thus being responsible for the state of chaos and anarchy which can be ruled only by power politics or a collective hypocrisy, used as a temporary device to keep everybody satisfied under the self-deceptive illusion of a true value democracy.

The philosophy of culture, inspired and supported by axiology, considers the presentation of at least the fundamental dimensions of culture with a view toward the goal of its structural and ethical integration as part of its duty. The diagram presented below offers such a preliminary attempt at integration between the three regions of reality: man, values, and culture (civilization included).

Since the problem of personal integration was already presented, here we give only the ascending scale of man's basic psychic functions which are present in his value experiences and cultural activities. The totality of this psycho-somatic organism is identified as (1) the subjective sub-structure, underlying the objective spirit of culture (2), and the normative hierarchy of values as well (3). This schematic design could also be received as the guiding system for the diagnosis and prognosis of the many forms of human culture known to us from history. It is, therefore, the key to cultural understanding.

The schematic outline of the three fundamental aspects of

civilization and culture does not offer any specific criteria for the understanding of the differentiated forms of cultural life. It is well understood that human culture is rather heterogeneous than homogeneous in its forms of manifestation, depending on many extraneous elements — geography, climate, natural resources, the prevalent form of occupation, ethnico-racial characteristics — which lend a rather individualized form of a typical, almost exclusive organization to life. We feel, however, that it is the business of the science of anthropology and comparative ethnology to concern themselves with these specific problems and interpret their meaning in the light of their original significance. Nevertheless, the general value categories will still be present in all individualized forms of cultural life and they can be used for the interpretation thereof.

Due to the significance of understanding culture, insofar as it belongs to the purpose of the philosophy of culture, it must be emphasized that it rests on certain specific requirements. In the first place, the knowledge about man's psycho-somatic nature and functioning is the prerequisite for understanding his values which make up the meaning of his economic, socio-political, artistic, moral, and religious progress. In this sense philosophic anthropology or psychology must precede the philosophy of culture. It should now appear more clearly than before, why the mere factual and descriptive account of man's cultural achievements has to fall short of man's legitimate desire to understand it by developing an insight into its meaningful relationships.

Thus it is impossible to understand the meaning of science, the scientist, and his values without possessing at least some knowledge of man's innate curiosity, the nature of knowledge (sensate and intellectual), and its contribution to the wholeness of cultural life. Similarly, philosophy understood as the quest for ultimate meaning, will become meaningful only on the condition that the experience of "wonder" becomes part of the person's life experiences in the process of understanding. Perhaps the objectised facts of society, economics, and politics may appear easier to understand for belonging to everybody's daily experience and

**Schematic Illustration of (1) the Subjective, (2) Trans-Subjective or Objective, and (3) Normative Structure of Civilization and Culture**

Morality and Religion
Philosophy and Science
Aesthetics: the World of arts
Society: Human Relations
Politics: State, Government, Law
Economics: Material Securities

God - The Absolute
Truth - Insight
Beauty
Love: Community Communication
Will to organized power and security
The Useful

Man's bio-physical needs and instincts Vegetation
Imagery Sense Perception
Imagination Learning Associative Processes
Desires, interests Emotions
Preferences Feelings
Value Symbolism Reasoning, Intuition Idization Judgment
Self Appropriation Action Self determination

practical concerns. On the other hand, the understanding of the "science" and of the "meaning" of the above segments of human civilization requires the same intellectual qualifications as suggested above. By the same token, man may experience the beauty of nature in a spontaneous, natural form; but it takes much more than simple looking, should someone try to understand the hidden meaning behind the "desire for a free and symbolic interpretation of life." Finally, there is an immediate awareness of morality and religion due to the process of early conditioning and learning. It should be understood, however, that this does not exhaust the noumenal significance of religion and self-imposed morality. Let us repeat, therefore, once more, that understanding presupposes meaning which can be disclosed or revealed only by the philosophic interpretation of values themselves to the extent that they became part of man's personal experiences.

> "Undoubtedly human culture," says E. Cassirer, "is divided into various activities proceeding along different lines and pursuing different ends. It we content ourselves with contemplating the results of these activities — the creations of myth, religious rites or creeds, works of art, scientific theories — it seems impossible to reduce them to a common denominator. But a philosophic synthesis means something different. Here we seek not a unity of effects but a unity of action; not a unity of products but a unity of the *creative process.* If the term 'humanity' means anything at all, it means that, in spite of all the differences and oppositions existing among its various forms, these are, nevertheless, all working toward a common end. In the long run there must be found an outstanding feature, a universal character, in which they all agree and harmonize. If we can determine this character the divergent rays may be assembled and brought into a focus of thought.... Philosophy cannot, on the other hand, stop here. It must seek to achieve an even greater condensation and centralization. In the boundless multiplicity and variety of mythical images, of religious dogmas, of linguistic forms, of works of art, philosophic thought reveals the unity of a general function by which all these creations are held together. Myth, religion, art, language, even science, are now looked upon as so many variations on a common theme — and it is the task of philosophy to make this task audible and understandable." (*E. Cassirer,* in "An Essay on Man," p. 96, Doubleday, 1944).

The different fields of culture and civilization, such as presented in our schematic outline, should be regarded as integral parts of the whole organic structure of the world created by man through his imagination, intuitive reflection, and action. The degree of their prominence and weight should be assessed according to their intrinsic meaning and the impact they have left on the global meaning of existence. It should be kept in mind, however, that this difficult task of cultural assessment cannot be had by any quantitative or statistical procedure. For one thing, history testifies to the fact that the majority of people of all generations are only the beneficiaries of culture, while the number of benefactors is limited to a few outstanding geniuses. This remark should be taken as defending the qualitative differences not only among values as such but also among people at large. Culture is not the achievement of the masses, and it cannot be mass-produced either. While it is true, that no single individual can produce the wealth of human culture, it is also true that there has always been in every generation, a handful of outstanding minds who make up the cultural *élite* or the intellectual aristocracy of all times. An indirect proof for this restrictive appeal — besides the reference already made to the testimony of history — can be seen in the "popularization" rather than "massification" of cultural values by the media of collective communication, resulting in the "degradation" of the original values, reduced to a common standard of mediocrity in order to fit everybody's frame of mind. This situation bears out the truth about quantity and quality being inversely proportional.

Finally, a word should be said on the decline and death of cultures as attested to by universal history. Besides the physical, material, and economic factors, it is mainly the ethical aspect which answers our question. As Ed. Spranger expresses it quite forcibly: "The disappearance of the experience of moral commitment and responsibility implies the extinction of the culture." What this ethical commitment should mean, will be answered in the following chapter.

## CHAPTER VII

## THE ABSOLUTE: THE MORAL-RELIGIOUS VALUE

The analysis of the moral-religious value is necessarily directed at man's desire to assess "the value of morality and religion." But whenever the question about the value of anything is moved, it is the significant "quest for meaning" which underlies man's inquisitive curiosity. In this sense we should actually speak of "the meaning of the moral and religious value."

The quest for meaning is not the exclusive concern of the philosophers. In fact, due to man's rational and self-conscious nature, the desire to understand is a universal human disposition and the root of all philosophy as well. Man's innate curiosity may be directed at the three different regions of reality, that is, the objective order of things (the world), the subjective order of the human self (the person), and the metaphysical and transcendental order of the universal and absolute Being. Consequently, man's philosophic reflection embraces the many, the self, and the One, as the three fundamental fields of the act of philosophizing.

Because of man's bio-physical and earthbound condition, it is natural that — both chronologically and developmentally — man's attention is first extroverted, that is, concerned with his physical environment, called nature, the world, and, finally, the universe. The cosmological stage is then replaced by the psychological one, insofar as man now directs his curiosity toward his own reality (introversion), being moved by the desire to know and understand his own self, the inwardness of his existence. Finally, the conjugation of the objective and the subjective points of view may lead to a metaphysical, transcendental or supra-natural concern in order to discover a superior insight and wisdom which make the previous stages appear more meaningful than ever before.

Since man cannot abstract from his own self, it is quite natural that he occupy the central position between the other two poles of reality, the world and the invisible reality behind it. However, the above classification of universal reality into three distinct regions is rather academic and, to that extent, also artificial in the sense that it does not hold true in the global act of philosophizing which necessarily includes — besides man's whole soul, in the saying of Plato — man's fundamental relation to his world and, at least implicitly, to its ultimate reason as well. The fragmentation of the whole of reality into particular segments is due, therefore, to the imperfection of man's discoursive reason which can proceed but from particular insights to the problem of the ultimate meaning of the whole.

The methodical partition of reality into objective, subjective, and transcendental regions must be used also with regard to our present concern with the value and meaning of morality and religion, both considered from the natural point of view only. In fact, ethics and religion can be viewed objectively when considering the external, visible manifestations (historical, individual, and collective) in the many forms of natural and positive systems of religion and mores. The study of the objective spirit of morality and religion is, however, the proper object of cultural anthropology, ethnology, sociology, and history, as descriptive sciences, presenting their rich material for further clarification for the philosopher. The subjective approach is the standpoint of those psychologists who concern themselves with the visible forms of moral and religious behavior and the underlying invisible patterns of thinking, feeling, and acting which identify the proper character of man's ethico-religious attitudes (psychology of religion). The materials accumulated by the methods of psychological inquiry must again be evaluated from the philosophic point of view (philosophy of religion), which should answer the questions relative to the foundations, inner essence or nature, and the ultimate meaning or value of religion and morality. Obviously, the explicit interest in this set of questions identifies our present point of view, which naturally presupposes the descriptive or phenomenological standpoints too.

Since the philosophy of religion, taken in its traditional sense, used to be named "natural theology" or "theodicy" — discussing the problems of God's existence, nature, attributes and His relation to the created world or creatures, especially man — we must make it clear that it is not our intention here to present the sketch of another variation on the same old theme of either theodicy or moral philosophy. While recognizing their validity and significance, we restrict ourselves to the axiological point of view, according to which we shall discuss religion and morality as the first and supreme value, belonging to man's ideal hierarchy of values. On the other hand, however, this restricted point of view presupposes the wealth of knowledge proper to both natural theology and ethics. In this sense our approach may be called psycho-ontological insofar as it is derived from philosophic anthropology and value ontology. Finally, the problem of the ultimate foundation of all human values in the Absolute and its qualitative significance has already been alluded to in chapters I and II, respectively. Those who do not share our conviction on God's existence and man's spirituality, will have to find the following considerations devoid of real foundation and validity. Nevertheless, since even the professed atheists or old-fashioned materialists are, in a way, convinced believers in their unproven positions, they might profit from studying this chapter dedicated to the universal phenomenon and reality of religion and morality.

Man is the only being known to us directly as rational, self-conscious, and free. He is a person. He finds himself as given to himself, living as a stranger in a strange world. Unlike other living beings, man is not predetermined by the necessity of instinctual reflex reactions to lead a pre-established form of life. The meaning of his life is not printed on his birth certificate. Even though he is being told very early in life by his fellow man many things about himself and his life, still it is up to him to accept or to reject this formal or informal indoctrination. He will accept it only on the condition that it "makes sense," that is, it has a meaning for him; otherwise it will be rejected as nonsensical or meaningless. Furthermore, the pre-established program man finds in his socio-cultural environment — positive religion and morality — may not appeal to him because of its rather impersonal, universal, general, and maybe even antiquated or conservative character, without expressing the problems of his unique and singular mode of being as an original individual. Consequently, the individual still must face the challenge of giving a meaning (*Sinngebung*) to himself as an existent in the world.

Man goes about this existential task by making use of his innate, and, possibly, trained intelligence. In the very intricate processes of sensing, feeling, and thinking, his constant interpretation is motivated by the desire to know, that is, to evaluate the impact of his experiences on him in terms of their intelligibility, significance, and contribution to his incessant desire for a meaningful (happy) life. Since he possesses only a general or unspecified desire for happiness (meaningful life), he is bound to go through a long series of illusions and disillusions, partial satisfactions, and partial frustrations. Very often he may question even the possibility of reaching a meaning which would offer a satisfactory justification for his life (*raison d'être*) with all the implicit activities he must carry on from day to day in a rather mechanized and repetitious form. Thus it appears that the quest for meaning is necessarily subordinated to the need for justification and the desire for a life worth living. Since man's value-directed condition was already described to some considerable extent in the first chapter of this study in values, we can limit the following presentation to the specific problem of the meaning to be attached to or derived from his ethico-religious attitudes.

It is well known from psychology that man's inner and outer behavior is motivated and goal-directed. Thus every act or attitude derives its meaning from its object (both material and formal), as well as from the specific purpose which may be either intrinsic to the act itself or not. There is a limited number of questions which can always be asked regarding the meaning of man's activities. Thus one may ask "what," "why," "how," "what for," "by what means" (*quis, quid, ubi, cur, quomodo, quando, quibus auxiliis*), in connection with any conation. These questions represent, therefore, the causal and the finalistic aspects — subjective and objective — of human endeavors. Should anyone fail to determine at least some partial aspects subsequent to these questions, the fundamental quest for meaning, knowing, understanding, insight, and value has to fall short of its objective.

The quest for meaning is restricted in axiology to man's fundamental value tendencies or to the basic dimensions of his value experiences. (The elementary psychic functions which make up the complete *"Gestalt"* of a meaningful act is here disregarded.) If we proceed now to examine the specific meaning of man's axiological attitudes, it appears that it is given with the specific value which constitutes its material and formal objects. Thus the meaning of man's theoretical concern is the appropriation of more knowledge, understanding, insight, or, in a word, the possession of truth. Similarly, the meaning of all aesthetic creation and contemplation is directly aimed at the possession of the beautiful. Love is the meaning and the justification for man's social behavior, just as the will to power — striving for superiority — is the motivating force underlying man's political attitudes. Finally, it is the value of the useful which identifies the meaning and the significance of man's economic interests.

If we compare the meanings proper to each value category with one another, the first noticeable thing will be the various degrees of mutual incompatibility, polarity or conflict among them. Consequently, the meaning of each value is limited in the sense that it discloses only a well-defined meaning of a particular act of valuing and finds thus its barrier at the point where the meaning of the other value begins. (Everyone must have experienced, for instance, not only the specific qualitative difference in the meaning of the aesthetic and economic values, but their mutual intolerance as well.)

Nonetheless, man is still interested in reaching a harmonious synthesis of partial meanings in order to derive the global meaning of the whole set of his values. This legitimate desire is the driving force behind the many attempts and, alas, failures to integrate the conflicting polarities of personal and cultural life. For man will never consider himself satisfied unless he can arrange the parts into a meaningful pattern (the whole) which is the imperative of any insight at all. The next step consists, therefore, in associating the particular meaning of values with the total meaning and value of human existence. No one will fail to notice at this point the new element present in this question whose formulation requires a standpoint which transcends all the particular interests, goals, meanings, and values that belong to man's day-to-day life. This new standpoint is truly philosophic and as such necessarily leads to the ultimate problems of metaphysics, religion, and morality. It is correct then to conclude that man's fundamental quest for meaning is a metaphysical act of philosophizing, necessitated by man's existential condition. To this extent man is metaphysically disposed and oriented whether or not he possesses an insight into the depths of his existence. Let us, therefore, specify the implications of this fundamental quest for meaning by formulating the questions pertinent to it.

1. What is the total and final or ultimate value of *my* existence?
2. What is the total and final or ultimate value of *human* existence?
3. What is my highest value for the world in which I live and its highest value for me?
4. What is the ultimate meaning and value of being as such?

Because these questions are aimed at the total and ultimate meaning of the wholeness of being, the answer cannot be derived from any particular segment of human life, no matter how meaningful or worthwhile it can otherwise be. Should someone overextend the restricted field of validity proper to any value category — save the moral and religious one — a unilateral interpretation and a tragical distortion of the meaning of existence would necessarily follow. History gives us some classical instances of cultural crisis and imbalance due to the abortive attempt to interpret the whole of human existence in terms of one or two value categories only. Thus the various forms of idealism or materialism — ancient, medieval, modern, and contemporary — could serve as convincing illustrations.

*C. G. Jung* in his book *The Undiscovered Self* (New American Library, 1959), offers a profound analysis and illustration for the condition of polarity existing between the political and the religious values:

> The State has taken the place of God; that is why, seen from this angle, the socialist dictatorships are religions and State slavery is a form of worship. But the religious function cannot be dislocated and falsified in this way without giving rise to secret doubts, which are immediately repressed so as to avoid conflict with the prevailing trend toward mass-mindedness. The result, as always in such cases, is overcompensation in the form of fanaticism, which in its turn is used as a weapon for stamping out the least flicker of opposition. Free opinion is stifled and moral decisions ruthlessly suppressed, on the plea that the end justifies the means, even the vilest. The policy of the state is exalted to a creed, the leader or party boss becomes a demigod beyond good and evil, and his votaries are honored as heroes, martyrs, apostles, and missionaries. There is only one truth and beside it no other. It is sacrosanct and above criticism. Anyone who thinks differently is a heretic, who, as we know from history, is threatened with all manner of unpleasant things. Only the party boss, who holds the political power in his hands, can interpret the State doctrine authentically, and he does so just as suits him. (p. 35) Furthermore, the State, like the Church, demands enthusiasm, self-sacrifice and love, and if religion requires or presupposes the 'fear of God,' then the dictator State takes good care to provide the necessary Terror. Even a dictator thinks it necessary not only to accompany his acts of State with threats but to stage them with all manners of solemnities. Brass band, flags, banners, parades, and monster demonstra-

tions are no different in principle from ecclesiastical processions, cannonades and fireworks. (p. 37) Words like 'society' and 'State' are so concretized that they are almost personified. In the opinion of the man in the street, the 'State,' far more than any king in history, is the inexhaustible giver of all goods; the 'State' is invoked, made responsible, grumbled at, and so on and so forth. Society is elevated to the rank of a supreme ethical principle; indeed, it is credited with positively creative capacities. (p. 88) Faith and belief in the State becomes credulity, and the word itself becomes an infernal slogan capable of any deception. With credulity come propaganda and advertising to dupe the citizen with political jobbery and compromise, and the lie reaches proportions never known before in the history of the world. (p. 88) Thus the constitutional State drifts into the situation of a primitive form of society, namely the communism of a primitive tribe where everybody is subject to the autocratic rule of a chief or an oligarchy. (p. 27)

Whenever any particular segment of life is made into the universal principle, used for the interpretation of the whole, there must appear different forms of radical "isms" which, though claiming a universal validity and meaning, cannot be accepted as such. In this sense it would be much more correct to call all "totalitarian" or "radical" systems of socio-political life as "unilateralism" and, of course, fanatic. For the whole (*totum*) is the integration of parts into a meaningful structure without violently distorting, eliminating or simply ignoring the significant meaning proper to each integrating element.

From another point of view, it would still be incorrect to attempt the final and ultimate integration of existence by a simple arithmetic device of adding up or lumping together all the particular meanings into some universal category or class without even trying to name or identify the nature of this unknown container. Although the democratically inclined egalitarian progressivists may advocate such a wholesale procedure, we must point to the resulting chaos and anarchy which must ensue as long as the parts are only thrown together without a common denominator or principle by which order or harmonious integration could be achieved, and without doing harm to the legitimate meaning and relative validity of the composing elements. Anarchy calls for dictatorial intervention as the only emergency to keep the disintegrated whole in a forced, that is, artificial semblance of equilibrium and unstable peace. It is history again which explains the rise of dictatorships as the necessary outcome of the absence of a unified system of integrated human values from which men could derive meaning, justification, order, peace, and happiness. The disintegrated elements being kept in one place by the artificial device of power and violence, anyone may foresee and predict its necessarily short duration as attested again by history as the "*magistra vitae*" (the master of life). The conflicting elements must bring forth the natural process of inner unrest and fermentation to the point of forcing the slats and the rings of the barrel into explosion.

Since there can be no order, unity, integration, and harmony in the person, in society and its culture without an inner principle of organization, it is necessary to look for a reality which, being at the same time both immanent in and transcendent to the parts, can offer the needed foundation from which the quest for ultimate meaning of the whole and its parts can be derived. This supreme reality and value is the Absolute.

This last statement could be interpreted as a simple postulate, dictated, perhaps, by man's practical reason after the Kantian fashion of dealing with the problem of transcendence. Such an interpretation, however, would be false, inconclusive, and devoid of any weight to carry man's rational consent. For it is of the nature of any postulate to establish a functional device only of a purely theoretical and abstract character, to be used for the interpretation of a certain class of phenomena. Herein consists its only value without, however, enjoying any degree of objective evidence. Consequently, it does not represent any reality and it can be replaced at any time if another, equally workable postulate, should be born out of the thinker's mind. Even granting a logical validity for the postulate in the order of thought and reasoning, it would again be fatal to fall into the well-known danger of ontological argumentation by arbitrarily jumping from the intentional order of knowledge to the objective one. Consequently, should there appear in the following considerations some degree of a "must" with reference to the reality of the absolute Being and Value, it should also be known that this "must" is forced upon the mind not only because of its pure logical validity, but also on grounds of an indirect, objective, that is, psycho-ontological evidence, derived from reflections on the human condition in the world.

The evidence claimed is only an indirect one; for the very idea of transcendence and metaphysics suggests the transition from the immediate reality, given in man's experiences, to a new reality, which lies beyond the realm of phenomena. It is exactly because of this indirect evidence that there has to appear some degree of myth and mystery—in *R. Otto's* saying: *"mysterium fascinosum et tremendum"* (a fascinating and fearful mystery) — commanding the use of a new vocabulary and language whose meaning can be interpreted only symbolically. The symbolic character of religion and morality can be seen also in their visible manifestations such as myth, rite or rituals, and liturgy, prescribing a new and rather formal pattern of attitude and behavior. The varied aspects of the religious experience will be briefly touched upon when coming to the encounter between man's self and the Other.

The starting point for this metaphysical journey into the noumenal regions of this "hidden God" (*"Deus absconditus"*) is man's psycho-ontological condition.

From the many existential categories of man's being we shall take that which we consider to be the most fundamental one and the source of all other secondary traits. This attribute is man's paradoxical condition to exist as an *"imperfect perfection"* or a *"demigod."* These expressions, however, may sound quite unfamiliar to a great number of people who have always been either too naive or too busy to spend some time with an Augustine or a Pascal and to reflect on the coexisting mystery and greatness in the human person. Those who lead the well-established life of good adjustment, happy conformity, and philistine narrow-mindedness, may even take pride and pleasure in their being the "top" of the universe due to their title of a "rational animal." (I think that being a "top" well expresses their condition of unperturbed ignorance; for no cover-"top" knows that which is either "below"—in the pot—or "above" itself.) Let us now dwell into the dimensions of man's antithetical situation.

Man's "imperfect perfection" expresses the coexistence of two opposite elements, that is, of a positive value (perfection) and of a negative one (imperfection). The positive elements of perfection can be found in man's personal mode of being as a self-conscious, rational, and free self. Since the Greeks man's highest perfection was identified with his fundamental power of thought, reflection, contemplation, and insight. The power of ideation, judgment, and reasoning bring man very close to the immaterial and even spiritual mode of being insofar as man's intellect—theoretically speaking—transcends the limitations of matter, time, and space in virtue of its unlimited object, the possession of truth. This quality of cognitive transcendence allows man the possibility and the freedom to assimilate the perfections of all other beings which belong to the field of his unlimited desire to know. Intellectual knowledge, therefore, offers man the opportunity for enlarging the limitations of his actual being to the extent of becoming "everything as it were" in the saying of Aquinas *quodammodo omnia.* In this sense knowledge is the means for an unrelenting process of ascending insights, a truly dynamic and creative progress and development whose final stage is set at the contemplation and intentional possession of Truth and Goodness unlimited. In a word, man—unlike other inferior beings—is truly unlimited in his intellectual and volitive powers; he is almost divine, enjoying the freedom of thought and action.

To be almost divine means to be godlike, but not God; it also suggests the mode of being proper to a "demigod" whereby is given man's negative value, rooted in his actual limitation or imperfection. For what we have just said on the possibility of a cognitive and volitive emancipation and transcendence holds true only in the ideal order of a theoretical possibility without any promise or guarantee for its actual or real achievement or possession (*ars longa, vita brevis*). While granting that the adequate object of man's intellect is truth unlimited (measured by being unlimited), still it is quite another question whether man really possesses this transcendent value by which he could quench his unlimited thirst for knowledge. And, alas, the answer is no; there has never been any human genius — without mentioning the condition of the average man who succeeded in overcoming the curse of half or learned ignorance. The same conclusion applies also to man's freedom of action by which he could realize the ideal values, known to him in the light of reflective meditation and contemplation. Unfortunately, there is always a barrier or wall put up against man's legitimate desire to know and to act, without always falling back to the ground in consequence of being held captive by the forces of his overall and actual limitations. There is an insurmountable gap between the ideal and the real order of being. Plato's ideas have never become man's possession whose trouble, therefore, is being only real. (In the language of metaphor we could name man as a spark held prisoner in a pile of dirt, the reason why he always becomes muddy and dirty.)

If we want to account for the chasm between the ideal order of "ought to be" and the real order of imperfect beings, we must bring up the full metaphysical meaning and implications of limitation in the order of existence. The meaning of ontological limitation or finitude can be introduced, as a preliminary attempt, by enumerating the list of the ideas which are implicit to its comprehension. Thus being limited implies the imperfections of being relative, dependent, and captive; the relation of dependence is first experienced on the material level, suggesting the situation of an earthbound existence with all its negative consequences in the struggle for life and subsistence. It is here that man is bound to suffer the first frustrating blows while trying to dominate a hostile nature, as matter, energy, space, and time. The condition of being earthbound is made worse by adding to it man's fundamental contingency, that is, his being indifferent toward being or not-being. In fact, man knows only too well that he is participating in existence only for a very short while, as if he were here on a short-lived vacation loaded with unforeseen threats, frustrations, and sufferings. In other words, man is always running out of time because time is running against him. The awareness of being in the world and facing the approaching hour of death must, of necessity, add a basic tragical note to man's short-lived existence. Besides knowing that he does not necessarily exist — actually this means some degree of not being necessary, needed, or, if you please, being superfluous — man also knows that each moment of life is also the moment of dying; while he is, he is becoming less in the sense that he is spending the uncertain amount of being until he ends up in total existential bankruptcy — death.

Furthermore, while spending his unguaranteed life and critically examining the quality and the kind of being he has for a while, man also has to discover that the existential qualities of his being and nature are not unspoiled perfections. On the contrary, whatever perfections he possesses, he owns them in an "imperfect" form because of their limitations. To be limited in the order of existence is the metaphysical root for man's misery. It simply means that he has only this much or so much of whatever he has and not more. Naturally, this is no problem at all to those limited beings which are *not aware* of their condition. For they simply are without realizing what they are, how they are, what mode of being they possess and what are the red tapes wrapping up their being. On the other hand, it is a painful experience and the constant source of frustration, the conscious feeling and awareness of representing only some broken fragments of perfections without promise and hope for ever recovering from this condition.

Take, for instance, any perfection, power or value which belongs to man's nature. Whatever it is — be it physical health, integrity, power, and beauty; intelligence, imagination, feelings, emotions, and instincts; knowledge, truth, beauty, goodness, virtue, freedom, love, justice; in sum, all values of the organic, psychic, social, cultural, and moral dimensions of existence — all display one common element of being only imperfect, limited, and to that extent also false. The theologians, philosophers, scientists, artists, all human leaders and economists spend their limited energies overcoming the limitations of human existence. Even common sense wisdom underlines the universal presence of the "human element" even in man's highest endeavors.

A realistic mind, therefore, will never subscribe to the religion of unlimited progress because of the evident contradiction in assuming that the "limited" will reach the "unlimited" by himself only. In fact, it takes a great deal of naive optimism and more emotional involvement to pick up everyday anew the imperfect tools of existence and continue the vain effort to reach the impossible. Since there is no rational justification for man's ambitious efforts from a purely natural point of view, most energetic persons must have grown forgetful of their true human condition and "pretend" as if they were going to succeed. Many others — mainly the mourners of human existence — would like to bury man alive.

Considering man's condition from a rational point of view, everyone must admit some degree of tragical element in human existence whose reason lies in the fact of "being limited," an "imperfect perfection" or a "demigod." There are, of course, the cynics who make fun out of man's condition and give birth to the comical, clownish aspect of life. The more serious persons, however, may dwell upon this antithetical character of human destiny and reason their way toward some possible solution before committing a moral or physical suicide.

There is no doubt as to the frustrating and even painful experience of being a "demigod" in the sense that man becomes extremely conscious of both his limitations and his concomitant desire for transcending them. One possible reaction to this state of things could be the desire to "revolt" against this injustice, a revolt inspired by the spirit of resentment for being "trapped" or "caged-in" a contradictory form of being. This existential revolt may have two specific aims: first, to refuse to accept the condition of metaphysical limitation, imperfection, and dependence by proclaiming the fateful *"non serviam"*—I shall not serve. This refusal rests on the assumption that limitation equals the state of slavery or disdainful servility. This is the demoniac spirit of Lucifer and of his rebels; second, besides refusing to serve, the limited and imperfect being may entertain the folly of taking over the place of the Infinite and the Absolute. The "demigod" wants to dethrone God. This is an abortive and irrational move, the metaphysical root of defiance or original sin; for we saw above the impossibility of the "limited" to become "unlimited" on his own account and effort. It must necessarily fail and result in self-condemnation. It is the result of the strongest temptation any limited being can experience when presented with the prospect of becoming God (*eritis sicut Dii*—you shall be like God). The deification of the limited is, in a way, both tragical and comical; its name is devil; its deed is sin, understood as the attempt at the metaphysically impossible; its result, once more, is condemnation and hell.

Another possible reaction on the part of the limited being to his condition of imperfection and fundamental dependence moves in the right direction, namely, to the infinite source of all being, to the absolute Being and Value. Should this fortunate move occur, there appears on the horizon of human existence the promise of his metaphysical redemption or salvation. Its end result consists in the encounter of the limited human self with the Other. Let us attempt a possible sketch of this transition from immanence toward transcendence.

The experience of frustration, failure, defeat, suffering, anguish, dread, and of the certainty of death must necessarily appear in human life because of the ambivalent condition of "being and not being," that is, being limited, imperfect, contingent, relative, dependent, etc., etc. However, these experiences could also be interpreted as the symptoms for a basic *"hunger for more being"* or the evidence for the metaphysical necessity of a certain redemption. Before going any further into this question, it serves our purpose if we make it clear that the problem of redemption is approached here from a metaphysical point of view, thus disregarding, for the moment, its ethical or moralistic interpretation.

In this restricted sense, then, redemption means man's rescue from his condition of finitude and imperfection. It is not suggested, however, that this redemption can be had by stretching man's existential dimensions into the indefinite. We saw, time and time again, that it is simply contradictory and irrational to attempt man's deification. Man can never become God or the absolute Being and Value. There can be no more than one Infinite. Consequently, man cannot redeem himself; similarly, there can be no redemption of the finite being outside the Infinite. Thus we conclude that man's metaphysical redemption can be had only in, through, and with the Infinite. There can be no sensible thought on being "apart from" the absolute Being. In scholastic terms we would say that *"ens"* necessarily gravitates toward *"esse"* thus making the redemption equal to *"co-esse."* This "being with" (*co-esse*) should, again, not be taken as existing side by side; on the contrary, the Infinite allows only one form of *"esse"* for limited beings and that should be called *"in-esse"* or being in God in the form of participation (taking part in) God's infinite perfection without losing one's relative self-identity.

This intimate mode of being in God naturally presupposes the opposite of revolt, hatred, resentment, and secession; it must necessarily rest upon the act of love or the intimate co-existence, maybe even co-penetration or union of two selves in the communion (union, unity in common, common union) of being. Thus redemption may come only through the personal act of love in which the limited being transcends his metaphysical imperfections by participating in God's divine mode of being (*particeps divinae naturae*). In a word, redemption is the communion in *"esse"* through the act of love.

There can be no doubt that this line of thinking is necessarily inspired by the act of philosophic faith. Should one expect a purely "rational" — maybe even "scientific" — proof for the problem of metaphysics, religion, and morality, such a person has never experienced the mysterious depths of being. Due to its overwhelming importance and far-reaching consequences, we must elaborate further on this act of philosophic faith.

Faith on both the natural and supernatural levels is the necessary outcome of man's psycho-ontological constitution viewed from the angle of his overall limitations. In fact, had man an adequate insight by his reason alone into the meaning and value of being — both subjective and trans-subjective — plus the power and guarantee to carry out his ideals through creative action and feeling, he would need no faith. In other words, adequate knowledge and power, based on immediate and direct evidence, derived from facts, could dispense with the necessity of faith. Unfortunately, however, there is no region of human existence which could claim the fullness of knowledge and the guarantee of success through action. On the contrary, the fatal limitation is all pervasive even in the "positive" or "exact" sciences and much more so in the field of "humanities" or "liberal arts." As far as the power of human action is concerned, the long list of human failures in politics, economics, ethics, etc. — as documented by history — should suffice as proof of man's limitations in his practical endeavors. Consequently, faith is an all-pervasive or universal phenomenon, subsequent to man's psycho-ontological limitation or to the condition of his "imperfect perfection."

Faith emerges whenever man runs out of funds, and, since he is almost always on the verge of bankruptcy, faith must hasten to his rescue. Therefore, it is much more correct and realistic to associate any of man's functions — vegetative, sensitive, cognitive, affective, and volitive — with the underlying reassurance he derives from his acts of believing in the meaning, value, and success of his dynamic tendencies. Thus man lives by faith and there is no going beyond this fact. He can carry on the burden of his existence only by believing in himself (self-confidence), in his fellow man (faith in humanity or humanism), and in an ultimate, global meaning in and value of his world. In this sense, therefore, even the most extreme forms of rationalism, positivism, naturalism, empiricism, materialism, etc., are indirect symptoms for the transfer of man's metaphysical or religious faith down to the "natural" order of a man-made reality. The validity of human values — scientific, aesthetic, moral, political, social, and economic — also rests upon and is guaranteed by the act of believing in their ideal or normative character. Whenever a crisis in this act of faith occurs, it necessarily brings about an accompanying crisis in the life of the individual, of society, and of culture as well. Faith is, therefore, the answer for man's psycho-ontological imperfection. Its dimensions embrace all regions of reality.

One should not create the impression that the act of believing necessarily implies or leads to a naive, primitive, irrational, and blind faith. Due to man's rational disposition and freedom, even the act of believing demands justification in order to make it acceptable by man's reason. As we mentioned elsewhere, there is a coexistence and a co-penetration between the acts of rational attitude and that of faith. It is, therefore, not wise to separate reason (*ratio*) from faith (*fides*) or to try to assess certain priority and prominence to either member of the pair. In this sense all attempted formulae (*credo ut intelligam* — I believe in order to understand; *intelligo ut credam* — I understand in order to believe; *credo quia absurdum* — I believe because it is absurd) should be regarded as the outcomes dictated by certain psychological and axiological premises more or less congenial with the frame of mind of a particular thinker without imposing a universal assent to it.

In view of this situation, we would like to suggest a better formula — *credo quia homo sum* — I believe because I am a man — which expresses the psycho-ontological necessity of faith and also allows sufficient room for the particular formulations of the same fundamental principle. One should also understand that neither is faith completely blind (irrational) nor is man altogether rational. Instead of calling faith an *Ersatz* for man's ignorance, it seems much better to identify it as man's fundamental existential act, needed for the enactment of and justification for his thought, feeling, and action. The *"homo arbiter"* —man the judge—introduced in the foregoing chapters appears now as *"homo fidens"*—man the believer—to the extent that all his value judgments necessarily include the act of believing in its validity and meaning. The loss of this existential act of commitment through faith leads to Sartre's "absurdism" which presupposes a preceding psycho-ethical bankruptcy and suicide.

The philosophic and scientific systems, paraded under the banner of rationalism and agnosticism—a really antithetic combination of incompatible attitudes—rests upon a distorted view of man's ontological condition which does not fit his finite, limited, contingent, and imperfect being. On the other hand, the act of philosophic faith—as opposed to immature credulity of the child and of the primitive—represents the attempt on man's part to expand and thus overcome the conditions of his limitations. There is no place for any pure *"cogito," "intelligo,"* and *"scio"* (I think, I understand, I am confident). Let us conclude, therefore, this discussion on the justification of the acts of faith by the dictum: *Credo quia homo sum*—I believe because I am a man, or, being a man, I must believe. Faith is a universal—natural and supernatural—phenomenon because it is rooted in man's existential condition.

It would be a great error, however, to put religious faith side by side and on the same footing with the acts of natural belief. For faith is of as many forms and degrees as the number of distinct human concerns is. Self-confidence, the faith in the fellow human being, faith in the validity and the benefits of human science and culture, cannot be equated with the genuine character of religious experiences. Consequently, let us introduce a bipartite division of faith according to its specific object and purpose. There is, first, the belief related to the meaning and value or success of all intramundane affairs which do not necessarily entail any immediate reference to the act of believing in an extramundane, metaphysical order, meaning, and value. Second, the religious value experience occurs only in the act of inquiring into the ultimate, final, and global meaning of existence in general.

On the other hand, it is quite natural that this metaphysical act should occur only as subsequent to the state of world-immanence. Religion, therefore, appears to us as the transition from world-immanence to world-transcendence. Hence the character of the other-worldliness in all forms of religious beliefs. The meaning of the latter, however, can be derived only from the experiences man had in the domain of the intramundane regions of reality.

The metaphysical and transcendental character of the religious value experience can be known only by starting with the analysis of the act involved in the basic religious attitude understood as a quest for ultimate meaning and redemption. There are three basic stages we can identify in this search for the absolute Value and Being. First, man will sooner or later become aware of: 1) his unrelented desire for happiness, that is, for a meaningful life, founded upon his need for security, direction, guidance, creative effort, and the promise of ultimate success; 2) his condition of psycho-ontological limitation as the source of his existential unrest, uneasiness, tension, anguish, loneliness, failure, and the immanent threat of death; 3) his awareness of being unable to change his ontological status by himself and thus overcome the condition of moral impotence, renunciation, resignation, and final despair.

Having thus arrived at the crucial point of existential crisis, there are only two things man can do with himself. Should man be totally blinded by the powers of his selfish desires and pride (*concupiscentia et superbia,* in the words of St. Augustine), he may desperately try to save himself by clinging to the limitations of his own self and subsistence. Since the limited necessarily involves some degree of separation and loneliness — individuation also means separation, that is, being divided from all other beings — man's egocentric self-concern necessarily results in self-condemnation in the forms of isolation and loneliness. While trying to save himself, he actually chooses the path of isolation from the ultimate source of unlimited perfection in which he could find the solution for his imperfect condition. There remains now the other alternative of understanding that redemption can be achieved only through the metaphysical act of offering up one's own limited being to be reunited with the unlimited, infinite being and perfection of the Absolute.

There must be a considerable struggle within the conscious and free self of the human person when challenged by the possibility and necessity of giving himself up in order to find himself again, redeemed from the excruciating experiences of imperfection and finitude. This struggle can be best described as a typical case of ambivalent behavior, consisting of the conflict between two opposite emotions, that is, the desire for happiness on the one hand, and the fear of losing oneself by embarking on the road toward the encounter with the Absolute Being. As long as the emotion of fear, inspired by natural self-centeredness, has the upper hand, there is no hope for such an encounter. In religious terms, we would say that man's selfish concern stands in his own way toward redemption. The self-loving self condemns itself to the condition of isolation, separation, loneliness, and despair. This condition is usually dealt with in the form of the well-known compensation mechanisms which provide a symptomatic relief for man's existential anguish and dread. Naturally, this escape from God and the adoration of the self in the many forms of self-gratification will sooner than later lead to the state of nausea and boredom (*ennui*). Many states of mental imbalance, according to *C. G. Jung,* are due simply to the cramped and compulsive attachment of the human self to the little world of his neurotic egotism, autism, or egocentrism.

The opposite of "self-preservation" is the act of "self-sacrifice" as the inner essence of the religious experience. Man comes to understand that the ultimate and global meaning of his limited being consists in the act of recollecting himself (*re-legere*) and reuniting himself (*re-ligare*) with the source of his origin and destiny. Man must lose his life in order to regain it after the process of a psychic and ethical rebirth (*metanoia*). The devestment from the state of petty selfishness may be a painful experience only as long as the individual does not realize that the act of self-sacrifice actually results in a psycho-ontological gain because of his being one with the only One, thus ending the condition of his restless, uneasy, and anguished despair. The union of the limited with the Unlimited and the Infinite brings with it the promise of immortality and eternity. This promise represents the release of man's mounting anxiety and dread in the face of death.

Before coming to the analysis of the psychic process which follows the act of religious conversion to the Absolute Being (*convertere* — to turn about), we must delve further into the nature of this first act from an ethical point of view. We hope to identify thereby the essence of the moral value and tie it up with the religious value experience.

It was made clear, on several occasions, that the personal mode of existence consists in the perfection of relative subsistence, self-consciousness, and autonomy, qualities which flow from man's reason and will, both rooted in the depths of his undefinable and mysterious self. Because of this self-conscious personal autonomy, it is up to man to give meaning, value, and direction to his own existence, thus determining for himself — to a relative degree only — his own fate or destiny. Now the act of self-determination or the exercise of freedom always occurs in the form of a value judgment whose fundamental elements are rational, emotional, and volitional.

Since there is nothing wanted unless previously known (*nihil volitum nisi praecognitum,* in the words of Aquinas), the process of valuing presupposes rational discourse, reflection, and subsequent insight into the meaning or perfection of the objects (motives) which happen to specify man's intellect. Considering, however, the inadequate or imperfect character of human knowledge, truth is never possessed in its fullness, thus allowing for the emergence of possible doubt or error which, in its turn, may also influence man's emotional dispositions, already aroused by the objects of his knowledge. In such wise, man is confronted with certain known perfections, saturated with his emotional involvements. Since no apprehended good or perfection exhausts man's intellect and will, there appears the state of indetermination, indecision, and ambivalence which demand from man the act of personal commitment in the form of deliberation, choice, and decision.

Whenever man exercises his power of decision, he must also experience some degree of personal responsibility in view of the consequences which follow his commitment. At the same time, there is present the element of doubt, fear or dread, due to his awareness of the imperfect character of his insights which do not exclude the possibility of error or fatal mistake. It is at this crucial point that man's will exercises his power of self-determination in the light of his reason and his faith as well. The element of faith is needed for overcoming the states of indecision and ambivalence which — in the long run — become psychologically intolerable. Since man cannot have an *a priori* guarantee for the absolute correctness of his decisions, for lack of an adequate insight and foresight, it is faith which adds the extra needed weight to take him out of the state of indetermination. Nevertheless, there will always be an element of doubt and fear in spite of the faith and hope which supplement the imperfection of preceding knowledge.

This situation of uncertainty becomes even more aggravated whenever man has to deal with realities which surpass the possibility of objective validation. Such is the case of man's metaphysical decision to offer himself to the Absolute Being whose existence and nature do not allow any direct proof or demonstration. This justifies the unusually great amount of "philosophic faith" needed for the act of metaphysical self-sacrifice in the hope of achieving the ideal of happiness, peace, redemption, and immortality in the union with the hidden God of all being.

In the light of these reflections the inner essence of the religious value experiences consists in man's highest commitment to the highest reality and value (God) as the metaphysical locus for all perfections indirectly known by reason, sustained by faith, and chosen by the act of free self-determination as the highest good, perfection, and the only source of his redemption and happiness. On the other hand, every act of personal commitment through self-determination also discloses the essence of moral or ethical behavior.

Perhaps it should be made clear that in the present discussion on the essence of morality we constantly refer to the "self imposed" morality (*autonomos*) as being different—though not necessarily opposed to—the morality of sheer conformity (*heteronomos*). The latter, undoubtedly, belongs to the ethical behavior of human groups, large or small, and rests upon tradition, authority, and environmental conditioning which creates the desired set of inhibitions in a given group in order to establish certain uniformity and constancy of collective behavior. Self-imposed morality, on the other hand, requires an intellectually and emotionally mature individual who has passed beyond the level of "good adjustment" and tries to establish for himself the code of his own behavior, without necessarily rejecting or contradicting the collective norms of moral life. However, such an individual feels it necessary to justify or validate before himself the meaning of certain moral restrictions, prohibitions, laws, taboos, etc., before committing himself either for or against them.

The conditions for the establishment of ethical autonomy (self-imposed morality) consist in developing the qualities of personal awareness of the individual's freedom, founded upon his rational nature. Only the individual who possesses this lucid awareness of his personal autonomy and the will to accept and use it, is qualified for the self-imposed mode of moral behavior. Such an individual must possess, first, a rather critical knowledge concerning the limitations of human existence, mainly its relative, dependent, and imperfect character. Second, the knowledge of man's indigent nature is confronted with the knowledge of values, understood as the ideals of perfection and goodness. At the moment of personal confrontation with the hierarchy of values, our individual must become aware of their normative or ethical character insofar as he looks upon them as being necessary for him to overcome the limitations and imperfections of his own life. Thus he develops an insight into the exact relationship between his own mode of being and the meaning values represent for his existence. He must, therefore, conclude that he cannot assume an attitude of radical callousness toward values without which his life would be empty and meaningless.

The experience of being necessarily dependent upon values results in the acts of personal commitment, obligation, duty, and responsibility. And herein lies the essence of all genuine moral autonomy. Consequently, the normative or "ought to" character of values will not be interpreted as an intrusion on or limitation of personal freedom as may very often be the case whenever the "commandments" are imposed upon man from without. On the contrary, the mature human person realizes that the meaning of his existence consists in the process of incorporating within himself the perfections (values) which are necessary for the achievement of the ideals of self-realization, self-appropriation, and self-possession (autonomy). By the same token, ethics appears to man as the developmental process leading to self-enrichment and the means for surpassing the initial imperfections, limitations, and barrenness of his existence. We may, therefore, define the moral obligation and responsibility as man's self-imposed commitment to appropriate the values (perfections) needed for the fulfillment of his psycho-ontological destiny. In this interpretation values and the moral good appear to be synonymous in meaning and significance. This is also the foundation for an ideal humanism and cultured life. Immorality or unethical behavior consists in man's deliberate refusal to work on the development of his personal existence thus degenerating into practical hedonism and happy vegetation. We believe that this interpretation conveys the meaning Aquinas wanted to express when defining *"bonum"* (good) as *"perfectivum rei"* (perfecting, improving, being).

We saw throughout these pages that values themselves belong to different orders; according to their qualitative differences they occupy a definite position — higher or lower — in the ideal hierarchy of values. It follows, therefore, that the "normative impact" of values on personal existence varies with regard to the kind, quality, intensity, height, and the redeeming power intrinsic to their specific perfections. There are values which qualify only as a means (*bonum utile*) for the attainment of other values (*bonum honestum*) which are wanted for themselves. Besides, there are many other particular goods and goods of order which are not absolutely necessary for the actualization of the ideal form of personal existence. Consequently, we may conclude that the normative impact of any value is directly proportional to the perfection it represents for the human person. It also follows that the value which stands for the highest perfection and goodness (*summum bonum*) will command the highest ethical impact on the human person. Since God is the highest perfection and goodness (*ipsum esse subsistens*), man's ethical behavior necessarily gravitates towards and ends at the threshold of the religious experience. Thus the moral and religious values coincide in the experience of man's highest commitment to the highest Being Who is the transcendental source and foundation for all lesser perfections and values. This much should already suffice to show the impossibility of separating the order of morality from the religious one. Both of them disclose to man the ultimate meaning, value, and direction of his existence to be reunited with the Absolute as the only possibility for man's redemption and happiness. We have, therefore, sufficient reason to assert that man's existential condition is both ethical and religious because he is psychologically and ontologically destined to meet the supreme Being and Value.

The encounter of the human self with the absolute Self necessarily dictates the emergence of man's religious behavior whose essential moments are: faith, hope, and love, inspiring prayerful adoration, self-sacrifice, thanksgiving, and entreaty. Due to their spiritual nature most of man's religious attitudes and experiences must express themselves in symbolic form thus giving rise to rite, ritual, liturgy and cult, both individual, and collective. Religious symbolism, however, derives its meaning from actually lived personal experiences. Should this personal experience fade, the religious behavior must degenerate into sheer formalism and stereotyped action. Perhaps we should also mention the different types of religious experience and conduct. This, however, would take us into the field of religious psychology and typology for which we do not have either space or immediate concern in this study. We feel that it is much closer to our field to finish our discussion with some final remarks on the effects man derives from his ethico-religious commitment.

For the sake of simplicity we may divide the impact religion and morality have on man by using the distinction between the individual and the collective dimensions of life. From the point of the individual existent, religion and morality offer him all the resources to fight the conflicts and polarities built into his psycho-somatic nature, as well as the consequences of his ontological imperfections. In this sense we may suggest that the emphasis the existentialists put on the tragical and dreadful character of human existence should be interpreted as the symptom of a "split consciousness" or as the result of the modern, secular, intra-mundane, even anti-religious form of life. The language used by truly religious persons discloses, on the contrary, the wisdom of the saints (*scientia sanctorum*) as being diametrically opposed to the states of anguish, despair, boredom, loneliness, and total personal bankruptcy. For it is of the nature of religious experience to saturate man with faith, hope, love, peace, inner equilibrium and the joyous anticipation of a final *"requies"* as the substitute for the modern man's restless, tense, and imbalanced neurotic condition. It is only the religious man who may understand the meaning of the language spoken by Augustine when he refers to the *"recta voluntas et bonus amor"* (right will and good love) as opposed to the *perversa voluntas et malus amor"* (perverted will and wrong love) which identify the uninterrupted state of *inquies"* (restlessness) of the anti-religious man.

From the collective point of view, according to C. G. Jung, "religion acts as a counterpoise to the 'world' and its 'reason', providing the foundations for the freedom and autonomy of the individual." The individual needs a point of reference outside and above himself and society to build up a reserve against the drifting power of collectivism and the authority of the sovereign state, threatening his life with total submission and enslavement. Due to his perfection of personal autonomy, the individual belongs to himself and wants to be himself; the meaning of his life is not identical with public welfare and higher standards of living. However, the "resistance to the organized mass" can be effected only by the individual who is as well-organized in his individuality as the mass itself. It is religion which offers the individual the opportunity to develop an inner sense and power of personal integrity, equilibrium, and autonomy. Without it, man will necessarily become the prey of the omnipotent state or sovereign society. The organized unity of the human person comes into being by the act of an ultimate commitment to and union with the only One Who has the right to claim the individual as his own. Being possessed by God and belonging to Him in the state of *"in-esse"* (participation in divine nature) does not annihilate the individual's selfhood. For the encounter between man as a limited self with God as the Absolute Self (The One Who is) is the confrontation of two persons resulting in the "I -Thou" relationship found upon and inspired by the acts of mutual love and respect. Thus the unity, truth, and goodness of the limited self finds itself enriched in the *"Unum," "Verum"* and *"Bonum"* of the *"ipsum esse subsistens."* Man's redemption appears to consist, therefore, in the appropriation of the transcendentals of being from its original source, God, Who is the identity of all perfection on an infinite scale, manifested through the act of His infinite love.

# BIBLIOGRAPHY

## I. THE THEORY OF VALUE

### 1. Partial Survey of Works and Articles on Value in General

DASHIELL, J. FREDERIC: "The Philosophic Status of Values," N. Y., 1913; "Values and Experience" in the *Journal of Philosophy*, v. 11, 1914; "Values and the Nature of Science" in *The Philosophical Review*, v. 22, 1913.

DEWEY, JOHN: "The Meaning of Value" in *The Journal of Philosophy*, v. 23, 1925; "The Problem of Value" in *The Journal of Philosophy*, v. 23, 1925; "Valuation and Experimental Knowledge" in *The Philosophical Review*, v. 31, 1922; "Value, Objective Reference and Criticism" in *The Philosophical Review*, v. 24, 1925; "Values, Liking, and Thought" in *The Journal of Philosophy*, v. 20, 1923.

HASEROT, FRANCIS S.: "Essays on the Logic of Being," N.Y. The Macmillan Co., 1932.

LEPLEY, RAY: "Value — A Cooperative Inquiry," N.Y. Columbia University Press, 1949.

MACKENZIE, J.S.: "Ultimate Values," London and Toronto: Hodder and Stoughton, 1924.

MASLOW, A.H. (Ed.): "New Knowledge in Human Values," Harper & Bros., 1959.

MOORE, JARED S.: "Value in its Relation to Meaning and Purpose" in *The Journal of Philosophy*, v. 11, 1914.

MORRIS, CHARLES: "Varieties of Human Value," The University of Chicago Press, 1956.

MUKERJEE, RADHAKAMAL: "The Social Structure of Values," N.Y. Macmillan and Co., 1958.

OAKLEY, H.D.: "On the Meaning of Value" in *Philosophical Review*, v. 31, 1922.

PARKER, DEWITT H.: "The Notion of Value" in *Philosophical Review*, v. 38, 1929.

PERRY, RALPH B.: "The Definition of Value" in *The Journal of Philosophy*, v. 11, 1914; "General Theory of Value: Construed in Terms of Interest," N. Y. Longmans, 1926.

PICARD, MAURICE: "Metaphysics and Value" in the *Philosophical*

*Review,* v. 34, 1925; "The Psychological Basis of Values" in *The Journal of Philosophy,* v. 17, 1920; "Value and Worth" in *The Journal of Philosophy,* v. 20, 1923; "Values, Immediate and Contributory, and Their Interrelations," N. Y. University Press, 1920.

PRALL, DAVID W.: "A Study in the Theory of Value," University of California, 1921; "Metaphysics and Value" in Essays in Metaphysics, Berkeley, 1924.

SHELDON, W. H.: "An Empirical Definition of Value" in *The Journal of Philosophy,* v. 11, 1914.

SMART, WILLIAM: "An Introduction to the Theory of Value," London, Macmillan, 1914.

TAYLOR, H. OSBORN: "Human Values and Verities,"N. Y. Macmillan, 1928.

TURNER, J. E.: "The Problem of Values" in *Journal of Philosophical Studies,* v. 3, 1928.

URBAN, W. M.: "Ontological Problems of Value" in *The Journal of Philosophy,* v. 14, 1917; "What is the Function of a General Theory of Value?" in *The Philosophical Review,* v. 17, 1908; "Valuation: Its Nature and Laws," N. Y. Macmillan, 1918.

WARD, L. RICHARD; C.S.C.: "The Philosophy of Value," N. Y. The Macmillan Co., 1930.

## 2. The Neo-Kantian and Phenomenological Background

BAMBERGER, FRITZ: "Untersuchungen zur Entstehung des Wert—problems des 19. Jahrhunderts," Halle, 1924.

DASHIELL, J. FREDERIC: "An Introductory Bibliography in Value" in *The Journal of Philosophy,* v. 10, 1913.

DEAT, MARCEL: "Kant et le Probleme des Valeurs," in *Revue de Metaphysique et de Morale,* v. 32, 1925.

ENGERT, JOSEPH: "The Philosophical Movement in Germany" in *The New Scholasticism,* v. 2, 1928.

MESSER, AUGUST: "Deutsche Wertphilosophie der Gegenwart," Liepzig, 1926.

DILTHEY, WILHELM (1883-1911): "Einleitung in die Geisteswissenschaften," 1 Band, 1883; "Ideen über eine beschreibende und zergliedernde Psychologie," 1894; "Der Aufbau der geschichtlichen Welt in den Geisteswissenschaften," 1910; "Die Typen der Weltanschauung," 1911.

NIETZSCHE, FRIEDRICH W. (1884-1900): "Also sprach Zarathustra," 1883; "Jenseits von Gut und Böse," 1886; "Zur Genealogie der Moral," 1887; "Der Wille zur Macht," 1906.

LOTZE, R. HERMANN (1817-1881): "Metaphysik," 1841; "Logik," 1842;

"Mikrokosmos," 3 Bände, 1856-1864; "System der Philosophie," 2 Bände, 1874 and 1879.

WINDELBAND, WILHELM (1848-1915): "Präludien," 1911; "Lehrbuch der Geschichte der Philosophie," 1891; "Die Prinzipien der Logik," "Einleitung in die Philosophie."

MEINONG, A. (1853-1921): "Psychologisch-ethische Untersuchungen zur Wettheorie"; "Uber Gegenstände höherer Ordnung"; "Uber Annahmen"; "Stellung der Gegenstands Theorie"; "Uber Möglichkeit und Wahrschienlichkeit."

BRENTANO, FRANTZ (1838-1917): "Psychologie vom empirischen Standpunkt"; "Vom Urprung sittlicher Erkenntniss"; "Von der Klassification psychischer Phänomene."

HUSSERL, EDMUND (1859-1938): "Philosophie der Arithmetik"; "Logische Untersuchungen"; "Ideen zu einer reinen Phänomenologie und phänomenologische Philosophie"; "Formale und transzendentale Logik."

RICKERT, HEINRICH (1863-1936): "Der Gegenstand der Erkenntnis," 1892; "System der Philosophie," I., 1921; "Die Logik des Prädikats und die Ontologie," 1930; "Grundprobleme der philosophischen Methodologie, Ontologie, Anthropologie," 1934; "Kennen und Erkennen," 1934

SCHELER, MAX: "Der Formalismus in der Ethik und die Materiale Wertethik," Halle, 1921; "Von Ewigen im Menschen," Leipzig, 1935; "Philosophische Weltanschauung," "Vom Umsturz der Werte," Leipzig, 1919.

HESSEN, JOHANNES: "Wertphilosophie," Paderborn, 1937; "Die Begründung der Erkenntnis nach dem heiligen Ausgustinus," Münster, 1916; "Die unmittelbare Gotteserkenntnis nach dem heiligen Augustinus," Paderborn, 1919; "Die Werte des Heiligen," Regensburg, 1938.

HARTMANN, NICOLAI: "Ethik," Berlin, 1935; "Zur Grundlegung der Ontologie," Berlin, 1935; "Grundzüge einer Metaphysik der Erkenntnis," Berlin, 1935; "Möglichkeit und Wirklichkeit," Berlin, 1938.

SPRANGER, EDUARD: "Lebensformen," 1914; "Kultur und Erzeihung," 1923; "Die Psychologie des Jugendhalters," 1924; "Der Sinn der Vorausetzungslosigkeit in den Geisteswissenschaften," 1929; "Goethes Weltanschauung," 1940; "Lebenserfahrung," 1945; "Probleme der Kulturmorphologie," 1947; "Die Kultruzyklentheorie und das Problem des Kulturverfalls," 1947.

### 3. Neo-Scholastic Solutions

ENGERT, JOSEPH: "The Philosophical Movement in Germany" in *The New Scholasticism,* v. 2, 1928.

SHEEN, FULTON J.: "Religion without God," N. Y., Longmans, 1928;

"God and Intelligence," N. Y., Longmans, 1925.
GILSON, ETIENNE: "The Philosophy of St. Thomas Aquinas," tr. by Bullough, Cambridge, 1925; "Saint Thomas d'Aquin," 2nd ed., Paris, Lecoffre, 1925.
OLGIATE-ZYBURA: "The Key to the Study of St. Thomas," 2nd. ed., Paris, 1922.
BEHN, S.: "Philosophie der Werte," 1930.
GEYESER, J.: "M. Schelers Phänomenologie der Religion," Freiburg, 1924.
HONECKER, M.: "Logik," Berlin, 1927.
LENNERZ, H., S.J.: "Scheler's Konformitätssystem und die Lehre der Kath. Kirche," Münster, 1924.
WITTMANN, M.: "Max Scheler als Ethiker," Düsseldorf, 1923; "Die Ethik des Aristoteles," Regensburg, 1920; "Die Ethik des hl. Thomas von Aquin," München, 1933; "Die Werttheorie bei Aristoteles und Thomas von Aquin" in *Archiv für Geschichte der Philosophie*, Bd. 12, 1942.
SERTILLANGES, A.: "La Philosophie Morale de Saint Thomas," 2nd. ed., Paris, 1922.
KLENK, G. FRIEDRICH, S.J.: "Wert, Sein, Gott," Rome, 1942.
LONERGAN, J. F. BERNARD, S.J.: "Insight — A Study of Human Understanding," Philosophical Library, 1956.
PATKA, FRIEDRICH: "De Ontologica Fundatione Valorum, Respectu Habito ad Tehorias Confessas in Hodiernis Scientiis Spiritus (Gcisteswissenschaften)" in Revista da Universidade Catolica de Sao Paulo, v. 4, 1953 "O estructuralismo de Ed. Sprangers," Sao Paulo, 1954; "Die ideale Abstufung der Werte im Sinne Ed. Sprangers," in Revista Brasileira de Filosofia, 1954, Sao Paulo.

## II. THE HIERARCHY OF VALUES

### 1. On Cognitive Value

BAUCH, BRUNO: "Wahrheit, Wert und Wirklichkeit," Leipzig, 1923.
DURKHEIM, E.: "Jugements de Valeur et Jugements de Realité," in *Revue de Métaphysique et de Morale*, v. 19, 1911.
FISHER, D. W.: "Problem of the Value-Judgment," in *Philosophical Review*, v. 22, 1913.
GOEDEKE, PAUL: "Wahrheit und Wert," Hildburghausen, 1927.
MCINTYRE, J. L.: "Value-feelings and Judgments of Value" in *Proc. Artist. Soc.*, v. 5, 1904-5.

PERRY, R. B.: "Dewey and Urban on Value-Judgments" in *The Journal of Philosophy*, v. 14, 1917.
PRALL, D. W.: "Value and Thought-Process" in *The Journal of Philosophy*, v. 21, 1924.
RUSSELL, J. E.: "Truth as Value and Value as Truth," in *Mind*, v. 20, 1911.
SELLARS, R. W.: "Cognition and Valuation" in *The Philosophical Review*, v. 35, 1936.
STUART, H. P.: "Valuation as a Logical Process," Univ. of Chicago, 1918.
URBAN, W. M.: "The Knowledge of Other Minds and the Problem of Meaning and Value" in *The Philosophical Review*, v. 26, 1917; "Knowledge of Value and the Value-Judgment" in *The Journal of Philosophy*, v. 13, 1916; "The Objective and the Value-Judgment" in *The Journal of Philosophy*, v. 15, 1918; "Definition and Analysis of the Consciousness of Value" in *Psychological Review*, v. 14, 1907.
WRIGHT, H. W.: "Value, Subjective and Objective" in *The Journal of Philosophy*, v. 23, 1926.

## 2. On the Economic Value

SPRANGER, ED.: "Lebensformen" 1914 (See sections on Homo Economicus).
CALKINS, M.: "Biological or Psychological?" in *The Journal of Philosophy*, v. 24, 1927.
LINK, H. C.: "Instinct and Value" in *American Journal of Psychology*, v. 33, 1922.
SCHNEIDER, H. W.: "The Values of Pragmatic Theory," in *The Journal of Philosophy*, v. 14, 1917.
URBAN, W. M.: "The Pragmatic Theory of Value" in *The Journal of Philosophy*, v. 14, 1917.
WRIGHT, W. K.: "The Evolution of Values from Instincts" in *The Philosophical Review*, v. 24, 1915.

## 3. On the Aesthetic Value

SPRANGER, ED.: "Lebensformen" 1914. (See sections on Homo Aestheticus.)
BUSH, W. T.: "Esthetic Values and Their Interpretation" in *The Journal of Philosophy*, v. 20, 1923.
CALLAHAN, L.: "The Esthetic Principles of St. Thomas," Washington, 1960.

MARITAIN, J.: "The Responsibility of the Artist," Ch. Scribner's, N. Y., 1960; "Art and Scholasticism," Ch. Scribner's, N. Y., 1936.
REID, L. A.: "Beauty and Moral Betterment," in International Journal of Ethics, v. 37, 1927.
URBAN, W. M.: "Value Theory and Esthetics" in Philosophy Today (ed., E. L. Schaug, London, Open Court, 1924).
WHITMORE, Ch. H.: "The Scale of Esthetic Values" in *The Journal of Philosophy*, v. 21, 1924.

## 4. On the Socio-Political Values

ALLPORT, F. H.: "Social Psychology and Human Values" in *International Journal of Ethics,* v. 38, 1928.
DESMOND, H. J.: "The Larger Values," Chicago: McClurg, 1913.
DEWEY, J.: "Reconstruction in Philosophy," Chicago, 1920.
DURKHEIM, E.: "The Elementary Forms of the Religious Life" (Tr. by Swain, London: Allen, 1903).
HUMPHREY, S. K.: "The Racial Prospect," N. Y.: Scribners, 1920.
OVERSTREET, H. A.: "Conventional Economics and a Human Valuation" in *The Journal of Philosophy*, v. 12, 1915.
RENAULD, J.: "Observations sur l'Idée de Valeur Considérée dans ses Rapports avec la Société," in *Revue de Métaphysique et de Morale,* v. 32, 1925.
SELLARS, R. W.: "Principles and Problems of Philosophy," N. Y.: Macmillan, 1926.

## 5. On Moral and Religious Values

AMES, Ed. S.: "Religious Values and the Practical Absolute" in International Journal of Ethics, v. 32, 1922.
BIXLER, J. S.: "Religion in the Philosophy of William James," Boston: Jones, 1926.
EVERETT, W. G.: "Moral Values: A Study of the Principles of Conduct," N. Y. Holt, 1918.
MACKENZIE, J. S.: "Spiritual Values" in *International Journal of Ethics*, v. 33, 1923; "The Meaning of Good and Evil" in *International Journal of Ethics*, v. 21, 1911.
MOORE, J. S.: "The System of Transcendental Values" in *The Journal of Philosophy,* v. 10, 1913.
MUNSTERBERG, H.: "The Eternal Values," Boston: Houghton Mifflin, 1909.
PERRY, R. B.: "Religious Values" in *The American Journal of Theology*, v. 19, 1915.

REISNER, E. H.: "Religious Values and Intellectual Consistency," N. Y., Science Press, 1915.

SOLOMON, J.: "Is the Conception of 'Good' Indefinable?" in *Proc. Artist. Soc.*, v. 6, 1905-6.

SORLEY, W. R.: "The Moral Life and Moral Worth," Cambridge, 1920; "Moral Values and the Idea of God," Cambridge, 1918.

TSANOFF, R. A.: "The Problem of Immortality: Studies in Personality and Value," N. Y., Macmillan, 1924.

TUFTS, J. H.: "The Moral Life and the Construction of Values and Standards" in *Creative Intelligence*, N. Y., Holt, 1917.

WELLS, W. R.: "On Religious Values" in *The Journal of Philosophy*, v. 15, 1918.

WIEMAN, H. N.: "A Criticism of Coordination as Criterion of Moral Values" in *The Journal of Philosophy*, v. 14, 1917.

WRIGHT, W. K.: "The Objectivity of Moral Values" in *The Philosophical Review*, v. 32, 1922; "Does the Objective System of Values Imply a Cosmic Intelligence?" in *International Journal of Ethics*, v. 38, 1928; "A Student's Philosophy of Religion," N. Y.: Macmillan, 1926.

SPRANGER, E.: "Lebensformen," 1914. (See sections on the Homo Religiosus.)

# INDEX

C

R



S

T



U



V